GITĀ & BEYOND

A SPIRITUAL JOURNEY INTO HINDU PHILOSOPHY

PART II

Sarang Tilak

Clever Fox®
PUBLISHING
Chennai • Bangalore

CLEVER FOX PUBLISHING
Chennai, India

Published by CLEVER FOX PUBLISHING 2025

ISBN: 978-93-6707-892-1

Preface

by Dr. Deepak Tilak

Dr. Deepak Tilak is the great grandson of Lokmanya Bal Gangadhar Tilak and serves as the Chancellor of Tilak Maharashtra Vidyapeeth.

This book serves not only as an elucidation of the profound teachings of the Geetārahasya, or Karmayoga Shāstra by B. G. Tilak but also as a guide for understanding the path to self-realization and personal transformation. Following are some of my views and observations:

Geetārahasya, written by Lokmanya Tilak as the science of action; is a monument in Indian Moral philosophy. Philosophers and critiques like Shri Ādi Shankarāchārya, Madhvāchārya, and Vallabhāchārya commented on and interpreted Shrimad Bhagavad Gitā as a philosophy of detachment or withdrawal from action (Nivrutti or Sanyās). Lokmanya Tilak however, emphasized that on the battlefield of Kurukshetra, Arjun was demoralized to see his kith and kin among the enemy-warriors and was thus in extreme agony. He expressed his desire to withdraw and lay down his weapons and requested Lord Krishna to guide him in such a critical situation. He expressed his repentance in achieving the kingdom of Indraprastha for Swarājya.

Lord Krishna did not give consent to Arjun's request to withdraw from action as a warrior. Instead, Lord Krishna stopped Arjun from refraining from action and asked him to go to war, which was his social and ethical duty (Dharma) as a warrior.

It was believed that, like most Upanishads, Bhagavad Gitā also advocated resignation from action. Lokmanya Tilak did not agree with this interpretation because Gitā emerged in Mahābhārat times where the social system and family institutions were highly stable. In that period, concepts like Dharma (ethical action) and Adharma (unethical action), Good and Bad, Worthy and Unworthy etc. got deeply blended into the social fabric. Lord Krishna at the juncture of battle deliberated on the importance of performing action (karma).

Arjun by nature is knowledge itself. However, he raises several questions, which later have been answered by Lord Krishna. Gitā is in the form of a colloquy of knowledge, which applies not only to Arjun but also to people belonging to all religions and castes. Bhagavad Gitā after remaining inconspicuous for five thousand years re-emerged for making human beings action-oriented. Therefore, it provided an impetus to Lokmanya Tilak to write his commentary on Karmayog Shāstra, an action-oriented path towards attainment of oneness (Yog) with God.

Life is impossible without action. Even when a person remains silent, breathing continues. Bhagavad Gitā does not promulgate any particular religion but propounds the action-oriented society and following of Dharma to the world. It is the crux of Vedic Literature. It belongs to the entire human race. Lokmanya Tilak wrote his commentary on Gitā in Marathi Language so that it could percolate to the downtrodden sections and the masses of the society for their use. Other writings by Lokmanya are in the English language - except Geetārahasya. Lokmanya Tilak told all the Indian citizens to act instead of following inaction or Sanyās.

Human existence without Karma (action, function) cannot be imagined. Even in sleep, the function of breathing continues endlessly. Karma includes all types of actions – even remembrance (smaran), listening (shruti), routine Karma and occasional Karma. In the Karmayog Shāstra or Geetārahasya by Lokmanya Tilak, 'Yog' implies appropriate deployment of Karma wherein skill or proficiency is the best. Lord Krishna says to Arjun - "Arjun, employ your skill with maximum proficiency and diligence in executing the war-deed". Even the scholars, who preached inaction or Sanyās worked or acted to spread their thoughts in the society. In Bhagavad Gitā, the word Yog does not mean Pātanjal Yog, but it means performance of action.

However, the purity, righteousness or piousness of Karmayog has to be judged by the soul with its discriminating faculty. The method of this discrimination is the vital question posed to the entire human race.

In this preface, I encourage readers to explore the layers of meaning within Geetārahsya or Karmayog Shāstra by B.G. Tilak with patience and reverence. This book is not merely a word-for-word translation but a gist, which is written, in a clear and accessible language suitable for today's generation. This book helps you to translate complex philosophies into accessible concepts and has brought the ancient text of the Gitā into the modern consciousness with clarity and reverence. I wish the book and its author Shri. Sarang Tilak all the success in getting the recognition they deserve.

Dr. Deepak Tilak
Chancellor, Tilak Maharashtra Vidyapeeth
Editor & Trustee, Daily Kesari
Great Grandson of Lokmanya Tilak

Foreword by

Dr. Geetali Tilak

Dr. Geetali Tilak, who is the great, great granddaughter of Lokmanya Bal Gangadhar Tilak, serves as the **Vice-Chancellor of Tilak Maharashtra Vidyapeeth**, continuing the legacy of academic excellence and cultural preservation established by her family. Their efforts in preserving heritage and promoting progressive ideas have made an indelible mark on Indian society.

Gitā & Beyond: A Spiritual Journey into Hindu Philosophy, penned by Sarang Manohar Tilak, is a profound exploration of the timeless wisdom of the Bhagavad Gitā, presented with remarkable depth and clarity. Drawing inspiration from Lokmanya Tilak's seminal work *Shrimad Bhagavad Gitā Rahasya*, the book does justice to its core message by examining deeply into the philosophy of Karmayog, or the path of selfless action, as a guide for leading a purposeful and balanced life. Tilak expertly navigates the diverse interpretations of the Gitā by renowned scholars like Adi Shankarāchārya and Rāmānujāchārya, offering a comparative analysis that highlights the rich diversity of Hindu thought.

The book stands out for its meticulous verse-by-verse translation, enriched with detailed footnotes that make the ancient text accessible to modern readers. Tilak's engaging narrative seamlessly connects the spiritual teachings of the Gitā with contemporary dilemmas, demonstrating its relevance in today's complex world. By emphasizing the practical application of Gitā's principles, the author encourages readers to embrace their duties with detachment and equanimity, making this work a valuable resource for both spiritual seekers and those interested in Hindu philosophy. With its blend of scholarly rigour and relatable insights, Gitā & Beyond is an essential read for anyone looking to deepen their understanding of Gitā's enduring message.

Table of Contents

Original Verses, Verse By Verse Translation and Footnotes of Shrimad Bhagavad Gitā

Prelude

Till now we've explained in detail the essence of Bhagavad Gitā and how it recommends making one's intellect equanimous through knowledge and devotion. It also tells us that one must continue to perform all actions even after achieving this, for welfare of the universe. We also saw how the sequential alignment of the 18 Adhyāyas of Gitā is explained. After this, all that appears to be remaining is literal verse by verse translation from Sanskrit. However, it wasn't possible to cover certain things during the general explanation, such as – how verses have been grouped within an Adhyāya or how communalist commentators have singled out certain verses, twisting their meaning to support their sect. We've used some footnotes along with translation, to denote such comments wherever applicable. We've used square brackets [] for the said footnotes. Whenever we encountered topics that have been covered in detail already, we've written instructions to refer the concerned chapters. While we've tried to give word by word accurate translation, due to difference in languages we've been forced to use extra or different words to explain the gist. We've used such words in round brackets (). In Sanskrit, the number for the verse is written at the end while we've written the numbers first in our translation. We request the readers to make a note of this and read the matter succeeding a number to read translation of the corresponding verse. We've kept the translation in such a way that even if one omits the footnotes and keeps reading verse by verse, there would be no loss of meaning or context. Having said all this, translation is after all, a translation. Someone who wants to understand the true, straight and explicit meaning of Gitā must learn Sanskrit and read it in the original, loving, beautiful and comprehensive language of Bhagwān Shri Krishna. Before you start, I'd request you that if you can read Sanskrit, keep a copy in Sanskrit script by your side for seeing the verses in original to better understand the words and pronunciations more accurately. We can now see, that the chapters before this and the following translation are supplementary to each other. Whoever wants to truly understand our opinion is strongly advised to read both parts.

Shlokas (Verses)

Prathamodhyāyah (First Adhyāya)

Dhrutarashtra Uvacha

Dharma-Kṣhetre Kuru-Kṣhetre Samavetā Yuyutsavaḥ

Māmakāḥ Pāṇḍavāśhchaiva Kimakurvata Sañjaya II1II

Sañjaya Uvācha

Dṛiṣhṭvā Tu Pāṇḍavānīkaṁ Vyūḍhaṁ Duryodhanastadā

Āchāryamupasaṅgamya Rājā Vachanamabravīt II2II

Translation

Prathamodhyāyah (First Adhyāya)

[Before the beginning of the Great War, sage Vyās went to the blind king Dhrutarāshtra and offered to lend him the power of vision if he wished to witness the impending war. When he refused to watch the annihilation of his dynasty, Vyās gave a special power to the assistant Sanjay before leaving, by which he could fathom every event of the war and narrate it to Dhrutarāshtra. Later when Sanjay went to inform Dhrutarāshtra of Bheeshma's death, he asked Sanjay to narrate the story of the entire war. Sanjay then began by describing the armies of both sides and narrated Gitā as per Dhrutarāshtra's request. The same story was narrated by sage Vyās to his disciples. Later one of the disciples, Vaishampāyan, told it to Janamejay and finally Sauti narrated it to Shaunak. All editions of Mahābhārat include Gitā in Bheeshma Parva (book) between 25th and 42nd Adhyāyas.]

Dhrutarāshtra says – (1) Sanjay, what did Pandu's sons and my sons, intending to battle, do in the hallowed land of Kurukshetra?

[Kurukshetra is the field surrounding Hastināpur. Modern city of New Delhi is located on this field. Kuru, the ancestor of Pāndav and Kaurav, had ploughed the field for agriculture. This is why it is called Kshetra (field). Later, Indra blessed Kuru and said that whoever performs austerities or dies during war in this field would go to heaven. Subsequently, Kuru stopped ploughing the field. Parshuram has been said to have killed all progenies of Kshatriya class 21 times on this very field, for avenging his father. There have been many other battles that have ensued on this battlefield since.]

Sanjay said – (2) Once Duryodhan saw Pāndav army in formation, he went to (Drona) Āchārya (Guru) and said –

[As Pāndav army was smaller than that of Kaurav, they had arranged their army in the form of Vajra, a divine weapon; after Bheeshma (who had strategized the formation of Kaurav army) had organized theirs. This is described in the Adhyāya preceding Gitā in Mahābhārat. These formations would then change at the beginning of every day.]

Paśhyaitāṁ Pāṇḍu-Putrāṇām Āchārya Mahatīṁ Chamūm

Vyūḍhāṁ Drupada-Putreṇa Tava Śhiṣhyeṇa Dhīmatā II3II

Atra Śhūrā Maheṣhvāsā Bhīmārjuna-Samā Yudhi

Yuyudhāno Virāṭaśhcha Drupadaśhcha Mahā-Rathaḥ II4II

Dhṛiṣhṭaketuśhchekitānaḥ Kāśhirājaśhcha Vīryavān

Purujit Kuntibhojaśhcha Śhaibyaśhcha Nara-Puṅgavaḥ II5II

Yudhāmanyuśhcha Vikrānta Uttamaujāśhcha Vīryavān

Saubhadro Draupadeyāśhcha Sarva Eva Mahā-Rathāḥ II6II

Asmākaṁ Tu Viśhiṣhṭā Ye Tānnibodha Dwijottama

Nāyakā Mama Sainyasya Sanjñārthaṁ Tānbravīmi Te II7II

Bhavānbhīṣhmaśhcha Karṇaśhcha Kṛipaśhcha Samitiñjayaḥ

Aśhvatthāmā Vikarṇaśhcha Saumadattis Tathaiva Cha II8II

Anye Cha Bahavaḥ Śhūrā Madarthe Tyaktajīvitāḥ

Nānā-Śhastra-Praharaṇāḥ Sarve Yuddha-Viśhāradāḥ II9II

Aparyāptaṁ Tadasmākaṁ Balaṁ Bhīṣhmābhirakṣhitam

Paryāptaṁ Tvidameteṣhāṁ Balaṁ Bhīmābhirakṣhitam II10II

(3) Āchārya, behold the army of the sons of Pandu (Pāndav) organized by your wise disciple, the son of Drupad (Dhrushtadyumna). (4) The army includes brave, master archers and fighters equally capable as Bheem and Arjun – such as Yuyudhān (Satyaki), Virāt and Mahārathi Drupad, (5) Dhrushtaketu, Chekitān, Veeryavān Kāshirāj, Purujit Kuntibhoj and Narashreshtha (superior) Shaibya, (6) besides valiant Yudhāmanyu, masculine Uttamauja and Subhadrā's son (Abhimanyu) and Draupadi's (five) sons are all Mahārathi (accomplished warriors).

[One who can fight alone with 10,000 archers is called Mahārathi. Udyog Parva of Mahābhārat describes which Rathi, Atirathi and Mahārathi were present in armies on either side in 8 Adhyāyas, 164 through 171. Dhrushtaketu was Shishupāl's son. Purujit Kuntibhoj is a single person. Purujit was the son born to Kuntibhoj king, who had adopted Kunti. Kuntibhoj is their family name. He was the maternal uncle of Yudhisthir, Bheem and Arjun. Yudhāmanyu and Uttamauja were both from Pānchal while Chekitān was a Yādav. Yudhāmanyu and Chekitān were protectors of Arjun's chariot. Shaibya was the ruler of kingdom Shibi.]

(7) O great Brāhman (priest), pray listen as I now indicate the key leaders of my army. (8) You and Bheeshma, Karna, always victorious Krupa, Ashwatthāmā and Vikarna (one of the 99 brothers of Duryodhan) besides Somdatta's son (Bhoorishravā), (9) and many more brave warriors like these are willing to sacrifice their lives; all are masters of various weapons and are skilled in battle. (10) This way, our army protected by Bheeshma is aparyāpta (huge), while the army protected by Bheem is paryāpta (limited).

[There's debate about how to derive meaning of the words paryāpta and aparyāpta. While the literal meaning of paryāpta is enough, some claim that we must translate the 10th verse as "Pāndav army is enough while our army is not enough". However, we don't feel this is correct. Earlier in Udyog Parva, Duryodhan narrates to Dhrutarāshtra the key members of his army and boasts how he's certain of his victory thanks to such capable warriors.]

Ayaneṣhu Cha Sarveṣhu Yathā-Bhāgamavasthitāḥ

Bhīṣhmamevābhirakṣhantu Bhāvantaḥ Sarva Eva Hi II11II

Tasya Sañjanayan Harṣhaṁ Kuru-Vṛiddhaḥ Pitāmahaḥ

Siṁha-Nādaṁ Vinadyochchaiḥ Śhaṅkhaṁ Dadhmau Pratāpavān II12II

Tataḥ Śhaṅkhāśhcha Bheryaśhcha Paṇavānaka-Gomukhāḥ

Sahasaivābhyahanyanta Sa Śhabdastumulo 'Bhāvat II13II

Tataḥ Śhvetairhayairyukte Mahati Syandane Sthitau

Mādhavaḥ Pāṇḍavaśhchaiva Divyau Śhaṅkhau Pradadhmatuḥ II14II

Pāñchajanyaṁ Hṛiṣhīkeśho Devadattaṁ Dhanañjayaḥ

Pauṇḍraṁ Dadhmau Mahā-Śhaṅkhaṁ Bhīma-Karmā Vṛikodaraḥ II15II

Anantavijayaṁ Rājā Kuntī-Putro Yudhiṣhṭhiraḥ

Nakulaḥ Sahadevaśhcha Sughoṣha-Maṇipuṣhpakau II16II

Kāśhyaśhcha Parameṣhvāsaḥ Śhikhaṇḍī Cha Mahā-Rathaḥ

Dhṛiṣhṭadyumno Virāṭaśhcha Sātyakiśh Chāparājitaḥ II17II

Drupado Draupadeyāśhcha Sarvaśhaḥ Pṛithivī-Pate

Saubhadraśhcha Mahā-Bāhuḥ Śhaṅkhāndadhmuḥ Pṛithak Pṛithak II18II

Sa Ghoṣho Dhārtarāṣhṭrāṇāṁ Hṛidayāni Vyadārayat

Nabhaśhcha Pṛithivīṁ Chaiva Tumulo Vyanunādayan II19II

Atha Vyavasthitān Dṛiṣhṭvā Dhārtarāṣhṭrān Kapi-Dhwajaḥ

Pravṛitte Śhastra-Sampāte Dhanurudyamya Pāṇḍavaḥ II20II

Hṛiṣhīkeśhaṁ Tadā Vākyam Idam Āha Mahī-Pate

Arjuna Uvācha

Senayor Ubhayor Madhye Rathaṁ Sthāpaya Me 'Chyuta II21II

Yāvadetān Nirīkṣhe 'Haṁ Yoddhu-Kāmān Avasthitān

Kairmayā Saha Yoddhavyam Asmin Raṇa-Samudyame II22II

Yotsyamānān Avekṣhe 'Haṁ Ya Ete 'Tra Samāgatāḥ

Dhārtarāṣhṭrasya Durbuddher Yuddhe Priya-Chikīrṣhavaḥ II23II

(11) (Pray) all of you now stand at different entry points of the army and collectively defend Bheeshma from all sides.

[General Bheeshma was mighty, brave and unassailable. Yet Duryodhan requested that he be protected; because Bheeshma had vowed not to fight Shikhandi, a eunuch warrior on Pāndav side. Thus, there was a possibility that Bheeshma may be killed by him if he attacks]

(12) (at that moment) Veteran warrior Bheeshma, to Duryodhan's delight, gave a loud war cry like a lion (to mark the beginning of war) and blew his conch shell. (13) Following this, numerous conch shells, bheri (drums), Panav, Ānak and Gomukh (war instruments) began and the noise filled the atmosphere. (14) Later, Mādhav (Krishna) and Pāndav (Arjun) who were sitting in a big chariot with clear white horses blew their divine conch shells (to signal their readiness for the battle). (15) Hrishikesh (Shri Krishna) blew Pānchajanya (name of the conch shell), Arjun blew Devdatta, Bheem blew big Paundra; (16) Kunti's son Yudhisthir blew Anantvijay, Nakul and Sahadev blew Sughosh and Manipushpak, (17) whereas master archer Kāshirāj, Mahārathi Shikhandi and Dhrushtadyumna, Virat and impregnable Satyaki, (18) Drupad and (five) sons of Draupadi and Mahābāhu (magnificent) Saubhadra (Abhimanyu) and everyone, O king, blew their respective conch shells. (19) Such loud noise penetrating the sky and the earth, tore through the hearts of Kaurav (army).

(20) Later, after seeing Kaurav lined up in military formation for battle, just before the battle was about to begin, Arjun, the Pāndav whose chariot had Māruti (Hanumān) on its flag (21) O King Dhrutarāshtra, said to Shri Krishna – Arjun said – O Achyut, please take my chariot to the middle, in between the two armies (22) so that I lay my eyes on the people ready for battle and see those whom I've to fight in the battlefield and (23) let me see who all have assembled to help the cause of imprudent Duryodhan. Sanjay said –

Sañjaya Uvācha

Evam Ukto Hṛiṣhīkeśho Guḍākeśhena Bhārata

Senayor Ubhayor Madhye Sthāpayitvā Rathottamam II24II

Bhīṣhma-Droṇa-Pramukhataḥ Sarveṣhāṁ Cha Mahī-Kṣhitām

Uvācha Pārtha Paśhyaitān Samavetān Kurūn Iti II25II

Tatrāpaśhyat Sthitān Pārthaḥ Pitṝn Atha Pitāmahān

Āchāryān Mātulān Bhrātṝn Putrān Pautrān Sakhīṁs Tathā II26II

Śhvaśhurān Suhṛidaśh Chaiva Senayor Ubhayor Api

Tān Samīkṣhya Sa Kaunteyaḥ Sarvān Bandhūn Avasthitān II27II

Kṛipayā Parayāviṣhṭo Viṣhīdann Idam Abravīt

Arjuna Uvācha

Dṛiṣhṭvemaṁ Sva-Janaṁ Kṛiṣhṇa Yuyutsuṁ Samupasthitam II28II

Sīdanti Mama Gātrāṇi Mukhaṁ Cha Pariśhuṣhyati

Vepathuśh Cha Śharīre Me Roma-Harṣhaśh Cha Jāyate II29II

Gāṇḍīvaṁ Sraṁsate Hastāt Tvak Chaiva Paridahyate

Na Cha Śhaknomy Avasthātuṁ Bhramatīva Cha Me Manaḥ II30II

Nimittāni Cha Paśhyāmi Viparītāni Keśhava

Na Cha Śhreyo 'Nupaśhyāmi Hatvā Sva-Janam Āhave II31II

Na Kāṅkṣhe Vijayaṁ Kṛiṣhṇa Na Cha Rājyaṁ Sukhāni Cha

Kiṁ No Rājyena Govinda Kiṁ Bhogair Jīvitena Vā II32II

Yeṣhām Arthe Kāṅkṣhitaṁ No Rājyaṁ Bhogāḥ Sukhāni Cha

Ta Ime 'Vasthitā Yuddhe Prāṇāṁs Tyaktvā Dhanāni Cha II33II

Āchāryāḥ Pitaraḥ Putrās Tathaiva Cha Pitāmahāḥ

Mātulāḥ Śhvaśhurāḥ Pautrāḥ Śhyālāḥ Sambandhinas Tathā II34II

Etān Na Hantum Ichchhāmi Ghnato 'Pi Madhusūdana

Api Trailokya-Rājyasya Hetoḥ Kiṁ Nu Mahī-Kṛite II35II

(24) O Dhrutarāshtra, when Gudākesh (one who's defeated laziness, a name for Arjun) said this, Hrishikesh (master of the senses, a name of Shri Krishna) took the superior chariot (of Arjun) to the center of the battlefield; and (25) said in front of all kings, Bheeshma and Drona – "Arjun, look at the Kaurav assembled here."

(26) Then Arjun realized that everyone assembled there are (his) fathers, grandfathers, gurus, uncles, sons, grandsons and friends, (27) and fathers in law and dear ones. Seeing all his kith and kin having assembled there, Kunti's son Arjun, (28) with heavy heart and feeling immense compassion, started speaking. Arjun said – O Krishna, looking at my fellow countrymen being ready for war (29) my limbs go lifeless and mouth dries up, my body trembles and I get goosebumps; (30) Gāndeev (bow) slips and my whole body burns up; I can't stand and my mind goes delusional. (31) Also, O Keshav, (I see) every sign ominous, I don't see any good coming out of killing my own kind in war. (32) O Krishna, I don't want victory, kingdom or pleasures. O Govind, what good is the kingdom, enjoyment or even life itself for us? (33) Those, for whom we ought to yearn this kingdom, enjoyment and pleasure; are themselves ready for war without hope for life and wealth.

(34) Gurus, fathers, sons along with grandfathers, uncles, in-laws, grandsons and kin (35) are ready to kill (us) and still, O Madhusudan, I don't wish to kill them even for monarchy of entire universe; what is this earth then?

Nihatya Dhārtarāṣhṭrān Naḥ Kā Prītiḥ Syāj Janārdana

Pāpam Evāśhrayed Asmān Hatvaitān Ātatāyinaḥ II36II

Tasmān Nārhā Vayaṁ Hantuṁ Dhārtarāṣhṭrān Sa-Bāndhavān

Sva-Janaṁ Hi Kathaṁ Hatvā Sukhinaḥ Syāma Mādhava II37II

Yadyapyete Na Paśhyanti Lobhopahata-Chetasaḥ

Kula-Kṣhaya-Kṛitaṁ Doṣhaṁ Mitra-Drohe Cha Pātakam II38II

Kathaṁ Na Jñeyam Asmābhiḥ Pāpād Asmān Nivartitum

Kula-Kṣhaya-Kṛitaṁ Doṣhaṁ Prapaśhyadbhir Janārdana II39II

Kula-Kṣhaye Praṇaśhyanti Kula-Dharmāḥ Sanātanāḥ

Dharme Naṣhṭe Kulaṁ Kṛitsnam Adharmo 'Bhibhāvaty Uta II40II

Adharmābhibhavāt Kṛiṣhṇa Praduṣhyanti Kula-Striyaḥ

Strīṣhu Duṣhṭāsu Vārṣhṇeya Jāyate Varṇa-Saṅkaraḥ II41II

Saṅkaro Narakāyaiva Kula-Ghnānāṁ Kulasya Cha

Patanti Pitaro Hy Eṣhāṁ Lupta-Piṇḍodaka-Kriyāḥ II42II

Doṣhair Etaiḥ Kula-Ghnānāṁ Varṇa-Saṅkara-Kārakaiḥ

Utsādyante Jāti-Dharmāḥ Kula-Dharmāśh Cha Śhāśhvatāḥ II43II

Utsanna-Kula-Dharmāṇāṁ Manuṣhyāṇāṁ Janārdana

Narake 'Niyataṁ Vāso Bhāvatītyanuśhuśhruma II44II

Aho Bata Mahat Pāpaṁ Kartuṁ Vyavasitā Vayam

Yad Rājya-Sukha-Lobhena Hantuṁ Sva-Janam Udyatāḥ II45II

Yadi Mām Apratīkāram Aśhastraṁ Śhastra-Pāṇayaḥ

Dhārtarāṣhṭrā Raṇe Hanyus Tan Me Kṣhemataraṁ Bhavet II46II

(36) O Janārdan! What good is going to come to us by killing these Kaurav? Even though they're stubborn, we'd commit sin by killing them. (37) Hence, we must not kill Kaurav, our own family. As, O Madhav, how would we be happy by killing our own? (38) While those with greed have their prudence destroyed and don't see the sin of devastating their dynasty and betraying their own, (39) O Janārdan, how can we avoid the thought of distancing ourselves from this sin, when we clearly see the imminent blunder?

[We've discussed the essence of this predicament faced by Arjun and its relation with the subsequent explanation in Gitā, in the 1st and 14th chapter. We've also discussed in 12th Chapter how one should behave when they realize their mistake (even if the opponent doesn't). Once we understand that the explanation in all subsequent Adhyāyas is for clearing the doubts in Arjun's mind which are narrated in the 1st Adhyāya, there's no confusion about the definitive moral of Gitā. Arjun now explains what tragedies arise by annihilation of one's own kind.]

(40) Annihilation of dynasties destroys eternal Dharma, and once Dharma gets destroyed, entire population gets influenced by evil; (41) O Krishna, once evil takes over, the women of the dynasty get spoilt; and once women are spoilt, O Vārshneya, the class gets degraded. (42) Once the class gets degraded, it destroys the dynasty and takes (all) dynasties definitely to hell; as knowledge of posthumous rituals is lost, even the ancestors get tarnished. (43) This blunder that destroys dynasties and degrades class also extinguishes traditional and dynastic customs; (44) and we've heard that those whose dynastic customs have been lost are definitely destined for hell.

(45) Behold! We (truly) prepared to commit a grave sin of killing our own, because of our greed for kingdom. Alas! (46) If I rather drop my arms and stop retaliating, Kaurav would kill me in the battlefield and it would be good for me. Sanjay said –

Sañjaya Uvācha

Evam Uktvārjunaḥ Saṅkhye Rathopastha Upāviśhat

Visṛijya Sa-Śharaṁ Chāpaṁ Śhoka-Saṁvigna-Mānasaḥ II47II

(47) After speaking this way on the battlefield, gloomy Arjun threw away the bow & arrow and sat down on his seat in his chariot!

[As it was customary to stand in chariots during the battle, Arjun sitting down aptly conveys his state of mind. Erstwhile chariot used to be with two wheels and four horses while the warrior and charioteer used to sit next to each other in the front section. Every chariot had a flag on top to denote who's riding in it. It's famous that Hanumān himself sat on the flag of Arjun's chariot.]

This concludes the first Adhyāya **Arjunvishādyog** from the dialogue between Shri Krishna and Arjun on Yog Shāstra (Karmayog Shāstra) within Brahmavidyā (knowledge of Brahman) in the Upanishad sung (narrated) by Shri Bhagwān (Shri Krishna).

[Gitā not only covers Brahma Vidyā but also Karmayog along with that. This is the meaning of this verse that appears at the end of every Adhyāya along with the name of the concluded Adhyāya. We've discussed this in 1st, 3rd and 11th chapters. While this verse is not in Mahābhārat, it must've been from before the commentary of ascetic critiques. It becomes clear from this that Gitā advocates Karmayog and not Sanyās.]

Dwiteeyodhyāyah (Second Adhyāya)

Sañjaya Uvācha

Taṁ Tathā Kṛipayāviṣhṭamaśhru Pūrṇākulekṣhaṇam

Viṣhīdantamidaṁ Vākyam Uvācha Madhusūdanaḥ II 1 II

Śhrī Bhagavān Uvācha

Kutastvā Kaśhmalamidaṁ Viṣhame Samupasthitam

Anārya-Juṣhṭamaswargyam Akīrti-Karam Arjuna II 2 II

Klaibyaṁ Mā Sma Gamaḥ Pārtha Naitat Tvayyupapadyate

Kṣhudraṁ Hṛidaya-Daurbalyaṁ Tyaktvottiṣhṭha Parantapa II 3 II

Arjuna Uvācha

Kathaṁ Bhīṣhmam Ahaṁ Sankhye Droṇaṁ Cha Madhusūdana

Iṣhubhiḥ Pratiyotsyāmi Pūjārhāvari-Sūdana II 4 II

Gurūnahatvā Hi Mahānubhāvān Śhreyo Bhoktuṁ Bhaikṣhyamapīha Loke

Hatvārtha-Kāmāṁstu Gurūnihaiva Bhuñjīya Bhogān Rudhira-Pradigdhān II 5 II

Dwiteeyodhyāyah (Second Adhyāya)

[Gitā uses various names to denote Arjun as well as Shri Krishna. We've used those names in the translation of the 1st Adhyāya. However, for simplicity and to focus more attention to the content, we've used the standard names viz. Shri Krishna/Shri Bhagwan and Arjun from now on despite different names used in Sanskrit verses. We request readers to note this while reading the translation hereon.]

Sanjay said – (1) To such compassionate, teary eyed and miserable Arjun, Krishna started narrating. Shri Bhagwān said – (2) O Arjun! Where did you get such regressive, defaming and dark thoughts from, at such a perilous time, which no great man has ever had? (3) O Arjun, don't be so impotent! It doesn't suit you. You are the scourge of enemies! Quit this pathetic weakness of mind and stand up (for war)!

Arjun said – (4) O Krishna! How do I fight such revered men as Bheeshma and Drona in the battle, with arrows? (5) Rather than killing these gurus, it's better to beg for alms in this world. While they (elders like Drona, Shalya etc. in Kaurav army) may be bound by wealth, I'd be tainted with their blood if I kill these gurus.

[By gurus, one should infer elderly people in this context; as only Drona was a guru to Arjun. When Yudhisthir went to touch the feet and take blessings of Bheeshma, Drona and Shalya before the war, all of them blessed him and explained why they're fighting alongside Duryodhan in these words – "Man is a slave of wealth. Wealth is enslaved by none. Hence, O Yudhisthir, Kaurav have bound us with wealth." The words used by Arjun in 5th verse have a reference to this statement.]

Na Chaitadvidmaḥ Kataranno Garīyo Yadvā Jayema Yadi Vā No Jayeyuḥ

Yāneva Hatvā Na Jijīviṣhāmas Te 'Vasthitāḥ Pramukhe Dhārtarāṣhṭrāḥ II 6 II

Kārpaṇya-Doṣhopahata-Svabhāvaḥ Pṛichchhāmi Tvāṁ Dharma-Sammūḍha-Chetāḥ

Yach-Chhreyaḥ Syānniśhchitaṁ Brūhi Tanme Śhiṣhyaste 'Haṁ Śhādhi Māṁ Tvāṁ Prapannam II 7 II

Na Hi Prapaśhyāmi Mamāpanudyād Yach-Chhokam Uchchhoṣhaṇam-Indriyāṇām

Avāpya Bhūmāv-Asapatnamṛiddhaṁ Rājyaṁ Surāṇāmapi Chādhipatyam II 8 II

Sañjaya Uvācha

Evam-Uktvā Hṛiṣhīkeśhaṁ Guḍākeśhaḥ Parantapa

Na Yotsya Iti Govindam Uktvā Tūṣhṇīṁ Babhūva Ha II 9 II

(6) We can't even make out whether we should win or be won. We're facing those Kaurav (in the battle) whom we don't wish to kill, (even) to survive!

[Moral of this verse is to point out how 'majority's happiness' can't be used as a yardstick to decide which action is right or wrong. Please refer to chapter 4 for further discussion on it.]

(7) Poverty destroyed my innate nature and made me unsure of what my Dharma or duty is, which is why I'm asking you. Please tell me definitively the right thing to do. I, your disciple, have surrendered to you. Pray guide me; (8) as I don't see any solution to alleviate my misery that sucks life out of my senses, even if I am granted wealth, unopposed kingdom or even monarchy of gods (heaven)! Sanjay said – (9) This way, Arjun spoke to Shri Krishna and stood still after saying to Shri Krishna, "I shall not fight"!

Tam-Uvācha Hṛiṣhīkeśhaḥ Prahasanniva Bhārata

Senayorubhayor-Madhye Viṣhīdantam-Idaṁ Vachaḥ II 10 II

Śhrī Bhagavān Uvācha

Aśhochyān-Anvaśhochas-Tvaṁ Prajñā-Vādānśh Cha Bhāṣhase

Gatāsūn-Agatāsūnśh-Cha Nānuśhochanti Paṇḍitāḥ II 11 II

Na Tvevāhaṁ Jātu Nāsaṁ Na Tvaṁ Neme Janādhipāḥ

Na Chaiva Na Bhaviṣhyāmaḥ Sarve Vayamataḥ Param II 12 II

(10) Then, O Dhrutarāshtra, Shri Krishna said with a smile to Arjun who was sitting sadly in between the two armies.

[On the one hand there's warrior duty while on the other there's risk of committing sin of killing gurus and one's own family. To Arjun who was facing such a predicament and was willing to quit the battlefield and beg for alms, Shri Krishna now provides an advice. Arjun was thinking that a deed like the bloody war wouldn't yield him any good. Hence, Shri Krishna now starts with the examples of men who have purified their mind and attained knowledge of Parabrahma. Bhagwān tells Arjun that if one observes history of the world, there are two paths adopted by enlightened people. While some, like Shuka, quit all familial life and beg for alms happily; others like Janak continue to strive for welfare of the universe even after attaining knowledge. First path is called Sānkhya while the second is called Yog or Karmayog. As Arjun had tilted towards Sānkhya path now, Krishna points out the mistake in this path first and then from 39th verse onwards begins explanation of Karmayog. Whichever path one takes (Sānkhya or Karmayog), knowledge remains the same. If even according to Sānkhya, Ātmā (soul) is indestructible and eternal, the argument of Arjun about "How do I kill them?" is proved pointless. This is what Shri Krishna intends to point out to Arjun a bit sarcastically.]

Shri Bhagwān said – (11) You're grieving about those you shouldn't grieve, and you speak of knowledge! Knowledgeable people don't grieve about who dies and who survives.

(12) See it this way – Not only is it that I never existed, it's not that you or these kings never existed, and it's not that we all wouldn't exist in future either.

[Rāmānujabhāshya claims that by treating Shri Bhagwān's soul as separate whereas Arjun and other kings' souls separately, Brahman and Ātman are proven to have separate existence. However, this dualistic view is wrong and purely communalistic. The only point being made here is that soul is eternal.]

Dehino 'Smin Yathā Dehe Kaumāraṁ Yauvanaṁ Jarā

Tathā Dehāntara-Prāptir Dhīras Tatra Na Muhyati II 13 II

Mātrā-Sparśhās Tu Kaunteya Śhītoṣhṇa-Sukha-Duḥkha-Dāḥ

Āgamāpāyino 'Nityās Tans-Titikṣhasva Bhārata II 14 II

Yaṁ Hi Na Vyathayantyete Puruṣhaṁ Puruṣharṣhabha

Sama-Duḥkha-Sukhaṁ Dhīraṁ So 'Mṛitatvāya Kalpate II 15 II

(13) Just as wearer of this body attains childhood, youth and old age in this body, it (subsequently) also attains another body. (Hence), knowledgeable people don't get deluded by this.

[Shri Krishna tells Arjun the philosophy of death and killing as he's deluded/scared about how he could kill someone. A person is not just their body but a combination of body and soul. Of the two, soul is eternal so dying or killing doesn't apply to it. Body is utterly perishable so it's bound to perish today or sometime later. Moreover, even if one body dies, another body is attached to the soul. Thus, either way, there's no point in grieving about human life. Even if one understands this, there's pain in death. Bhagwān now explains the nature of bodily happiness and sorrow, before explaining why grieving about it is not advisable.]

(14) O Arjun! The union of senses with its objects in the outside world, that leads to heat and cold or happiness and sorrow, keeps coming and going so it's impermanent. O Arjun, you bear with it (without getting sad).

(15) O Arjun! The knowledgeable person who considers happiness and sorrow to be equal, becomes worthy of attaining immortality or state of eternal Brahman.

[Someone who hasn't realized that only Brahman is true while the universe is Mithya or Māyā (appearance), gets affected by the dualistic nature of the universe. They consider the dualistic experiences as true and feel happy or sad, heat or cold etc. However, one who understands that all these manifestations are of Prakruti whereas the soul is inert and detached, considers both sides of this duality equal and doesn't get affected by them. Now Shri Krishna explains the same meaning through Adhyātmik method.]

Nāsato Vidyate Bhāvo Nābhāvo Vidyate Sataḥ

Ubhayorapi Dṛiṣhṭo 'Nta Stvanayos Tattva-Darśhibhiḥ II 16 II

Avināśhi Tu Tadviddhi Yena Sarvam Idaṁ Tatam

Vināśham Avyayasyāsya Na Kaśhchit Kartum Arhati II 17 II

Antavanta Ime Dehā Nityasyoktāḥ Śharīriṇaḥ

Anāśhino 'Prameyasya Tasmād Yudhyasva Bhārata II 18 II

Ya Enaṁ Vetti Hantāraṁ Yaśh Chainaṁ Manyate Hatam

Ubhau Tau Na Vijānīto Nāyaṁ Hanti Na Hanyate II 19 II

Na Jāyate Mriyate Vā Kadāchin Nāyaṁ Bhūtvā Bhavitā Vā Na Bhūyaḥ

Ajo Nityaḥ Śhāśhvato 'Yaṁ Purāṇo Na Hanyate Hanyamāne Śharīre II 20 II

Vedāvināśhinaṁ Nityaṁ Ya Enam Ajam Avyayam

Kathaṁ Sa Puruṣhaḥ Pārtha Kaṁ Ghātayati Hanti Kam II 21 II

Vāsānsi Jīrṇāni Yathā Vihāya Navāni Gṛihṇāti Naro 'Parāṇi

Tathā Śharīrāṇi Vihāya Jīrṇānya Nyāni Sanyāti Navāni Dehī II 22 II

Nainaṁ Chhindanti Śhastrāṇi Nainaṁ Dahati Pāvakaḥ

Na Chainaṁ Kledayantyāpo Na Śhoṣhayati Mārutaḥ II 23 II

Achchhedyo 'Yam Adāhyo 'Yam Akledyo 'Śhoṣhya Eva Cha

Nityaḥ Sarva-Gataḥ Sthāṇur Achalo 'Yaṁ Sanātanaḥ II 24 II

(16) That which is not (Asat) doesn't manifest and that which is (Sat) doesn't disappear; this is how philosophers have concluded, or decided by looking at their (Sat and Asat) ultimate form.

[Sat means Brahman and Asat means Perceptible universe made up of Nāmroope (name-forms) in this verse. One must note that while the statement 'that which is, doesn't disappear' may seem like the principle of causation; it's slightly different. Theory of causality says that only a seed becomes a tree. However, this verse attempts to state both phenomenon – One, the existence of that which is (Sat) and two, absence of that which is not (Asat) – are independently eternal. Once we understand the separate nature of both, we infer that Sat doesn't get destroyed to form Asat. However, this inference is different from the principle of causation which says that characteristics of the effect must be pre-existent in some form within the cause.]

(17) Remember that what (primordial Ātman or Brahman) occupies this (universe) is indestructible. No one is capable of destroying this imperishable principle.

(18) This body, endowed to the eternal, indestructible and unthinkable master (soul), is declared perishable or impermanent. Therefore, O Arjun, you go to war! (19) One who considers it (soul) to be the killer as well as one who considers that it can be killed are both not truly knowledgeable. (Since) it (soul) neither kills nor does it get killed. (20) It (soul) is neither born nor does it die; it is not that having existed once it would not exist again; it's unborn, permanent, eternal and ancient. Even if body is killed, it doesn't die. (21) O Pārth, how would a man, who recognizes this soul to be indestructible, permanent, primordial and eternal, kill someone or get someone killed? (22) Just as a person gives up old clothes and wears new ones; soul gives up old bodies and unites with new ones. (23) Weapons don't break it (soul), fire doesn't burn it, water doesn't wet it and neither does wind dry it.

(24) This (soul) that can't be broken, burned, wet or dried is permanent, omnipresent, stable, firm and timeless.

Avyakto 'Yam Achintyo 'Yam Avikāryo 'Yam Uchyate

Tasmādevaṁ Viditvainaṁ Nānuśhochitum Arhas II 25 II

Atha Chainaṁ Nitya-Jātaṁ Nityaṁ Vā Manyase Mṛitam

Tathāpi Tvaṁ Mahā-Bāho Naivaṁ Śhochitum Arhasi II 26 II

Jātasya Hi Dhruvo Mṛityur Dhruvaṁ Janma Mṛitasya Cha

Tasmād Aparihārye 'Rthe Na Tvaṁ Śhochitum Arhasi II 27 II

Avyaktādīni Bhūtāni Vyakta-Madhyāni Bhārata

Avyakta-Nidhanānyeva Tatra Kā Paridevanā II 28 II

(25) This soul is also called Avyakta (imperceptible to senses), Achintya (unfathomable) and Avikārya (something that can't be tainted with anything). Hence, it's important that you understand it (soul) and not grieve about it.

[This description is borrowed from Upanishads and describes the Nirguna (without attributes) soul, as Avikārya and Achintya are not the adjectives one can use for Saguna (with attributes). This explains the final conclusion of Vedānta about the soul. Someone may now object saying that they don't consider soul permanent and try to deny this explanation. Hence, Bhagwān now mentions this objection and answers it –]

(26) Or even if you consider this (soul) to take birth and death (along with body and is impermanent), still O Arjun! It's not prudent that you grieve about it. (27) As, whatever takes birth is destined to die and whatever dies is destined to take birth again; hence, it's not appropriate (even as per your logic) to grieve about (this) unavoidable phenomenon.

[The explanation given in above two verses isn't part of Gitā's principles. It's merely an answer to a possible doubt raised. The point is only to convince Arjun that it's unnecessary to grieve, whether he considers soul permanent or impermanent. Explained further is another explanation as per Sānkhya philosophy.]

(28) If all living beings are Avyakta (unmanifest) at the start, Vyakta (manifest) in the middle and Avyakta again after death, then O Arjun, where's the (question of) grief?

[Avyakta itself denotes that it is 'imperceptible to senses'. The argument is based on the Sānkhya idea that an unmanifest manifests itself sequentially to become the entire universe while everything turns back into unmanifest at the time of pralay (dissolution). We've discussed this in detail in 7th and 8th chapters. If the manifest state is perishable for any object, there's no point in grieving about it. Thus, by both philosophies, Vedānta and Sānkhya, it is imprudent to grieve. Why is it that people still grieve about death? Ignorance about the soul is the only reason, because –]

Āśhcharya-Vat Paśhyati Kaśhchid Enan Āśhcharya-Vad Vadati Tathaiva Chānyaḥ

Āśhcharya-Vach Chainam Anyaḥ Śhṛiṇoti Śhrutvāpyenaṁ Veda Na Chaiva Kaśhchit II 29 II

Dehī Nityam Avadhyo 'Yaṁ Dehe Sarvasya Bhārata

Tasmāt Sarvāṇi Bhūtāni Na Tvaṁ Śhochitum Arhasi II 30 II

Swa-Dharmam Api Chāvekṣhya Na Vikampitum Arhasi

Dharmyāddhi Yuddhāch Chhreyo 'Nyat Kṣhatriyasya Na Vidyate II 31 II

(29) Someone perceives it as if it's mysterious, someone else describes it as mysterious while yet someone else listens to it as if it's mysterious. However, despite (seeing, saying or) hearing it, (among them) no one knows it (essentially).

[Although most people consider the soul to be mystical and debate about it voluminously, very few know its true nature. Hence, most people grieve about death. However, Shri Krishna is asking Arjun to gain comprehensive knowledge of the soul and knowingly quit grieving. The description is similar to the one in Kathopanishad.]

(30) Residing in every body, this master of the body (soul) is eternally immortal. Hence, O Arjun, it's unadvisable for you to grieve about any living being.

[It's been thus proven as per Sānkhya and Vedānta philosophy that soul is immortal and body is perishable. Thus, there's no point in grieving about anyone killing or being killed. However, from this if one tries to infer that killing someone isn't a sin, they'd be sorely mistaken. The context in which it's being said is extremely important. The explanation given is only to reduce the fear of killing or getting killed in battle. However, this doesn't answer the question of whether one should engage in a battle to kill someone. While soul is immortal and body is perishable, body is still the only tool to achieve welfare of the soul and hence, committing suicide or killing anyone without substantial cause is still considered a sin. While grieving anyone's death is not advisable, it needs to be reasoned why someone should kill someone. This is called Dharmādharmavivek (decision between what's right and what's wrong) and it's the principal subject of Gitā. Therefore, Bhagwān now tries to explain Arjun by reminding his duties as per his profession, based on Sānkhya philosophy.]

(31) Moreover, even if we consider duty, you should not falter (at this moment); because there's nothing more prudent for a warrior than a righteous war.

Yadṛichchhayā Chopapannaṁ Swarga-Dvāram Apāvṛitam

Sukhinaḥ Kṣhatriyāḥ Pārtha Labhante Yuddham Īdṛiśham II 32 II

Atha Chet Tvam Imaṁ Dharmyaṁ Saṅgrāmaṁ Na Kariṣhyasi

Tataḥ Sva-Dharmaṁ Kīrtiṁ Cha Hitvā Pāpam Avāpsyasi II 33 II

Akīrtiṁ Chāpi Bhūtāni Kathayiṣhyanti Te 'Vyayām

Sambhāvitasya Chākīrtir Maraṇād Atirichyate II 34 II

Bhayād Raṇād Uparataṁ Mansyante Tvāṁ Mahā-Rathāḥ

Yeṣhāṁ Cha Tvaṁ Bahu-Mato Bhūtvā Yāsyasi Lāghavam II 35 II

Avāchya-Vādānśh Cha Bahūn Vadiṣhyanti Tavāhitāḥ

Nindantastava Sāmarthyaṁ Tato Duḥkhataraṁ Nu Kim II 36 II

Hato Vā Prāpsyasi Swargaṁ Jitvā Vā Bhokṣhyase Mahīm

Tasmād Uttiṣhṭha Kaunteya Yuddhāya Kṛita-Niśhchayaḥ II 37 II

Sukha-Duḥkhe Same Kṛitvā Lābhālābhau Jayājayau

Tato Yuddhāya Yujyasva Naivaṁ Pāpam Avāpsyasi II 38 II

(32) And this war, which is like an easily opened door to heaven, O Arjun, is only accessible to fortunate warriors. (33) Therefore, if you don't engage in this war which is your duty; you'd lose out on responsibility and fame, and commit a sin; (34) not only that, (all) people would forever narrate tales of your dishonor. And dishonor is worse than death for a man.

(35) (All) Mahārathi would feel that you've returned from the war scared, and those who consider you worthy would start devaluing you. (36) Besides, they'd condemn your strength and your enemies would speak unspeakable things (about you). What could be worse!

(37) If you die, you'd go to heaven, and if you win then you'd enjoy ruling the earth! Therefore O Arjun! Make up your mind for war and get up!

[After explaining about pointlessness of grief and duty of going to war, Bhagwān now explains whether or not one would be tainted with sin due to the killing involved in the war. Practically speaking, this rationale belongs to Karmayog and its narration virtually begins here.]

(38) Consider happiness and sorrow, profit and loss, victory and defeat as equal and begin the battle. Once you do this, you'd not be tainted with any sin.

[There are two paths of leading life – Sānkhya and Yog. Of these, the Sānkhya path, considering which Arjun wanted to quit war and go begging for alms, does explain why it's not advisable to grieve about the soul or the body. However, as the path is essentially ascetic, it doesn't explain why Arjun shouldn't quit war and adopt renunciation immediately. It also doesn't explain why Arjun must perform his duties. This would leave Arjun's question unanswered comprehensively. Hence Bhagwān now says –]

Eşhā Te 'Bhihitā Sānkhye Buddhir Yoge Tvimāṁ Śhṛiṇu

Buddhyā Yukto Yayā Pārtha Karma-Bandhaṁ Prahāsyasi II 39 II

Nehābhikrama-Nāśho 'Sti Pratyavāyo Na Vidyate

Svalpam Apyasya Dharmasya Trāyate Mahato Bhayāt II 40 II

(39) I explained to you the Buddhi (here means knowledge or explanation) as per Sānkhya (Sanyās). Now O Arjun, let me explain to you that Buddhi (knowledge), the one in (Karma) Yog, which would eliminate the bondage of (your) actions.

[It's critical to understand the meaning of this verse. By Sānkhya, not only Kāpilsānkhya philosophy is intended. Similarly, by Yog, Pātanjalyog isn't intended. Sānkhya means Sanyās (asceticism) and Yog means Karmayog. This is clear once we read Gitā 3.3 later. People from Sānkhya philosophy insist on quitting karma at least at some stage in life and hence their philosophy can't explain why Arjun should go to war. Hence knowledge of Karmayog (briefly denoted as Yog), which insists that one must never renounce and keep performing one's duties with detachment till you're alive, is what is initiated from here till the last Adhyāya with different reasons and to answer different doubts so as to justify its aptitude. Once we understand this logic used by Bhagwān Shri Krishna here, there's not an ounce of doubt that Karmayog is advocated in Gitā. He begins by narrating core principles of Karmayog now –]

(40) Here (in this path of Karmayog) the Karma that begins (once) doesn't get destroyed and doesn't get interrupted (later). Even a little (conduct) of this Dharma (path) protects from grave fear.

[The importance of this principle is explained in detail in chapter 10. Even if you don't attain Moksha in this birth while practicing Karmayog, the Karma doesn't go waste but gets utilized in the next birth and every birth keeps adding up and ultimately leads you to Moksha in some birth. This is the meaning of this verse. Now Bhagwān tells the second important principle –]

Vyavasāyātmikā Buddhir Ekeha Kuru-Nandana

Bahu-Śhākhā Hyanantāśh Cha Buddhayo 'Vyavasāyinām II 41 II

Yāmimāṁ Puṣhpitāṁ Vāchaṁ Pravadanty-Avipaśhchitaḥ

Veda-Vāda-Ratāḥ Pārtha Nānyad Astīti Vādinaḥ II 42 II

Kāmātmānaḥ Swarga-Parā Janma-Karma-Phala-Pradām

Kriyā-Viśheṣha-Bahulāṁ Bhogaiśhwarya-Gatiṁ Prati II 43 II

Bhogaiświarya-Prasaktānāṁ Tayāpahṛita-Chetasām

Vyavasāyātmikā Buddhiḥ Samādhau Na Vidhīyate II 44 II

Trai-Guṇya-Viṣhayā Vedā Nistrai-Guṇyo Bhavārjuna

Nirdvandvo Nitya-Sattva-Stho Niryoga-Kṣhema Ātmavān II 45 II

(41) O Arjun, professional intellect (organ that decides right and wrong) must be focused in this path. As, whoever doesn't achieve (such) resolve of intellect, their intellect (desires) is diverse and endless.

[The word Buddhi has many meanings in Sanskrit. In the 39th verse, it's used as 'knowledge'. Later in 41st verse, it is used as desire, mindset, wish or intent. However, in the first line, it assumes the meaning 'organ that decides right and wrong', due to the prefix 'professional'. One must understand the different meanings used in different contexts in order to fully fathom the true explanation of Karmayog.]

(42) O Arjun! The fools who are mystified by (ritualistic) Vedic verses (from Falashruti) and who consider it as the only truth, proclaim with pride that – (43) "Different (ritualistic) Karma leads to (re) birth and yields pleasure and wealth (in every birth)," These desirous people running after heaven, (44) pay attention only to the above statement and hence immerse themselves in pleasure and wealth, thus their professional intellect never gets stabilized into Samādhi (focused on one thing).

(45) O Arjun! (Ritualistic) Vedas are (thus) filled with topics about the three Gunas (attributes) and hence you make yourself detached from these Gunas, forever stable in solemn thoughts, free from the dualities of happiness and sorrow, disconnected from the selfish thoughts of gains and immerse yourself in Ātman (soul).

[The world is made up of three Gunas – Sattva, Raja and Tama and hence worldly cravings are indicated by three Gunas. As these thoughts are full of dualistic contradictions, Arjun is advised to divert his attention from these ritualistic desirous Karma and focus it on Parabrahma to attain Moksha. One may raise a doubt as to how would the universe run (if everyone starts paying attention to Parabrahma instead of worldly possessions). This question is answered in detail in 9th Adhyāya. Here, the only message conveyed is that Arjun must quit the desirous actions, detach himself from the duality of happiness and sorrow, and quit the desire and attachment associated with actions. One must note that quitting actions themselves is not suggested in Karmayog but only the attachment. This is why Bhagwān has later insisted on performing all these actions (ritualistic and others) later in

Yāvān Artha Udapāne Sarvataḥ Samplutodake

Tāvānsarveṣhu Vedeṣhu Brāhmaṇasya Vijānataḥ II 46 II

Karmaṇy-Evādhikāras Te Mā Phaleṣhu Kadāchana

Mā Karma-Phala-Hetur Bhūr Mā Te Saṅgo 'Stvakarmaṇi II 47 II

Yoga-Sthaḥ Kuru Karmāṇi Saṅgaṁ Tyaktvā Dhanañjaya

Siddhy-Asiddhyoḥ Samo Bhūtvā Samatvaṁ Yoga Uchyate II 48 II

Dūreṇa Hy-Avaraṁ Karma Buddhi-Yogād Dhanañjaya

Buddhau Śharaṇam Anvichchha Kṛipaṇāḥ Phala-Hetavaḥ II 49 II

Buddhi-Yukto Jahātīha Ubhe Sukṛita-Duṣhkṛite

Tasmād Yogāya Yujyasva Yogaḥ Karmasu Kauśhalam II 50 II

18th Adhyāya. This makes it clear that the message is only pertaining to intention and not the actual action.]

(46) Just as useful a well is when it's flooded everywhere (obviously of no use), as much are (ritualistic) Vedas to a knowledgeable Brāhman (meaning he doesn't need desirous Vedic rituals).

(47) You have the right only to perform Karma; fruit (whether you get it or not) is never under your purview (within your rights); (hence) don't be someone who performs karma by keeping an intention of the fruit (of your karma); and neither should you insist on abstaining from karma.

[As the four lines of this verse are complementary to each other, this verse briefly narrates the entire meaning of Karmayog. In fact, we can call this verse one of the most fundamental tenets of Karmayog. While it states initially that performing Karma is one's right, second line immediately clarifies that if one starts thinking that they have equal rights of getting the intended outcome, it is not so. Third line follows up with the principle that one must not become a doer keeping the desire of fruits in their mind. However, fourth line immediately clarifies that, if one assumes that quitting desire of fruits inevitably means quitting the fruits, then they're sorely mistaken. One is asked to not quit Karma. In essence, doing Karma doesn't mean keeping the desire whereas quitting desire doesn't mean quitting Karma.]

(48) O Arjun! While quitting attachment and being equanimous about achievement or non-achievement of the goal, be Yogastha (established in Yog) and perform Karma. Equanimity (of mind about success or failure) is called (Karma) Yog. (49) Because, compared to the Yog of Buddhi (equanimous mind), Karma is very insignificant. (Hence,) surrender to Buddhi (mind which is equanimous). Those who perform Karma with eyes on the fruit are of the lower order. (50) Whoever is endowed with (equanimous) Buddhi, is detached from good or bad effects of karma; therefore, resort to Yog. The skill of performing Karma (being detached to its effects) is called (Karma) Yog.

Karma-Jaṁ Buddhi-Yuktā Hi Phalaṁ Tyaktvā Manīṣhiṇaḥ

Janma-Bandha-Vinirmuktāḥ Padaṁ Gachchhanty-Anāmayam II 51 II

Yadā Te Moha-Kalilaṁ Buddhir Vyatitariṣhyati

Tadā Gantāsi Nirvedaṁ Śhrotavyasya Śhrutasya Cha II 52 II

Śhruti-Vipratipannā Te Yadā Sthāsyati Niśhchalā

Samādhāv-Achalā Buddhis Tadā Yogam Avāpsyasi II 53 II

Arjuna Uvācha

Sthita-Prajñasya Kā Bhāṣhā Samādhi-Sthasya Keśhava

Sthita-Dhīḥ Kiṁ Prabhāṣheta Kim Āsīta Vrajeta Kim II 54 II

Śhrī Bhagavān Uvācha

Prajahāti Yadā Kāmān Sarvān Pārtha Mano-Gatān

Ātmany-Evātmanā Tuṣhṭaḥ Sthita-Prajñas Tadochyate II 55 II

Duḥkheṣhv-Anudvigna-Manāḥ Sukheṣhu Vigata-Spṛihaḥ

Vīta-Rāga-Bhaya-Krodhaḥ Sthita-Dhīr Munir Uchyate II 56 II

Yaḥ Sarvatrānabhisnehas Tat Tat Prāpya Śhubhāśhubham

Nābhinandati Na Dveṣhṭi Tasya Prajñā Pratiṣhṭhitā II 57 II

(51) Once a knowledgeable person is endowed with (equanimous) Buddhi, they're free of the bondage of birth by giving up the fruits of Karma, and attain the state beyond all sorrow. (52) When your Buddhi (mind) overcomes the murky envelope of delusion, you'd be indifferent about what's been heard and what's yet to be heard.

[It means that you'd not feel like listening to anything more, as you'd already have attained whatever knowledge is supposed to be accomplished by listening to these things. This is predominantly pertaining to the ritualistic actions in Vedas described earlier, which shall be cleared in following verses.]

(53) When your Buddhi (mind) baffled by (different) statements from the Vedas becomes stable and steadfast in Samādhi (consciousness), you'd attain (the equanimous) Yog then.

[In summary – Doing each karma for some particular achievement, as told in Falashruti of Vedas, confuses your Buddhi (mind) instead of making it steady. Therefore, instead of listening to these varied discourses, stabilize your mind into Samādhi; so that you attain equanimous Karmayog. You'd then need no more advice and would also be free of any sins of the actions. Such a person whose mind has become equanimous is called a Sthitapradnya (someone firm in wisdom or someone with stoic calm). Arjun now asks how the behavior of such a person is –]

Arjun said – (54) O Krishna, who should be called a Sthitapradnya immersed in consciousness? How does this Sthitapradnya speak, sit and walk? (Pray tell me).

Shri Bhagwān said – (55) O Arjun! One who quits all desires in mind and stays happy within themselves, is called a Sthitapradnya. (56) One who's not sad during suffering, who doesn't crave for pleasure and who's free of attachment, fear and anger is called a Sthitapradnya sage. (57) One who's detached from everything and is indifferent about good fortune or bad; is (said to be) with steady intellect.

Yadā Sanharate Chāyaṁ Kūrmo 'Ṅgānīva Sarvaśhaḥ

Indriyāṇīndriyārthebhyas Tasya Prajñā Pratiṣhṭhitā II 58 II

Viṣhayā Vinivartante Nirāhārasya Dehinaḥ

Rasa-Varjaṁ Raso 'Pyasya Paraṁ Dṛiṣhṭvā Nivartate II 59 II

Yatato Hyapi Kaunteya Puruṣhasya Vipaśhchitaḥ

Indriyāṇi Pramāthīni Haranti Prasabhaṁ Manaḥ II 60 II

Tāni Sarvāṇi Sanyamya Yukta Āsīta Mat-Paraḥ

Vaśhe Hi Yasyendriyāṇi Tasya Prajñā Pratiṣhṭhitā II 61 II

Dhyāyato Viṣhayān Puṁsaḥ Saṅgas Teṣhūpajāyate

Saṅgāt Sañjāyate Kāmaḥ Kāmāt Krodho 'Bhijāyate II 62 II

Krodhād Bhavati Sammohaḥ Sammohāt Smṛiti-Vibhramaḥ

Smṛiti-Bhranśhād Buddhi-Nāśho Buddhi-Nāśhāt Praṇaśhyati II 63 II

Rāga-Dveṣha-Viyuktais Tu Viṣhayān Indriyaiśh Charan

Ātma-Vaśhyair-Vidheyātmā Prasādam Adhigachchhati II 64 II

Prasāde Sarva-Duḥkhānāṁ Hānir Asyopajāyate

Prasanna-Chetaso Hyāśhu Buddhiḥ Paryavatiṣhṭhate II 65 II

(58) One who restrains their senses from the (sensory) pleasures, just as a tortoise restrains its limbs in its shell, is said to be firm in wisdom. (59) Those abstaining from eating may be free from Vishay (the objects of pleasure), yet their taste for the object persists. However, once someone experiences Parabrahma (Absolute) they're free of (objects and) their taste as well. (60)

As these mighty senses forcibly pull the mind away, even of a scholar who merely takes efforts (trying to douse their senses); (61) (therefore) one must restrain their senses into moderation, immerse themselves (in Yog) and become one with me. Whoever masters their senses this way, is said to be firm in wisdom.

[The essence of this verse is that someone who's in pursuit of true knowledge must maintain moderate diet and focus on attaining Brahmadnyān (knowledge of Brahman). Once someone gains this knowledge, their mind becomes truly detached. Severe physical strains (on senses) are superficial and not truly effective.]

(62) A person who thinks about the objects of pleasure develops an attachment to these objects. This attachment leads to desire and desire leads to anger (when there's hindrance to satisfying these desires).

(63) Anger leads to error of judgment which further leads to delusions of memory. Delusion of memory leads to destruction of intellect and when intellect is destroyed, the person is ruined. (64) However, one who has a control over their mind, is blissful and in control of their senses which become free of attachment and hatred; despite being among objects of pleasure. (65) As their mind is blissful, all sorrows end; because for someone whose mind is blissful, their Buddhi (mind) immediately becomes firm in wisdom.

[The above two verses describe how a Sthitapradnya only quits the attachment in Karma without actually quitting Karma. This is the fundamental difference between this Sthitapradnya and a Sanyāsi. Other aspects like restraint of senses, apathy and tranquility are common to both. Now by describing someone who's not blissful, the state of a Sthitapradnya is emphasized –]

Nāsti Buddhir-Ayuktasya Na Chāyuktasya Bhāvanā

Na Chābhāvayataḥ Śhāntir Aśhāntasya Kutaḥ Sukham II 66 II

Indriyāṇāṁ Hi Charatāṁ Yan Mano 'Nuvidhīyate

Tadasya Harati Prajñāṁ Vāyur Nāvam Ivāmbhasi II 67 II

Tasmād Yasya Mahā-Bāho Nigṛihītāni Sarvaśhaḥ

Indriyāṇīndriyārthebhyas Tasya Prajñā Pratiṣhṭhitā II 68 II

Yā Niśhā Sarva-Bhūtānāṁ Tasyāṁ Jāgarti Sanyamī

Yasyāṁ Jāgrati Bhūtāni Sā Niśhā Paśhyato Muneḥ II 69 II

Āpūryamāṇam Achala-Pratiṣhṭhaṁ Samudram Āpaḥ Praviśhanti Yadvat

Tadvat Kāmā Yaṁ Praviśhanti Sarve Sa Śhāntim Āpnoti Na Kāma-Kāmī II 70 II

Vihāya Kāmān Yaḥ Sarvān Pumānśh Charati Niḥspṛihaḥ

Nirmamo Nirahankāraḥ Sa Śhāntim Adhigachchhati II 71 II

(66) One who's not accomplished as above doesn't possess stable Buddhi (mind) and Bhāvanā (emotions). One who doesn't have (stable) emotions doesn't get peace; and how would one, who doesn't possess peace, be happy? (67) Just as wind pushes a boat off its course, the mind that follows senses which are roaming (among objects of senses) leads the person's Buddhi (intellect) astray. (68) Hence, O Arjun, one whose senses are restrained from the objects of pleasure, is to be considered to have their Buddhi firm in wisdom.

(69) When it is night for everyone, a Sthitapradnya is awake, and where everyone is awake it seems like night to this knowledgeable person.

[This paradox is used figuratively. Ignorance is darkness and Knowledge is light. What ignorant don't want (what they consider darkness) is favored by the knowledgeable and what they want (what they consider light) is what knowledgeable doesn't want. This is evident when you see that knowledgeable people consider those actions miserable that common people are busy doing whereas the detached action which a knowledgeable person follows is rejected by common people.]

(70) Just as the ocean remains within its boundaries despite so much water (from rivers) flowing into it; similarly, the person within whom all objects of desire enter (without disturbing him) attains (true) peace, not (possible for) the one who desires these objects. (71) One who gives up (attachment to) all desire, who lives free of greed and who doesn't possess ego and vanity is the one who attains (true) peace.

Eṣhā Brāhmī Sthitiḥ Pārtha Naināṁ Prāpya Vimuhyati

Sthitvāsyām Anta-Kāle 'Pi Brahma-Nirvāṇam Ṛichchhati II 72 II

(72) O Arjun! This is what is called Brāhmi (enlightened) state. One who attains this is never deluded; and being in this state even at the time of death enables them to attain Brahmanirvāna (Moksha or liberation where they become one with the Absolute).

This concludes the second Adhyāya **Sānkhyayog** from the dialogue between Shri Krishna and Arjun on Yog Shāstra (Karmayog Shāstra) within Brahmavidyā (knowledge of Brahman) in the Upanishad sung (narrated) by Shri Bhagwān (Shri Krishna).

[This Adhyāya begins with explanation of Sānkhya philosophy and hence is called Sānkhyayog. While many Adhyāya often have multiple topics covered, yet the name given is from the topic at the beginning or one that covers majority of the Adhyāya. Yet, a few critics try to forcibly derive meaning of each word in Adhyāya to fit the title. It's an incorrect way of interpretation and should not be followed.]

Truteeyodhyāyah (Third Adhyāya)

Arjuna Uvācha

Jyāyasī Chet Karmaṇas Te Matā Buddhir Janārdana

Tat Kiṁ Karmaṇi Ghore Māṁ Niyojayasi Keśhava II 1 II

Vyāmiśhreṇeva Vākyena Buddhiṁ Mohayasīva Me

Tad Ekaṁ Vada Niśhchitya Yena Śhreyo 'Ham Āpnuyām II 2 II

Śhrī Bhagavān Uvācha

Loke 'Smin Dvi-Vidhā Niṣhṭhā Purā Proktā Mayānagha

Jñāna-Yogena Sāṅkhyānāṁ Karma-Yogena Yoginām II 3 II

Na Karmaṇām Anārambhān Naiṣhkarmyaṁ Puruṣho 'Śhnute

Na Cha Sannyasanād Eva Siddhiṁ Samadhigachchhati II 4 II

Na Hi Kaśhchit Kṣhaṇam Api Jātu Tiṣhṭhatyakarma-Kṛit

Kāryate Hyavaśhaḥ Karma Sarvaḥ Prakṛiti-Jair Guṇaiḥ II 5 II

Karmendriyāṇi Sanyamya Ya Āste Manasā Smaran

Indriyārthān Vimūḍhātmā Mithyāchāraḥ Sa Uchyate II 6 II

Yas Tvindriyāṇi Manasā Niyamyārabhate 'Rjuna

Karmendriyaiḥ Karma-Yogam Asaktaḥ Sa Viśhiṣhyate II 7 II

Niyataṁ Kuru Karma Tvaṁ Karma Jyāyo Hyakarmaṇaḥ

Śharīra-Yātrāpi Cha Te Na Prasiddhyed Akarmaṇaḥ II 8 II

Truteeyodhyāyah (Third Adhyāya)

Arjun said – (1) O Krishna! If you opine that (equanimous) Buddhi is superior to Karma, then O Krishna, why do you make me engage in this terrible act (of war)? (2) You're making my Buddhi (mind) go delusional with your apparently ambiguous advice. Pray tell me one definitive (path) which would be the best for me.

Shri Bhagwān said – (3) O sinless Arjun! Earlier (in second Adhyāya) I told you about two paths (leading to Moksha) in this world – Dnyān Yog (path of knowledge) for Sānkhya (those inclined towards only knowledge) and Karma Yog (path of action) for (karma) Yogi (those inclined towards active life). (4) (However), mere abstinence from action doesn't lead to Naishkarmya (freedom from fruits of karma); neither can mere renunciation from action lead to Siddhi (true knowledge). (5) Because, no one can remain without action, even for a moment. Every person is compelled to act by Gunas (attributes) of Prakruti.

[Three important messages are given in the above verses which are extremely important in the context of Karmayog and Gitā as a whole – 1. Naishkarmya (freedom from fruits of action) doesn't mean inaction. 2. Even if one tries their best, they cannot completely abstain from action. And 3. Mere quitting of Karma doesn't lead to true knowledge. It's duly explained in the subsequent Adhyāyas how quitting attachment to action is the only way to escape the fruits while continuing to perform all actions without any binding. This is the essence of Bhagavad Gitā.]

(6) Whoever restrains the action organs but continues to think about the objects of sensory pleasure, is called delusional and their behavior hypocritical. (7) However, one who understands the senses through mind and begins Karmayog (path of action) by performing actions with organs (but) without any attachment, is definitely superior. (8) You perform the actions which are your duties (as per Dharma), as action is superior to inaction. You see, by quitting action even your bodily sustenance wouldn't be possible.

Yajñārthāt Karmaṇo 'Nyatra Loko 'Yaṁ Karma-Bandhanaḥ

Tad-Arthaṁ Karma Kaunteya Mukta-Saṅgaḥ Samāchara II 9 II

Saha-Yajñāḥ Prajāḥ Sṛiṣhṭvā Purovācha Prajāpatiḥ

Anena Prasaviṣhyadhvam Eṣha Vo 'Stviṣhṭa-Kāma-Dhuk II 10 II

Devān Bhāvayatānena Te Devā Bhāvayantu Vaḥ

Parasparaṁ Bhāvayantaḥ Śhreyaḥ Param Avāpsyatha II 11 II

Iṣhṭān Bhogān Hi Vo Devā Dāsyante Yajña-Bhāvitāḥ

Tair Dattān Apradāyaibhyo Yo Bhuṅkte Stena Eva Saḥ II 12 II

Yajña-Śhiṣhṭāśhinaḥ Santo Muchyante Sarva-Kilbiṣhaiḥ

Bhuñjate Te Tvaghaṁ Pāpā Ye Pachantyātma-Kāraṇāt II 13 II

Annād Bhavanti Bhūtāni Parjanyād Anna-Sambhavaḥ

Yajñād Bhavati Parjanyo Yajñaḥ Karma-Samudbhavaḥ II 14 II

Karma Brahmodbhavaṁ Viddhi Brahmākṣhara-Samudbhavam

Tasmāt Sarva-Gataṁ Brahma Nityaṁ Yajñe Pratiṣhṭhitam II 15 II

Evaṁ Pravartitaṁ Chakraṁ Nānuvartayatīha Yaḥ

Aghāyur Indriyārāmo Moghaṁ Pārtha Sa Jīvati II 16 II

(9) All actions except those performed as Yadnya (Vedic rituals) are binding in this world. Therefore, O Arjun, you perform (even prescribed) duties without any attachment.

[First line of the verse indicates the principle of Mimāmsaks while the second line explains that of Gitā. The precise essence of this verse is that when one performs all actions as duties and without attachment, 1. They're not binding as per Mimāmsak principle and 2. They're done without attachment and so don't yield any binding and lead to Moksha (liberation).]

(10) Initially, Brahmadev created humanity along with Yadnya (sacrificial rituals) and said to them, "Prosper while performing these duties. May this be the cause that fulfils all your wishes. (11) With these Yadnya (rituals), achieve welfare of the celestials (and) May the celestials yield opulence to you. Achieving each other's welfare may (both) attain great prosperity." (12) Because, the celestials, pleased by your Yadnya (rituals), would reward you with all the pleasures you wish. Those who enjoy the pleasures without offering anything (in return) to them are truly thieves.

(13) The noble people – who eat the food left after making the sacrifices – are liberated from all sins. However, those sinners who cook (food) only for themselves, truly consume sin. (14) All living beings subsist on food, food comes from rains, rain comes from Yadnya (sacrificial rituals) and Yadnya comes from Karma (action). (15) Karma has evolved from Brahmadev or Prakruti (primordial element) and Brahmadev has arisen from Akshar (Parmeshwar or Almighty). Hence, (understand that) all pervasive Brahman is what every Yadnya (sacrificial duty) is devoted to. (16) O Arjun! The life of those who do not perpetuate this cycle (the cycle of Yadnya or sacrificial rituals for continuance of the universe) is sinful and the life of these who live only to satiate their senses (without sacrificing anything for the celestials) lays waste.

[These verses try to emphasize the fact that Brahmadev (not humans) has initiated this cycle of sacrificial rituals for perpetuation of the universe including of humans. Thus, it is imperative that we play our part assisting it. This shows how Gitā preserves performing of rituals

Yas Tvātma-Ratir Eva Syād Ātma-Tṛiptaśh Cha Mānavaḥ

Ātmanyeva Cha Santuṣhṭas Tasya Kāryaṁ Na Vidyate II 17 II

Naiva Tasya Kṛitenārtho Nākṛiteneha Kaśhchana

Na Chāsya Sarva-Bhūteṣhu Kaśhchid Artha-Vyapāśhrayaḥ II 18 II

Tasmād Asaktaḥ Satataṁ Kāryaṁ Karma Samāchara

Asakto Hyācharan Karma Param Āpnoti Pūruṣhaḥ II 19 II

prescribed by Mimāmsak path by way of detached action so that they don't become binding. However, some ascetics raise a query that knowledgeable people attain Moksha (liberation) here itself and thus don't need to perform any more actions. To show how Gitā answers this, Bhagwān now continues –]

(17) However, for those who rejoice by themselves, feel satiated by themselves and become content by themselves; have no more duties to be performed (for themselves).

(18) Moreover, they have nothing to gain or lose by doing anything here (in this world). They have no interest or involvement pertaining to other living beings any more (for themselves). (19) Therefore, (just as a knowledgeable person doesn't keep any expectations) you too continue to perform (your) duties without keeping any attachment (to the fruits thereof); because one who performs actions without attachment attains the ultimate.

[These three verses are very crucial and have been misinterpreted often. People who follow Sanyās (path of asceticism) argue that as someone who's attained Moksha while being alive has nothing more to be achieved, they need not perform any Karma any more, even for welfare of others as they are no longer attached to anything or anyone. To this, Gitā counters by debating that if they are neutral to performing action or practicing inaction, why not continue performing all actions as duties without attachment? As bodily actions are anyway unavoidable how much ever you try, there's no point in avoiding other actions stubbornly. Rather, one must perform these actions without the mindset of seeking anything for oneself. Once the selfish motive is removed, the actions become selfless and thus non-binding. The definitive word 'Therefore' used in the 19th verse clarifies what Gitā stands for and upholds that Gitā encourages performing actions without attachment; and not inaction as attempted to be proven by many communalistic commentators.]

Karmaṇaiva Hi Sansiddhim Āsthitā Janakādayaḥ

Loka-Saṅgraham Evāpi Sampaśhyan Kartum Arhasi II 20 II

Yad Yad Ācharati Śhreṣhṭhas Tat Tad Evetaro Janaḥ

Sa Yat Pramāṇaṁ Kurute Lokas Tad Anuvartate II 21 II

Na Me Pārthāsti Kartavyaṁ Triṣhu Lokeṣhu Kiñchana

Nānavāptam Avāptavyaṁ Varta Eva Cha Karmaṇi II 22 II

Yadi Hyahaṁ Na Varteyaṁ Jātu Karmaṇyatandritaḥ

Mama Vartmānuvartante Manuṣhyāḥ Pārtha Sarvaśhaḥ II 23 II

Utsīdeyur Ime Lokā Na Kuryāṁ Karma Ched Aham

Sankarasya Cha Kartā Syām Upahanyām Imāḥ Prajāḥ II 24 II

Saktāḥ Karmaṇyavidvānso Yathā Kurvanti Bhārata

Kuryād Vidvāns Tathāsaktaśh Chikīrṣhur Loka-Saṅgraham II 25 II

Na Buddhi-Bhedaṁ Janayed Ajñānāṁ Karma-Saṅginām

Joṣhayet Sarva-Karmāṇi Vidvān Yuktaḥ Samācharan II 26 II

(20) The likes of Janak attained Siddhi (true knowledge) through Karma (action). Likewise, it's appropriate for you to continue with Karma looking at welfare of the universe.

(21) Others (common people) follow what greats (enlightened Karmayogi) do. Whatever standards they accept, people imitate them.

(22) O Arjun! I have no duty (for myself) left across the three worlds (heaven, earth or hell), neither do I have anything left to gain or attain; yet I continue to perform Karma. (23) Because if I ever fail to continue performing Karma, then O Arjun! Everyone would follow my path. (24) If I don't perform Karma, then these worlds would be destroyed. I would be responsible for their annihilation and the cause of destruction of all people.

[Through his own example, Bhagwān Shri Krishna has shown how the way of Karmayogi is definitively the most superior one as even he chooses to follow it. It's shown that even if one is not left with any duties to be performed for themselves, they must dutifully strive for welfare of the entire universe. Now he explains the difference between the actions of knowledgeable and those of ignorant with tips for ignorant to follow in order to improve –]

(25) O Arjun! A wise (knowledgeable) person who intends to achieve welfare of the universe must behave as ignorant people attached to their actions do, albeit without any attachment.

(26) A wise should not attempt to disturb the Buddhi (mind) of the ignorant who are attached to the fruits of their actions. (Rather) by gracefully performing (their own) duties, they should inspire people do theirs willingly.

[This verse tells that while wise people must achieve development of the ignorant, leading them by example to tread on the right path; they must avoid arguing with them about their mistakes. This is said because of two things – As the ignorant are not habituated to behave in a good way, mere preaching may not achieve the desired result, while also risking misinterpretation. Secondly, if a wise person practices inaction, it sets the wrong precedent for the ignorant to be lazy. Now Bhagwān explains the difference between the seemingly similar behavior of an ignorant and a wise –]

Prakṛiteḥ Kriyamāṇāni Guṇaiḥ Karmāṇi Sarvaśhaḥ

Ahankāra-Vimūḍhātmā Kartāham Iti Manyate II 27 II

Tattva-Vit Tu Mahā-Bāho Guṇa-Karma-Vibhāgayoḥ

Guṇā Guṇeṣhu Vartanta Iti Matvā Na Sajjate II 28 II

Prakṛiter Guṇa-Sammūḍhāḥ Sajjante Guṇa-Karmasu

Tān Akṛitsna-Vido Mandān Kṛitsna-Vin Na Vichālayet II 29 II

Mayi Sarvāṇi Karmāṇi Sannyasyādhyātma-Chetasā

Nirāśhīr Nirmamo Bhūtvā Yudhyasva Vigata-Jvaraḥ II 30 II

Ye Me Matam Idaṁ Nityam Anutiṣhṭhanti Mānavāḥ

Śhraddhāvanto 'Nasūyanto Muchyante Te 'Pi Karmabhiḥ II 31 II

Ye Tvetad Abhyasūyanto Nānutiṣhṭhanti Me Matam

Sarva-Jñāna-Vimūḍhāns Tān Viddhi Naṣhṭān Achetasaḥ II 32 II

Sadṛiśhaṁ Cheṣhṭate Svasyāḥ Prakṛiter Jñānavān Api

Prakṛitiṁ Yānti Bhūtāni Nigrahaḥ Kiṁ Kariṣhyati II 33 II

Indriyasyendriyasyārthe Rāga-Dveṣhau Vyavasthitau

Tayor Na Vaśham Āgachchhet Tau Hyasya Paripanthinau II 34 II

(27) While all Karma is manifested owing to the Gunas (attributes) of Prakruti, those (ignorant people) deluded with ego consider themselves to be the doers. (28) However, O Arjun, the wise knows that Gunas (attributes) and Karma (actions) are both separate from the soul. They understand that it's nothing but a play of the Gunas (attributes) and don't get attached to it. (29) Those deluded with Gunas of Prakruti get attached to the Gunas and Karma. A knowledgeable person (who understands this) should not disturb such ignorant dimwits. (30) (Hence, O Arjun,) by spiritually dedicating all Karma to me; and by giving up desire (for fruits) and ego, go to war without hesitation!

(31) Those devoted (people) who follow my advice without trying to find faults, they too free themselves from (the bondage of) Karma.

(32) However, those who find faults in my tutelage and don't follow my guidelines; all those fools ruin themselves while being devoid of knowledge and bereft of discretion.

(33) Even the wise act as per their nature. When all living beings behave as per (their respective) nature, what's the point of being stubborn? (34) Senses and their love and hate for their objects are (both) naturally predefined. We should not be enslaved by them as they're way layers and our foes.

[The word 'Nigraha' in 33rd verse indicates stubbornness shown by many ascetics while practicing severe bodily practices. While Gitā advocates appropriate restraint of the senses, it's against such severity as it's pointless. Even a knowledgeable ascetic steps out to beg for alms when pressed by hunger. Thus, however enlightened one is, basic necessities would continue, necessitating action. Hence, it's prudent to control your senses to keep them in check. Moreover, 34th verse shows that happiness and sorrow are two separate emotions and one is not defined as the absence of the other. We're often compelled to do something we don't like. Gitā advises that a wise person should do those things dutifully and stay aloof from their repercussions where a fool gets attached to them and gets sad. This is shown as the main difference between a wise person and a fool.]

Śhreyān Swa-Dharmo Viguṇaḥ Para-Dharmāt Sv-Anuṣhṭhitāt

Swa-Dharme Nidhanaṁ Śhreyaḥ Para-Dharmo Bhayāvahaḥ II 35 II

Arjuna Uvācha

Atha Kena Prayukto 'Yaṁ Pāpaṁ Charati Pūruṣhaḥ

Anichchhann Api Vārṣhṇeya Balād Iva Niyojitaḥ II 36 II

Śhrī Bhagavān Uvācha

Kāma Eṣha Krodha Eṣha Rajo-Guṇa-Samudbhavaḥ

Mahāśhano Mahā-Pāpmā Viddhyenam Iha Vairiṇam II 37 II

Dhūmenāvriyate Vahnir Yathādarśho Malena Cha

Yatholbenāvṛito Garbhas Tathā Tenedam Āvṛitam II 38 II

Āvṛitaṁ Jñānam Etena Jñānino Nitya-Vairiṇā

Kāma-Rūpeṇa Kaunteya Duṣhpūreṇānalena Cha II 39 II

Indriyāṇi Mano Buddhir Asyādhiṣhṭhānam Uchyate

Etair Vimohayatyeṣha Jñānam Āvṛitya Dehinam II 40 II

Tasmāt Tvam Indriyāṇyādau Niyamya Bharatarṣhabha

Pāpmānaṁ Prajahi Hyenaṁ Jñāna-Vijñāna-Nāśhanam II 41 II

Indriyāṇi Parāṇyāhur Indriyebhyaḥ Paraṁ Manaḥ

Manasas Tu Parā Buddhir Yo Buddheḥ Paratas Tu Saḥ II 42 II

Evaṁ Buddheḥ Paraṁ Buddhvā Sanstabhyātmānam Ātmanā

Jahi Śhatruṁ Mahā-Bāho Kāma-Rūpaṁ Durāsadam II 43 II

(35) Even though it's possible to happily perform someone else's duties, it's advisable to perform our own prescribed duties even if they're flawed. It's preferable to die while performing our own duties but performing someone else's duties is ghastly!

Arjun said – (36) O Shri Krishna! Now (tell me), with whose influence does one unwillingly commit sins, as if by force?

Shri Bhagwān said – (37) In this respect, consider the greedy and sinful lust and anger as the enemy that arises out of Raja Guna (attribute). (38) Just as smoke engulfs the fire, dust layers the mirror or womb engulfs the embryo; it (lust) has enveloped everything. (39) O Arjun! It is this arch nemesis of the wise in the form of lust which, like the insatiable fire, masks their knowledge. (40) Senses, mind and intellect are called its abode (or fortress). With their support, it clouds knowledge and deludes a person. (41) Therefore, O Arjun, by first restraining your senses, you must slay this sinner that destroys Dnyān (Spiritual knowledge) and Vidnyān (Special knowledge).

(42) It is said that, senses are beyond gross body, mind is beyond the senses, Buddhi (professional intellect) is beyond the mind and soul is even beyond the Buddhi. (43) Thus, by recognizing the one beyond Buddhi and by restraining yourself, O Arjun, vanquish this formidable enemy called lust.

This concludes the third Adhyāya **Karmayog** from the dialogue between Shri Krishna and Arjun on Yog Shāstra (Karmayog Shāstra) within Brahmavidyā (knowledge of Brahman) in the Upanishad sung (narrated) by Shri Bhagwān (Shri Krishna).

Chaturthodhyāyah (Fourth Adhyāya)

Śhrī Bhagavān Uvācha

Imaṁ Vivasvate Yogaṁ Proktavān Aham Avyayam

Vivasvān Manave Prāha Manur Ikṣhvākave 'Bravīt II 1 II

Evaṁ Paramparā-Prāptam Imaṁ Rājarṣhayo Viduḥ

Sa Kāleneha Mahatā Yogo Naṣhṭaḥ Parantapa II 2 II

Sa Evāyaṁ Mayā Te 'Dya Yogaḥ Proktaḥ Purātanaḥ

Bhakto 'Si Me Sakhā Cheti Rahasyaṁ Hyetad Uttamam II 3 II

Arjuna Uvācha

Aparaṁ Bhavato Janma Paraṁ Janma Vivasvataḥ

Katham Etad Vijānīyāṁ Tvam Ādau Proktavān Iti II 4 II

Śhrī Bhagavān Uvācha

Bahūni Me Vyatītāni Janmāni Tava Chārjuna

Tānyahaṁ Veda Sarvāṇi Na Tvaṁ Vettha Parantapa II 5 II

Ajo 'Pi Sannavyayātmā Bhūtānām Īśhvaro 'Pi San

Prakṛitiṁ Svām Adhiṣhṭhāya Sambhavāmyātma-Māyayā II 6 II

Chaturthodhyāyah (Fourth Adhyāya)

Shri Bhagwān said – (1) I told this eternal and timeless (path of Karma) Yog to Vivaswān (the Sun god). Vivaswān told it to Manu (his son) and Manu in turn narrated it to Ikshvāku (his son). (2) Through this tradition, it was made available to the saintly kings. However, O Arjun, over a long period of time this Yog got lost in this world. (3) It is the same ancient Yog (path of Karma) I revealed to you today as the best secret, as you're my friend and devotee.

[We've highlighted in 3rd chapter how the word 'Yog' is used in these verses as Karmayog, referring to the two paths 'Sānkhya' and 'Yog' where Sānkhya is the ascetic path while Yog is the action-oriented path. It's amply clear from many anecdotes from Mahābhārat, Bhāgwat Purān, Manu Smruti and Gitā itself that the 'Yog' described here is Karmayog and is distinctly different and an alternate path to Sānkhya path of the ascetic. Arjun raises a chronological doubt here –]

Arjun said – (4) You've been born recently whereas Vivaswān is from way before; then how should I understand that you told this beforehand to him?

Shri Bhagwān said – (5) O Arjun! You and I have had many previous births. I know them all while you don't.

(6) I'm the lord of (all) living beings, I am unborn and my spirit never perishes. Yet, I take birth by mastering my own Prakruti (nature) and with my own Māyā (appearance).

[This verse combines Sānkhya and Vedānta schools. Sānkhya believe that Prakruti creates the universe by itself. However, Vedānti believe Prakruti to be a form of Parmeshwar whereby Parmeshwar masters Prakruti which then gives birth to the universe. The unfathomable power of Parmeshwar to create the universe from its unmanifest form is called 'Māyā' (appearance) in Gitā. We've elaborated on the concept of Māyā in the 9th chapter.]

Yadā Yadā Hi Dharmasya Glānir Bhavati Bhārata

Abhyutthānam Adharmasya Tadātmānaṁ Sṛijāmyaham II 7 II

Paritrāṇāya Sādhūnāṁ Vināśhāya Cha Duṣhkṛitām

Dharma-Sansthāpanārthāya Sambhavāmi Yuge Yuge II 8 II

Janma Karma Cha Me Divyam Evaṁ Yo Vetti Tattvataḥ

Tyaktvā Dehaṁ Punar Janma Naiti Mām Eti So 'Rjuna II 9 II

Vīta-Rāga-Bhaya-Krodhā Man-Mayā Mām Upāśhritāḥ

Bahavo Jñāna-Tapasā Pūtā Mad-Bhāvam Āgatāḥ II 10 II

Ye Yathā Māṁ Prapadyante Tāns Tathaiva Bhajāmyaham

Mama Vartmānuvartante Manuṣhyāḥ Pārtha Sarvaśhaḥ II 11 II

Kāṅkṣhantaḥ Karmaṇāṁ Siddhiṁ Yajanta Iha Devatāḥ

Kṣhipraṁ Hi Mānuṣhe Loke Siddhir Bhavati Karmajā II 12 II

(7) O Arjun! Whenever righteousness declines and evil dominates, I manifest by myself (as an avatar or incarnation). (8) To protect the sages, to vanquish the wicked and for reestablishing Dharma (righteousness), I take birth age after age.

[While we've mentioned righteousness as the meaning of Dharma in this verse, the actual meaning is broader; covering social norms, justice, ethics etc. It's central to these verses that whenever evil begins to dominate, Parmeshwar assumes an incarnation or avatar in the form of a glorious and courageous human being and restores order.]

(9) Whoever recognizes and understands the principle behind such divine births and actions I undertake, don't take birth again after leaving the body and become one with me.

(10) Many people have quit attachment, fear and anger; devoted themselves to me and taken refuge in me. Many such (people) have purified themselves with power of my knowledge and become one with me.

[To understand the avatars/incarnations of Parmeshwar, it's necessary to understand how it manifests itself through Māyā (appearance). Once we understand this, we attain spiritual knowledge. Once we understand divine action, we decipher the idea of performing action without attachment. Thus, by knowing divine births and divine actions, we obtain spiritual knowledge as well as Karmayog. As Moksha requires one to understand this, such a person definitely becomes one with the Parmeshwar. Once someone does this, no other knowledge is required. Now Bhagwān explains other slightly inferior forms of worship.]

(11) The way one worships me, I reward them accordingly. O Arjun! Whichever path they take, everyone (ultimately) converges onto my path. (12) Those who wish for fruits of their actions in material world (not the extinction of the fruits) worship celestial deities, as (these) fruits of actions manifest faster in this (material) world.

[The ultimate fruit of worship of Parmeshwar is Moksha and it is attained after arduous and persistent pursuit upon complete extinction of the bindings of Karma. However, very few people are so farsighted

Chātur-Varṇyaṁ Mayā Sṛiṣhṭaṁ Guṇa-Karma-Vibhāgaśhaḥ

Tasya Kartāram Api Māṁ Viddhyakartāram Avyayam II 13 II

Na Māṁ Karmāṇi Limpanti Na Me Karma-Phale Spṛihā

Iti Māṁ Yo 'Bhijānāti Karmabhir Na Sa Badhyate II 14 II

Evaṁ Jñātvā Kṛitaṁ Karma Pūrvair Api Mumukṣhubhiḥ

Kuru Karmaiva Tasmāttvaṁ Pūrvaiḥ Pūrvataraṁ Kṛitam II 15 II

Kiṁ Karma Kim Akarmeti Kavayo 'Pyatra Mohitāḥ

Tat Te Karma Pravakṣhyāmi Yaj Jñātvā Mokṣhyase 'Śhubhāt II 16 II

Karmaṇo Hyapi Boddhavyaṁ Boddhavyaṁ Cha Vikarmaṇaḥ

Akarmaṇaśh Cha Boddhavyaṁ Gahanā Karmaṇo Gatiḥ II 17 II

Karmaṇyakarma Yaḥ Paśhyed Akarmaṇi Cha Karma Yaḥ

Sa Buddhimān Manuṣhyeṣhu Sa Yuktaḥ Kṛitsna-Karma-Kṛit II 18 II

and persistent. Most people possess material ambitions from the actions that they perform. Such people revere celestial deities. This is the meaning of this verse.]

(13) I've created the Chāturvarnya system (four-tiered system consisting of Brāhman, Kshatriya, Vaishya and Shudra tiers) as per varying qualities and actions. While I am the creator of this, know that I'm also eternal and non-doer.

[Although Parmeshwar has created it, it's completely detached from the outcomes and hence is non-doer. This is conveyed through this verse.]

(14) I am not bound by the actions (because) I am not attached to the fruits of Karma. One who understands me so, doesn't get bound by Karma.

[Bhagwān is not bound by Karma as he doesn't act with a desire for the fruits. Someone who understands this and acts without attachment to the fruits of their action are similarly unbound.]

(15) Knowing this, ancient seekers of Moksha (liberation) continued with action. Therefore, following in the footsteps of these ancestors, you too continue to act (perform your duties).

(16) Even the wise are baffled about what Karma (action) is and what Akarma (inaction) is. (Hence), let me tell you the Karma, knowing which you should be free of all sins. (17) The way of Karma is profoundly difficult; (hence) it is important to understand what Karma is, what Vikarma (wrong action) is and what Akarma is.

(18) The person who sees Karma in Akarma and Akarma in Karma is the most knowledgeable, Yogi and performer of all actions.

[The 18th verse, along with subsequent five verses, explains in detail what Karma, Akarma and Vikarma mean. Later, 18th Adhyāya emphasizes on the three different types of Karmatyāg (giving up of Karma), Karma and Karta (doer). Once we understand the essence of Gitā in promoting selfless or detached action, we understand the meaning of inaction as envisaged by Bhagavad Gitā – Action without attachment, and not literal lack of action as Sanyāsis (ascetics) do. According to Gitā, literal

Yasya Sarve Samārambhāḥ Kāma-Saṅkalpa-Varjitāḥ

Jñānāgni-Dagdha-Karmāṇaṁ Tam Āhuḥ Paṇḍitaṁ Budhāḥ II 19 II

Tyaktvā Karma-Phalāsaṅgaṁ Nitya-Tṛipto Nirāśhrayaḥ

Karmaṇyabhipravṛitto 'Pi Naiva Kiñchit Karoti Saḥ II 20 II

Nirāśhīr Yata-Chittātmā Tyakta-Sarva-Parigrahaḥ

Śhārīraṁ Kevalaṁ Karma Kurvan Nāpnoti Kilbiṣham II 21 II

Yadṛichchhā-Lābha-Santuṣhṭo Dvandvātīto Vimatsaraḥ

Samaḥ Siddhāvasiddhau Cha Kṛitvāpi Na Nibadhyate II 22 II

Gata-Saṅgasya Muktasya Jñānāvasthita-Chetasaḥ

Yajñāyācharataḥ Karma Samagraṁ Pravilīyate II 23 II

Brahmārpaṇaṁ Brahma Havir Brahmāgnau Brahmaṇā Hutam

Brahmaiva Tena Gantavyaṁ Brahma-Karma-Samādhinā II 24 II

Daivam Evāpare Yajñaṁ Yoginaḥ Paryupāsate

Brahmāgnāvapare Yajñaṁ Yajñenaivopajuhvati II 25 II

Śhrotrādīnīndriyāṇyanye Sanyamāgniṣhu Juhvati

Śhabdādīn Viṣhayānanya Indriyāgniṣhu Juhvati II 26 II

inaction is impossible and hence it's infeasible to recommend it. Doing nothing may appear like inaction. Yet, it's a type of Karma of choosing not to do anything. Hence, Gitā says perform all Sāttvic actions as duty, simply without getting attached.]

(19) A person who performs all actions without desire for material gains is called by scholars as wise; whose actions are burnt with the fire of knowledge. (20) A person who has given up attachment to the fruits of their actions, is always satisfied and independent (of the feelings of having done something for someone); and is said to do nothing, despite being immersed in action. (21) A person who's given up expectations (for the fruits of their actions), controlled their mind and given up all attachment performs all actions with body but is untainted by any sin.

(22) The person who is content with whatever gain comes naturally, is free of dualities (of happiness and sorrow), is free of envy and is stoic about success or failure; is unbound by (fruits of) actions despite performing them. The actions of someone who's free of all attachments, stable with knowledge (of equanimity) and who performs all actions (only) as a Yadnya (sacrificial ritual); are thoroughly nullified.

[Here, the meaning of Yadnya is not limited to the sacrificial rituals mentioned in Vedas or by Mimāmsaks for attaining a place in heaven. Gitā goes beyond heaven and targets Moksha (liberation). It thus declares that actions performed aimed at attaining a place in heaven are not worthy of Moksha. It states that every action you perform as a duty and without any ownership, is a Yadnya as you're dedicating it to Brahman (the ultimate) and not claiming it for yourself.

(24) Someone who considers the act of sacrifice as Brahman, the oblation as Brahman, the sacrificial fire as Brahman and that the act is performed by Brahman; is bound to attain Brahman (Moksha) as their Buddhi (intellect) considers (every) action as Brahman. (25) Many (Karma) yogis perform Yadnya to worship celestial deities; others perform Yadnya (the ritual) offering Yadnya (sacrifice) to Yadnya (the god of sacrifice) in the fire of Brahman. (26) Some others offer senses like hearing etc. in the sacrificial fire of restraint; yet others offer objects of senses like sound etc. in the fire of senses.

Sarvāṇīndriya-Karmāṇi Prāṇa-Karmāṇi Chāpare

Ātma-Sanyama-Yogāgnau Juhvati Jñāna-Dīpite II 27 II

Dravya-Yajñās Tapo-Yajñā Yoga-Yajñās Tathāpare

Swādhyāya-Jñāna-Yajñāśh Cha Yatayaḥ Sanśhita-Vratāḥ II 28 II

Apāne Juhvati Prāṇaṁ Prāṇe 'Pānaṁ Tathāpare

Prāṇāpāna-Gatī Ruddhvā Prāṇāyāma-Parāyaṇāḥ II 29 II

(27) Still others offer all actions of the senses and the Prāna (life energy) in the fire of Yog of self-control lit with knowledge.

[There are 2-3 types of symbolic Yadnya described in the above verse – 1. Controlling the senses, which means letting senses function within limits. 2. Complete abstinence of the objects of senses and 3. Abstinence of not only the senses but also the life energy to attain a state of Samādhi (super consciousness or transcendence). Once we use the simile of Yadnya (sacrificial fire) with these, different entities are denoted as the sacrificial fire. In the first case of controlled senses, the boundary set is designated as the fire as everything within the boundary is said to be offered as sacrifice. In the second, the senses themselves and in the third, senses and life energy are both to be offered as sacrifice while abstinence is the fire. The term Yadnya has become a lot broader since the beginning of original Yadnya during Vedic times. Any sacrificial duty performed is considered a Yadnya.]

(28) Such Yati (people who live a life of restraint) following strict rules practice different types of Yadnya – Some offer their wealth as sacrifice, some practice austerity, some follow (Karma) Yog, some practice self-study (of the scriptures) while some practice pursuit of knowledge as sacrifice.

(29) By devotedly engaging in the act of Prāṇāyām (control over life energy) and by restraining the outgoing and incoming breaths, many sacrifice incoming breath into outgoing while others sacrifice outgoing breath into incoming.

[While Prāṇāyām indicates both incoming and outgoing breaths, when separately indicated Prāna means outgoing breath while Apān means incoming breath. When incoming breath is sacrificed in the outgoing, it's called Rechak Prāṇāyām. When outgoing breath is sacrificed in the incoming, it's called Poorak Prāṇāyām. When both are restrained, it's called Kumbhak Prāṇāyām. There are three other breaths – Vyān, Udān and Samān. Of these, Vyān is expressed when vigorous exercises are done by holding breath in the middle. Udān is the one that leaves the body at the time of death. Samān is the one which carries the nutrition in food to every part of the body. These are the meanings as explained in Vedānta.]

Apare Niyatāhārāḥ Prāṇān Prāṇeṣhu Juhvati

Sarve 'Pyete Yajña-Vido Yajña-Kṣhapita-Kalmaṣhāḥ II 30 II

Yajña-Śhiṣhṭāmṛita-Bhujo Yānti Brahma Sanātanam

Nāyaṁ Loko 'Styayajñasya Kuto 'Nyaḥ Kuru-Sattama II 31 II

Evaṁ Bahu-Vidhā Yajñā Vitatā Brahmaṇo Mukhe

Karma-Jān Viddhi Tān Sarvān Evaṁ Jñātvā Vimokṣhyase II 32 II

Śhreyān Dravya-Mayād Yajñāj Jñāna-Yajñaḥ Parantapa

Sarvaṁ Karmākhilaṁ Pārtha Jñāne Parisamāpyate II 33 II

(30) Many others regulate their diet and sacrifice Prāna (life energy) into Prāna itself. All these scholars of sacrifice purified with Yadnya

(31) (and) consumers of the remnants after sacrifice attain eternal Brahman. O Arjun! When those who don't perform Yadnya (sacrificial duties) don't attain this world, then how would they attain the other (world)?

[Bhagwān has explained that once all duties are treated as Yadnya, the rules of it become applicable too. E.g. In ritualistic sacrifices of ancient times, the offerings left after completing the sacrifice are called Amrut and are supposed to be consumed by the performers of sacrifice. Similarly, the above verse explains that those who consume what's left after performing their duties attain eternal Brahman. Moreover, like the ritualistic sacrifices in the eyes of Mimāmsaks, even these duties are non-binding for those who perform them without any attachment or expectations. They shall freely enjoy the natural outcomes of their actions consequently.]

(32) Many such different types of Yadnya are ongoing within the mouth of Brahman. Know that they all originate from Karma (action). Knowing this shall liberate you.

(33) O Arjun! Yadnya of knowledge is superior to Yadnya of wealth; because O Pārth! All actions of all kinds culminate in knowledge.

[While we may perform Yadnya (a sacrifice), offering wealth in order to attain Parmeshwar, this attainment isn't possible without knowledge of its true form. 'Yadnya of knowledge' means knowing the form of Parmeshwar and behaving according to this knowledge. This is achievable through Man (mind) and Buddhi (intellect) and is considered superior to a Yadnya of wealth. Even though it's said that all actions culminate in knowledge, one should not infer that one must quit all actions post knowledge. Gitā always emphasizes that once you attain knowledge, you must perform all actions with equanimity and without attachment whereby their outcomes don't become binding.]

Tad Viddhi Praṇipātena Pariprashnena Sevayā

Upadekṣhyanti Te Jñānaṁ Jñāninas Tattva-Darśhinaḥ II 34 II

Yaj Jñātvā Na Punar Moham Evaṁ Yāsyasi Pāṇḍava

Yena Bhūtānyaśheṣheṇa Drakṣhyasyātmanyatho Mayi II 35 II

Api Ched Asi Pāpebhyaḥ Sarvebhyaḥ Pāpa-Kṛit-Tamaḥ

Sarvaṁ Jñāna-Plavenaiva Vṛijinaṁ Santariṣhyasi II 36 II

Yathaidhānsi Samiddho 'Gnir Bhasma-Sāt Kurute 'Rjuna

Jñānāgniḥ Sarva-Karmāṇi Bhasma-Sāt Kurute Tathā II 37 II

Na Hi Jñānena Sadṛiśhaṁ Pavitramiha Vidyate

Tatsvayaṁ Yogasansiddhaḥ Kālenātmani Vindati II 38 II

Śhraddhāvānllabhate Jñānaṁ Tat-Paraḥ Sanyatendriyaḥ

Jñānaṁ Labdhvā Parāṁ Śhāntim Achireṇādhigachchhati II 39 II

Ajñaśh Chāśhraddadhānaśh Cha Sanśhayātmā Vinaśhyati

Nāyaṁ Loko 'Sti Na Paro Na Sukhaṁ Sanśhayātmanaḥ II 40 II

Yoga-Sannyasta-Karmāṇaṁ Jñāna-Sañchhinna-Sanśhayam

Ātmavantaṁ Na Karmāṇi Nibadhnanti Dhanañjaya II 41 II

(34) Remember that you should learn this knowledge from the wise through surrender, inquiry and service. (35) Upon acquiring this knowledge, O Arjun, you shall not be deluded this way; and through the Yog of this knowledge (attainment of this knowledge) you'd realize that all living beings are one with you and also with me.

[This describes the equanimity of intellect which is mentioned again later in the 6th Adhyāya. It is this knowledge through which you see everyone like yourself. As soul and Bhagwān are but two forms of the same principle, all beings are one with the soul and thereby one with Bhagwān as well. The illusion of finding the three entities as separate doesn't exist anymore. We've explained this in detail in 12th and 13th chapter.]

(36) Even if you're committing more sins than all sinners, you'd sail through all these sins with (this) ship of knowledge. (37) O Arjun! Just as a kindled fire incinerates (all) wood to ashes, (this) fire of knowledge incinerates (the binding of) all Karma likewise.

(38) There's truly nothing in this world as pure as knowledge. The person who attains (Karma) Yog obtains this knowledge by themselves. (39) (Even) a faithful person who pursues this knowledge by restraining their senses, attains it; and as soon as they obtain this knowledge, they attain ultimate peace.

[Here, Gitā states that the same knowledge and peace that's attained by the path of intellect is also attainable through path of devotion.]

(40) However, a person of skeptical nature who possesses neither knowledge nor devotion gets destroyed. For the disbelieving, it's not this world, the other or happiness.

(41) O Arjun! Karma doesn't bind that wise person who has knowledge of self, who's renounced (bindings of) action with the help of Yog and whose doubts have been dispelled by knowledge.

Tasmād Ajñāna-Sambhūtaṁ Hṛit-Sthaṁ Jñānāsinātmanaḥ

Chhittvainaṁ Sanśhayaṁ Yogam Ātiṣhṭhottiṣhṭha Bhārata II 42 II

(42) Therefore, O Arjun, sever the doubt that's appeared in your heart because of ignorance with the sword of knowledge, dedicate yourself to (Karma) Yog and stand up (for war)!

[In these two verses, Gitā demonstrates the significance of both Dnyān (knowledge) and Karma (action) separately first and then asks Arjun to practice Dnyānkarmasamucchay (combination of knowledge and action). By performing actions without attachment, they become non-binding and don't become a hindrance to Moksha. Knowledge clears doubts from the mind and bestows Moksha (liberation). Hence, Shri Krishna advices not to pursue knowledge or action in isolation but as a combination and conclusively asks Arjun to get ready for war.]

This concludes the fourth Adhyāya **Dnyānkarmasanyāsyog** from the dialogue between Shri Krishna and Arjun on Yog Shāstra (Karmayog Shāstra) within Brahmavidyā (knowledge of Brahman) in the Upanishad sung (narrated) by Shri Bhagwān (Shri Krishna).

Panchamodhyāyah (Fifth Adhyāya)

Arjuna Uvācha

Sannyāsaṁ Karmaṇāṁ Kṛiṣhṇa Punar Yogaṁ Cha Śhansasi

Yach Chhreya Etayor Ekaṁ Tan Me Brūhi Su-Niśhchitam II 1 II

Śhrī Bhagavān Uvācha

Sannyāsaḥ Karma-Yogaśh Cha Niḥśhreyasa-Karāvubhau

Tayos Tu Karma-Sannyāsāt Karma-Yogo Viśhiṣhyate II 2 II

Jñeyaḥ Sa Nitya-Sannyāsī Yo Na Dveṣhṭi Na Kāṅkṣhati

Nirdvandvo Hi Mahā-Bāho Sukhaṁ Bandhāt Pramuchyate II 3 II

Sānkhya-Yogau Pṛithag Bālāḥ Pravadanti Na Paṇḍitāḥ

Ekamapyāsthitaḥ Samyag Ubhayor Vindate Phalam II 4 II

Yat Sānkhyaiḥ Prāpyate Sthānaṁ Tad Yogair Api Gamyate

Ekaṁ Sānkhyaṁ Cha Yogaṁ Cha Yaḥ Paśhyati Sa Paśhyati II 5 II

Panchamodhyāyah (Fifth Adhyāya)

[In the 5th Adhyāya, Arjun has raised the same doubt that people from the path of Sanyās are likely to raise after the explanation given by Shri Krishna in the 4th. While Shri Krishna has first said that Yadnya of knowledge is superior to Yadnya of wealth, he's still gone ahead and recommended that Arjun follows his duty and gets ready for war, at the end of 2nd as well as 4th Adhyāya. While Krishna explained the concept of Dnyānkarmasamucchay (combination of knowledge and action) to clarify this, there's one question that still remains unanswered – If both Karmayog and Sānkhya are two paths accepted by the scriptures, why object someone choosing the path of Sānkhya as per their preference and quitting Karma? Arjun raises this question at the start of 5th Adhyāya.]

Arjun said – (1) O Krishna! Once you call Sanyās, while next you call (Karma) Yog as the best path; please tell me one path which is decisively the preferred one.

Shri Bhagwān said – (2) Karma Sanyās (path of renunciation) and Karma Yog (path of action) are both potent for achievement (of Moksha). However, Karmayog is especially superior to Karma Sanyās.

[Frankly, these two verses make it crystal clear that Bhagavad Gitā prefers Karmayog over Karma Sanyās. However, as this statement is not conducive for the sects following path of asceticism, they've tried to twist these verses unreasonably to suit them. Anyway, Bhagwān Shri Krishna and Gitā firmly say that Karmayog is the superior path among the two paths which are both capable of attaining Moksha. Now Shri Krishna shows how these two paths are not principally separate.]

(3) A person who neither hates nor desires anything, is an ascetic (despite performing Karma); because O Arjun! Someone who's free of the dualities (of happiness and sorrow), is naturally free of all bondages (of Karma). (4) Sānkhya (Karma Sanyās or renunciation) and Yog (Karmayog or action) are considered separate only by fools; not by the wise. Pursuing any one path appropriately yields the fruits of both. (5) The same place (Moksha) that Sānkhya go to is also reached by (Karma) yogi. One who sees both Sānkhya and Yog paths as the same (in principle) sees it (the true meaning, correctly).

Sannyāsas Tu Mahā-Bāho Duḥkham Āptum Ayogataḥ

Yoga-Yukto Munir Brahma Na Chireṇādhigachchhati II 6 II

Yoga-Yukto Viśhuddhātmā Vijitātmā Jitendriyaḥ

Sarva-Bhūtātma-Bhūtātmā Kurvann Api Na Lipyate II 7 II

Naiva Kiñchit Karomīti Yukto Manyeta Tattva-Vit

Paśhyañ Śhṛiṇvan Spṛiśhañjighrann Aśhnangachchhan Svapañśhvasan II 8 II

Pralapan Visṛijan Gṛihṇann Unmiṣhan Nimiṣhann Api

Indriyāṇīndriyārtheṣhu Vartanta Iti Dhārayan II 9 II

Brahmaṇyādhāya Karmāṇi Saṅgaṁ Tyaktvā Karoti Yaḥ

Lipyate Na Sa Pāpena Padma-Patram Ivāmbhasā II 10 II

Kāyena Manasā Buddhyā Kevalair Indriyair Api

Yoginaḥ Karma Kurvanti Saṅgaṁ Tyaktvātma-Śhuddhaye II 11 II

Yuktaḥ Karma-Phalaṁ Tyaktvā Śhāntim Āpnoti Naiṣhṭhikīm

Ayuktaḥ Kāma-Kāreṇa Phale Sakto Nibadhyate II 12 II

(6) O Arjun! Even Sanyās (renunciation) is difficult to attain without (Karma) Yog. One who follows Karmayog properly attains Brahman without delay.

[Even if someone pursues pure knowledge through renunciation, this knowledge can't be attained without Karma, while in Karmayog the actions are performed with knowledge and hence don't deter attainment of Brahman. The above verses thus call it pointless to fight over these two paths as separate.]

(7) Whoever is immersed in Karmayog, has pure mind, who's mastered their mind and senses and considers everyone's soul as his own; is free of all entanglements (of the consequences of their action) despite doing everything. (8) A Karmayogi philosopher must always consider "I'm not doing anything", (and) while seeing, hearing, touching, smelling, eating, walking, sleeping, breathing, (9) speaking, excreting, receiving and while opening or closing their eyes they must consider that the organs are (simply) being among their respective objects.

(10) Someone who performs Karma dedicating it to the Brahman and without attachment, remains untouched by sin; just as lotus leaf remains untouched by water. (11) (Hence), (Karma) Yogis perform actions only with their body, mind, intellect and senses forfeiting attachment; for purifying themselves.

[There are three types of Karma – Physical, verbal and psychological. This verse shows that while a Karmayogi performs all these Karma, they become non-binding as they're all done without ego and attachment. They all become merely the actions of the respective components of their body and are not bound to the soul.]

(12) A (Karma) Yogi attains everlasting peace by giving up the outcomes of their actions; (while) those who're not immersed (in Karmayog) get bound by attaching themselves to the fruits of their actions owing to their desires.

Sarva-Karmāṇi Manasā Sannyasyāste Sukhaṁ Vaśhī

Nava-Dvāre Pure Dehī Naiva Kurvan Na Kārayan II 13 II

Na Kartṛitvaṁ Na Karmāṇi Lokasya Sṛijati Prabhuḥ

Na Karma-Phala-Saṅyogaṁ Svabhāvas Tu Pravartate II 14 II

Nādatte Kasyachit Pāpaṁ Na Chaiva Sukṛitaṁ Vibhuḥ

Ajñānenāvṛitaṁ Jñānaṁ Tena Muhyanti Jantavaḥ II 15 II

Jñānena Tu Tad Ajñānaṁ Yeṣhāṁ Nāśhitam Ātmanaḥ

Teṣhām Āditya-Vaj Jñānaṁ Prakāśhayati Tat Param II 16 II

Tad-Buddhayas Tad-Ātmānas Tan-Niṣhṭhās Tat-Parāyaṇāḥ

Gachchhantyapunar-Āvṛittiṁ Jñāna-Nirdhūta-Kalmaṣhāḥ II 17 II

Vidyā-Vinaya-Sampanne Brāhmaṇe Gavi Hastini

Śhuni Chaiva Śhva-Pāke Cha Paṇḍitāḥ Sama-Darśhinaḥ II 18 II

(13) By renunciating all actions through mind (not literally), the person (who's mastered their senses) resides happily in the city of nine gates (the body) neither doing anything nor getting anything done.

[This shows that soul is not the doer of anything and as he knows that all the happenings are but a play of nature, it happily lies indifferently. Nine gates indicate the nine openings of human body viz. two eyes, two nostrils, two ears, mouth, genitals and anus.]

(14) Parmeshwar (almighty) doesn't create capability, actions or the fruits of these actions. They're all manifested as per their nature (Prakruti or composition). (15) Brahman (all pervasive universal soul or Parmeshwar) accepts neither anyone's virtues nor sin. All living beings are deluded due to the envelope of ignorance over their knowledge (Māyā or appearance). (16) However, for those whose ignorance has been dispelled by knowledge, this knowledge enlightens (them) with supreme wisdom like the sun. (17) Those whose Buddhi (intellect) is engrossed in this supreme wisdom, whose mind is absorbed in the wisdom, and who have become devoted to it and one with it; get all their sins washed away by knowledge and reach a place from where they don't return (attain Moksha or liberation).

[Verses 14 and 15 speak about Sānkhya philosophy of Prakruti and Purush where Prakruti is considered the doer while Purush is inert. Vedānti however, go one step ahead and consider Nirguna (without attributes) Parmeshwar to be the original principle behind both Prakruti and Purush of Sānkhya. Parmeshwar is inert like the Purush while Prakruti or Māyā is considered the doer. Common people don't understand this. However, a Karmayogi knows this and is thus aloof from the results of Karma despite performing them.]

(18) The view of someone who has become wise, is the same about a learned yet humble scholar, a cow, an elephant, a dog and even a wicked!

Ihaiva Tair Jitaḥ Sargo Yeṣhāṁ Sāmye Sthitaṁ Manaḥ

Nirdoṣhaṁ Hi Samaṁ Brahma Tasmād Brahmaṇi Te Sthitāḥ II 19 II

Na Prahṛiṣhyet Priyaṁ Prāpya Nodvijet Prāpya Chāpriyam

Sthira-Buddhir Asammūḍho Brahma-Vid Brahmaṇi Sthitaḥ II 20 II

Bāhya-Sparśheṣhvasaktātmā Vindatyātmani Yat Sukham

Sa Brahma-Yoga-Yuktātmā Sukham Akṣhayam Aśhnute II 21 II

Ye Hi Sansparśha-Jā Bhogā Duḥkha-Yonaya Eva Te

Ādyantavantaḥ Kaunteya Na Teṣhu Ramate Budhaḥ II 22 II

Śhaknotīhaiva Yaḥ Soḍhuṁ Prāk Śharīra-Vimokṣhaṇāt

Kāma-Krodhodbhavaṁ Vegaṁ Sa Yuktaḥ Sa Sukhī Naraḥ II 23 II

Yo 'Ntaḥ-Sukho 'Ntar-Ārāmas Tathāntar-Jyotir Eva Yaḥ

Sa Yogī Brahma-Nirvāṇaṁ Brahma-Bhūto 'Dhigachchhati II 24 II

Labhante Brahma-Nirvāṇam Ṛiṣhayaḥ Kṣhīṇa-Kalmaṣhāḥ

Chhinna-Dvaidhā Yatātmānaḥ Sarva-Bhūta-Hite Ratāḥ II 25 II

Kāma-Krodha-Viyuktānāṁ Yatīnāṁ Yata-Chetasām

Abhito Brahma-Nirvāṇaṁ Vartate Viditātmanām II 26 II

(19) Those whose mind has become stable in equanimity like this, win over the material world here itself (without having to wait for death). As the Brahman is flawless and equal, therefore the (equanimous) persons are one with the Brahman (then and there itself).

[Upanishads say that whoever recognizes the inertness of Parmeshwar and the play of Prakruti gets 'established in Brahman' and attains Moksha. These verses are drawn from this statement in Chhāndogya Upanishad. However, Gitā opines that even after attaining Moksha one can't escape Karma. Even Upanishads seem to be communicating that one must continue with the Karma of 3 ashrams (from the four-stage system).]

(20) One should not rejoice on getting something desirable and should not grieve on getting something unpleasant. One whose intellect is stable (this way) and who doesn't get deluded, is the truly knowledgeable person who is one with the Brahman. (21) The one whose mind is not attached to the interaction (of their senses) with the outer world (material pleasures) finds the happiness within; and this person who's one with the Brahman experiences eternal bliss. (22) The pleasures born out of interactions (of senses with the outer world) are the cause of misery as they possess a beginning and an end. O Arjun, a wise person doesn't indulge with them. (23) One who's capable of sustaining the impact of lust and anger before leaving the body (while being alive) is a Yogi and is truly happy.

[The definition of a true Yogi is the one who's capable of surviving the impact of happiness as well as sorrow with the same stoic calm. This definition is elaborated and explained in the above verses.]

(24) The one who's thus happy within, finding comfort within and attains the light within; is the Yogi who gets liberated from the world and becomes united with the Brahman. (25) The sages whose mind is free from duality (recognize the unity of Parmeshwar), who're free from all the sins and who strive for universal welfare with a disciplined mind attain this Moksha (liberation). (26) For Sanyāsis (ascetics) who are free of lust and anger, are self-disciplined and are self-realized; Moksha surrounds them (they get liberated then and there).

Sparśhān Kṛitvā Bahir Bāhyānśh Chakṣhuśh Chaivāntare Bhruvoḥ

Prāṇāpānau Samau Kṛitvā Nāsābhyantara-Chāriṇau II 27 II

Yatendriya-Mano-Buddhir Munir Mokṣha-Parāyaṇaḥ

Vigatechchhā-Bhaya-Krodho Yaḥ Sadā Mukta Eva Saḥ II 28 II

Bhoktāraṁ Yajña-Tapasāṁ Sarva-Loka-Maheśhvaram

Suhṛidaṁ Sarva-Bhūtānāṁ Jñātvā Māṁ Śhāntim Ṛichchhati II 29 II

(27) Someone while keeping out interactions with the external world (sensory pleasures and sorrow), focusing attention to (the space) between the eyebrows and equalizing the incoming and outgoing breaths; (28) who's controlled senses, mind and intellect, ridding themselves of desire, fear and anger; such sage worthy of Moksha is liberated forever! (29) One who recognizes me as the enjoyer of Yadnya (sacrifices) and Tapa (austerities), the master of all worlds and a true friend of all living beings; attains peace.

This concludes the fifth Adhyāya **Sanyāsyog** from the dialogue between Shri Krishna and Arjun on Yog Shāstra (Karmayog Shāstra) within Brahmavidyā (knowledge of Brahman) in the Upanishad sung (narrated) by Shri Bhagwān (Shri Krishna).

Shashtodhyāyah (Sixth Adhyāya)

Śhrī Bhagavān Uvācha

Anāśhritaḥ Karma-Phalaṁ Kāryaṁ Karma Karoti Yaḥ

Sa Sannyāsī Cha Yogī Cha Na Niragnir Na Chākriyaḥ II 1 II

Yaṁ Sannyāsam Iti Prāhur Yogaṁ Taṁ Viddhi Pāṇḍava

Na Hyasannyasta-Saṅkalpo Yogī Bhavati Kaśhchana II 2 II

Ārurukṣhor Muner Yogaṁ Karma Kāraṇam Uchyate

Yogārūḍhasya Tasyaiva Śhamaḥ Kāraṇam Uchyate II 3 II

Shashtodhyāyah (Sixth Adhyāya)

After explaining what Karmayog is and how it is better than Karma Sanyās (path of renunciation), Bhagwān Shri Krishna now proceeds with explanation of the tools necessary for practicing Karmayog. This covers Pātanjalyog. However, to emphasize that it is not explained separately but as a means of attaining Moksha through Karmayog, Shri Krishna starts with the description of a true Sanyāsi as the one who performs all actions (Karmayogi) as iterated in earlier Adhyāyas.

Shri Bhagwān said – (1) One who performs all actions as duties without resorting to the fruits of the actions (keeping no expectations for the fruits) is to be called a true Sanyāsi and a true (Karma) Yogi; not the one who quits all fire rituals (ritualistic duties) or who gives up action. (2) O Arjun! Consider what's called Sanyās as (Karma) Yog; because without Sanyās (renunciation) of the worldly desires no one becomes a (Karma) Yogi.

[A familial person is advised practicing Agnihotra (the fire rituals). In Manu Smruti it's said that whoever wants to renounce should quit the fire rituals, leave town and stay in the forest subsisting on alms. First line of the 2nd verse refers to this description in Manu Smruti and says that this is not the sign of a true Sanyāsi (ascetic). A Sanyāsi should give up the desire for material pleasures, not the actions themselves.]

(3) For an aspirant who wishes to attain (Karma) Yog, Karma becomes the tool (for peace). Once this person becomes a Yogi, peace is said to become the tool (for Karma).

[While communalistic critics of Gitā have twisted the meaning of this verse in different ways, the true meaning is clear if one keeps an unbiased view. As is evident from earlier verses as well as the overall tone of the message in Gitā, the above meaning fits perfectly here. Followers of Karma Sanyās state that while Karma Yog is the tool for an aspirant to attain enlightenment, there's no need for Karma post that. However, this seems far-fetched as it doesn't agree with the message in Gitā. The second line of the verse says that 'peace become the tool'. According to Sanyāsis, one who's attained Moksha has nothing left to do. How then would peace be the 'tool' for anything? If you take the obvious meaning however, it fits perfectly as mentioned above.]

Yadā Hi Nendriyārtheṣhu Na Karmasv-Anuṣhajjate

Sarva-Saṅkalpa-Sannyāsī Yogārūḍhas Tadochyate II 4 II

Uddhared Ātmanātmānaṁ Nātmānam Avasādayet

Ātmaiva Hyātmano Bandhur Ātmaiva Ripur Ātmanaḥ II 5 II

Bandhur Ātmātmanas Tasya Yenātmaivātmanā Jitaḥ

Anātmanas Tu Śhatrutve Vartetātmaiva Śhatru-Vat II 6 II

Jitātmanaḥ Praśhāntasya Paramātmā Samāhitaḥ

Śhītoṣhṇa-Sukha-Duḥkheṣhu Tathā Mānāpamānayoḥ II 7 II

Jñāna-Vijñāna-Tṛiptātmā Kūṭa-Stho Vijitendriyaḥ

Yukta Ityuchyate Yogī Sama-Loṣhṭāśhma-Kāñchanaḥ II 8 II

Suhṛin-Mitrāryudāsīna-Madhyastha-Dveṣhya-Bandhuṣhu

Sādhuṣhvapi Cha Pāpeṣhu Sama-Buddhir Viśhiṣhyate II 9 II

Yogī Yuñjīta Satatam Ātmānaṁ Rahasi Sthitaḥ

Ekākī Yata-Chittātmā Nirāśhīr Aparigrahaḥ II 10 II

(4) Because when (one) doesn't get attached to either the objects of the senses or the actions and renounces all desire for fruits of the actions, they're said to be established in Yog.

(5) (One should) elevate yourself. Never demotivate yourself. Because we're our own friend and we're our own enemy too. (6) One who wins over oneself becomes their own friend; however, one who doesn't recognize oneself, creates enmity with themselves.

[These two verses communicate the freedom of one's soul and state that one must chart their own progress themselves. However strong may the Prakruti (own nature) be, one can overcome its force and achieve development of their soul.]

(7) The soul of the one who's won over their mind and attained peace, remains equanimous and stable during heat or cold, happiness or sorrow, respect or disrespect. (8) The (Karma) Yogi whose soul is content with knowledge and science, who's won over their senses, who's rooted (in knowledge of Brahman) and who considers dirt, rock and gold as equal, is called enlightened. (9) That person who's equanimous towards well-wishers, friends, enemies, neutral, mediators, despicable, relatives, saints and sinners is to be considered distinguished.

[By enlisting various stakeholders, the intention is to cover everyone, not point out to anyone specific. These verses describe whom we could call a Yogi.]

(10) A (Karma) Yogi must concentrate by restraining their mind and soul while staying in isolation, keep no desire or bonds and continuously engage in study of Yog (meditation).

[It's clear from subsequent verses that the description in 10th verse is of Pātanjal Yog. However, this doesn't mean that Bhagwān Shri Krishna is advising a Karmayogi to spend their whole life practicing it. Pātanjal Yog is described as a tool to achieve the equanimity intended for a Karmayogi to attain Moksha (liberation). Similarly, the isolation is also suggested for a limited period. Often due to Prakruti (innate nature), many people are not able to attain Samādhi (Meditative Transcendence) in the same birth. At the end of this Adhyāya, Bhagwān Shri Krishna

Śhuchau Deśhe Pratiṣhṭhāpya Sthiram Āsanam Ātmanaḥ

Nātyuchchhritaṁ Nāti-Nīchaṁ Chailājina-Kuśhottaram II 11 II

Tatraikāgraṁ Manaḥ Kṛitvā Yata-Chittendriya-Kriyaḥ

Upaviśhyāsane Yuñjyād Yogam Ātma-Viśhuddhaye II 12 II

Samaṁ Kāya-Śhiro-Grīvaṁ Dhārayann Achalaṁ Sthiraḥ

Samprekṣhya Nāsikāgraṁ Svaṁ Diśhaśh Chānavalokayan II 13 II

Praśhāntātmā Vigata-Bhīr Brahmachāri-Vrate Sthitaḥ

Manaḥ Sanyamya Mach-Chitto Yukta Āsīta Mat-Paraḥ II 14 II

Yuñjann Evaṁ Sadātmānaṁ Yogī Niyata-Mānasaḥ

Śhāntiṁ Nirvāṇa-Paramāṁ Mat-Sansthām Adhigachchhati II 15 II

Nātyaśhnatastu Yogo 'Sti Na Chaikāntam Anaśhnataḥ

Na Chāti-Svapna-Śhīlasya Jāgrato Naiva Chārjuna II 16 II

has recommended stabilizing their mind as much as possible and practicing Karmayog which would reward you with Moksha after subsequent births, if not in this birth itself.]

(11) By placing Kush (a type of) grass, deer skin and a cloth one over the other and by placing a seat in a pure place undisturbed, neither too high nor too low (12) one must be seated to practice Yog, by restraining thoughts and senses, by concentrating their mind to purify themselves (their mind). (13) By aligning back, neck and head in a straight line and keeping it steady, stabilizing their gaze on the tip of their nose without letting the gaze wander around; (14) one must sit down immersed in Yog to become one with me by being fearless, keeping a stable mind, practicing celibacy, controlling thoughts and concentrating their mind on me.

[The phrases 'pure place' or 'aligning back, neck and head in a straight line' are borrowed from Shwetāshwatar Upanishad and the above description resembles the description of Yog from Upanishads and not Hatha Yog (a branch of Yog that emphasizes on pushing the body to extremes). Hatha Yog (literally meaning stubborn Yog) forcibly restrains senses. However, this Adhyāya (later in 24th verse) mentions restraining senses by controlling them with mind. Similarly, it's also stated later that one mustn't indulge in this practice 24x7. This makes it clear that Hatha Yog is not implicit in Bhagavad Gitā.]

(15) By practicing Yog in such manner regularly, a (Karma) Yogi stabilizes their mind and ultimately attains Nirvāna through a lasting peace that merges them with me.

[In this verse and earlier, one is advised to "become one with me" (Bhagwān Shri Krishna). There's a reason behind this. Pātanjalyog is an activity to restrain your mind. By performing this, one attains a stable mind which could be used for any activity. However, instead of wasting or misusing it, this must be put to good use in understanding the true form of Parmeshwar, according to Gitā.]

(16) O Arjun, this Yog is not attained by someone who eats excessively or who refrains from eating, someone who sleeps a lot or who doesn't sleep at all.

Yuktāhāra-Vihārasya Yukta-Cheṣhṭasya Karmasu

Yukta-Svapnāvabodhasya Yogo Bhavati Duḥkha-Hā II 17 II

Yadā Viniyataṁ Chittam Ātmanyevāvatiṣhṭhate

Niḥspṛihaḥ Sarva-Kāmebhyo Yukta Ityuchyate Tadā II 18 II

Yathā Dīpo Nivāta-Stho Neṅgate Sopamā Smṛitā

Yogino Yata-Chittasya Yuñjato Yogam Ātmanaḥ II 19 II

Yatroparamate Chittaṁ Niruddhaṁ Yoga-Sevayā

Yatra Chaivātmanātmānaṁ Paśhyann Ātmani Tuṣhyati II 20 II

Sukham Ātyantikaṁ Yat Tad Buddhi-Grāhyam Atīndriyam

Vetti Yatra Na Chaivāyaṁ Sthitaśh Chalati Tattvataḥ II 21 II

Yaṁ Labdhvā Chāparaṁ Lābhaṁ Manyate Nādhikaṁ Tataḥ

Yasmin Sthito Na Duḥkhena Guruṇāpi Vichālyate II 22 II

Taṁ Vidyād Duḥkha-Sanyoga-Viyogaṁ Yogasañjñitam

Sa Niśhchayena Yoktavyo Yogo 'Nirviṇṇa-Chetasā II 23 II

(17) This Yog proves beneficial for someone with a moderate diet, balanced action and moderate sleep.

[Even though Pātanjal Yog is described in this Adhyāya, the words balanced action indicate that Gitā still describes it as a subset of practicing Karma Yog. It is understood that one must follow this Yog while leading regular life of action.]

(18) When the restrained mind stabilizes on one's soul and there's no desire left (for any cravings or sensory pleasure), one is said to be immersed in Yog. (19) Just as the flame of a lamp kept in a quiet (windless) place burns steadily, a Yogi whose mind is restrained focuses themselves on the soul while practicing Yog.

(20) Where mind relishes being disciplined in Yog through restraint, we look at ourselves and stay blissful in our own soul; (21) where we experience the endless happiness unfathomable by our intellect or senses and where once established, it never deviates from the ultimate;

(22) attaining which state we don't consider anything to be better than it and where once established no sorrow can move (us) from there; (23) is the state which is considered as freedom from the bondage of sorrow or as 'Yog'. One must practice this Yog with determination, without getting deviated.

[The four verses (20-23) constitute a single sentence that describe 'Yog' or the state of Samādhi (Meditative transcendence). Like Pātanjal Yog describes Yog as 'restraint from the natural tendencies of the mind', Gitā describes it in the 20th verse. The ultimate stage attained in this journey is called Samādhi, alternatively known as Yog (literally union) where it's intended as union with the Brahman. This new description of the word Yog is mentioned in Gitā in this Adhyāya, just as the word 'Yog' is used with different meanings elsewhere. Understanding the contextual usage of this word is thus extremely critical, while trying to understand what Bhagavad Gitā intends to communicate. The endless happiness we experience in Samādhi is not because of the restraint of mind but because of union with the Brahman or the Parmeshwar (Absolute). This state of ultimate bliss is also called Brahmānand or Ātmānand. We shall see later that this state is also attainable through

Saṅkalpa-Prabhavān Kāmāns Tyaktvā Sarvān Aśheṣhataḥ

Manasaivendriya-Grāmaṁ Viniyamya Samantataḥ II 24 II

Śhanaiḥ Śhanair Uparamed Buddhyā Dhṛiti-Gṛihītayā

Ātma-Sansthaṁ Manaḥ Kṛitvā Na Kiñchid Api Chintayet II 25 II

Yato Yato Niśhcharati Manaśh Chañchalam Asthiram

Tatas Tato Niyamyaitad Ātmanyeva Vaśhaṁ Nayet II 26 II

Praśhānta-Manasaṁ Hyenaṁ Yoginaṁ Sukham Uttamam

Upaiti Śhānta-Rajasaṁ Brahma-Bhūtam Akalmaṣham II 27 II

Yuñjann Evaṁ Sadātmānaṁ Yogī Vigata-Kalmaṣhaḥ

Sukhena Brahma-Sansparśham Atyantaṁ Sukham Aśhnute II 28 II

Sarva-Bhūta-Stham Ātmānaṁ Sarva-Bhūtāni Chātmani

Īkṣhate Yoga-Yuktātmā Sarvatra Sama-Darśhanaḥ II 29 II

Yo Māṁ Paśhyati Sarvatra Sarvaṁ Cha Mayi Paśhyati

Tasyāhaṁ Na Praṇaśhyāmi Sa Cha Me Na Praṇaśhyati II 30 II

Sarva-Bhūta-Sthitaṁ Yo Māṁ Bhajatyekatvam Āsthitaḥ

Sarvathā Vartamāno 'Pi Sa Yogī Mayi Vartate II 31 II

Bhakti (Devotion) or Dnyān (Knowledge) just as it can be attained through Pātanjalyog. Now Bhagwān describes how to attain this state through Pātanjalyog.]

(24) By completely giving up all desires arising from resolution and moderating all senses from all sides; (25) (one should) slowly become peaceful with courage and by focusing mind on the soul, (one must) not let any thought come in their mind.

(26) (While focusing one's mind this way), one must restrain their wavering and unstable mind by controlling it with soul from wherever it may try to escape.

(27) Thus, the Yogi who's with peaceful mind, calmed passions, without sin and one with Brahman attains supreme happiness. (28) The Yogi who practices Yog regularly this way frees themselves from all sins, and happily experiences eternal bliss attained through union with Brahman.

[The word Yogi used in these two verses could be considered to denote Karmayogi as well as Pātanjal Yogi. Whichever meaning we take; we mustn't forget that the path advised by Gitā is beyond this Pātanjal Yog and definitively that of Karma (action). Pātanjal Yog is described as one of the tools of Karma Yog in Gitā.]

(29) The view of those whose soul is thus immersed in Yog becomes universal and they start seeing themselves in every living being, while seeing everyone within themselves. (30) I don't lose, nor am I lost; to someone who sees me (Parmeshwar or Parmātmā or Supreme soul) everywhere and everyone within me.

[In the first verse, the description is given using Adhyātma (spirituality) while in the second verse the same is given using Bhakti Yog (path of devotion). However, they both denote the same (read chapter 13). This view of oneness with Brahman is the basis of both Moksha as well as Karmayog.]

(31) The (Karma) Yogi who worships me (Parmeshwar) present in every living being while maintaining universality of soul, resides within me despite performing all actions.

Ātmaupamyena Sarvatra Samaṁ Paśhyati Yo 'Rjuna

Sukhaṁ Vā Yadi Vā Duḥkhaṁ Sa Yogī Paramo Mataḥ II 32 II

Arjuna Uvācha

Yo 'Yaṁ Yogas Tvayā Proktaḥ Sāmyena Madhusūdana

Etasyāhaṁ Na Paśhyāmi Chañchalatvāt Sthitiṁ Sthirām II 33 II

Chañchalaṁ Hi Manaḥ Kṛiṣhṇa Pramāthi Balavad Dṛiḍham

Tasyāhaṁ Nigrahaṁ Manye Vāyor Iva Su-Duṣhkaram II 34 II

Śhrī Bhagavān Uvācha

Asanśhayaṁ Mahā-Bāho Mano Durnigrahaṁ Chalam

Abhyāsena Tu Kaunteya Vairāgyeṇa Cha Gṛihyate II 35 II

Asaṅyatātmanā Yogo Duṣhprāpa Iti Me Matiḥ

Vaśhyātmanā Tu Yatatā Śhakyo 'Vāptum Upāyataḥ II 36 II

Arjuna Uvācha

Ayatiḥ Śhraddhayopeto Yogāch Chalita-Mānasaḥ

Aprāpya Yoga-Sansiddhiṁ Kāṅ Gatiṁ Kṛiṣhṇa Gachchhati II 37 II

Kachchin Nobhaya-Vibhraṣhṭaśh Chhinnābhram Iva Naśhyati

Apratiṣhṭho Mahā-Bāho Vimūḍho Brahmaṇaḥ Pathi II 38 II

Etan Me Sanśhayaṁ Kṛiṣhṇa Chhettum Arhasyaśheṣhataḥ

Tvad-Anyaḥ Sanśhayasyāsya Chhettā Na Hyupapadyate II 39 II

Śhrī Bhagavān Uvācha

Pārtha Naiveha Nāmutra Vināśhas Tasya Vidyate

Na Hi Kalyāṇa-Kṛit Kaśhchid Durgatiṁ Tāta Gachchhati II 40 II

(32) O Arjun! One who sees everyone like themselves, whether being happy or sad, is the (Karma) Yogi who's considered to be of the highest order.

Arjun said – (33) O Krishna! Owing to the fickle nature (of mind), I don't see the (Karma) Yog that you asked me to attain through universality of soul, to last forever. (34) Because, O Krishna, mind is unstable, mighty, powerful and tough to change. I perceive restraining it to be as difficult as taming the wind.

Shri Bhagwān said – (35) O Arjun! There's no doubt that mind is unstable and difficult to restrain; however, through practice and detachment, O Arjun! It's possible to contain. (36) Attaining this Yog is difficult for someone who doesn't have control over their mind. However, I opine that if one tries to persistently practice controlling their mind, consequently it's possible to attain this (Yog).

Arjun said – (37) O Krishna! For someone who trusts, but is deviated from the (Karma) Yog owing to natural inability (to try and control their mind); what are they destined for if they don't attain Yog?

(38) O Krishna! Doesn't this person, who becomes unable to persist on the path of attaining Brahman owing to delusion, get deprived of either side (Spiritual and Material), perishing like a broken cloud (in between)? (39) O Krishna! You must clear this doubt of mine; I wouldn't get anyone other than you who could answer this question.

[Someone who performs all actions with expectations but ethically is destined for heaven, whereas someone who performs all actions with a detached mind without any expectations is destined for Moksha (liberation). However, the doubt raised by Arjun is about someone who neither achieves total detachment nor follows exact methods as per scriptures. What is the fate of such a person, as they may be left with neither? This is the question asked by Arjun.]

Shri Bhagwān said – (40) O Arjun! Such a person is never destined for destruction, in this world or the next; because my friend, someone who performs good deeds is never fated to anything bad.

Prāpya Puṇya-Kṛitāṁ Lokān Uṣhitvā Śhāśhvatīḥ Samāḥ

Śhuchīnāṁ Śhrīmatāṁ Gehe Yoga-Bhraṣhṭo 'Bhijāyate II 41 II

Atha Vā Yogināṁ Eva Kule Bhavati Dhīmatām

Etad Dhi Durlabhataraṁ Loke Janma Yad Īdṛiśham II 42 II

Tatra Taṁ Buddhi-Sanyogaṁ Labhate Paurva-Dehikam

Yatate Cha Tato Bhūyaḥ Sansiddhau Kuru-Nandana II 43 II

Pūrvābhyāsena Tenaiva Hriyate Hyavaśho 'Pi Saḥ

Jijñāsur Api Yogasya Śhabda-Brahmātivartate II 44 II

Prayatnād Yatamānas Tu Yogī Sanśhuddha-Kilbiṣhaḥ

Aneka-Janma-Sansiddhas Tato Yāti Parāṁ Gatim II 45 II

(41) Such a person who has deviated from the path of Yog, reaches and spends many years in the place of the virtuous (heaven) before taking rebirth in a devout and prosperous family;

(42) otherwise taking birth in a family of intelligent Yogis. Such births are extremely difficult to attain in (this) world. (43) There, O Arjun! They're endowed with the wisdom earned in their previous birth and they strive to attain a higher degree of Yog.

(44) Owing to the practice performed in the previous births, they're drawn towards enlightenment definitely (even against their own will). One who develops aspiration for (Karma) Yog, goes beyond Shabda Brahma (ritualistic actions aimed at attaining a place in heaven). (45) Through practice and perseverance, a (Karma) Yogi while purifying their sins, through enlightenment achieved after many births attains perfection.

[In these verses, the words Yog, Yogi and Yogabhrashta (deviated from the path of Yog) are certainly used as Karmayog, Karma Yogi and Karmayogbhrashta), as being born in a wealthy and devout family is not favorable for either a Pātanjal Yogi or a Sānkhya Yogi. Shri Krishna advises that one must start small and as much as possible in the existing birth to practice Karmayog. Through one birth or many, you would definitely achieve enlightenment to attain Moksha. We've described this concept in detail in Chapter 10. Shabda Brahma indicates Vedic rituals which are performed with an expectation of earning something. It's said in Upanishads and Mahābhārat that one must understand that Brahma is of two types viz. Shabda Brahma and the one beyond that (Nirguna Brahma). One first attains Shabda Brahma and once they develop an expertise in that, they attain the one beyond. What this means in essence is that after turning weary of ritualistic actions one begins to perform the same actions with detachment and without expectations. This is the beginning of Karmayog. Once someone begins on this path, one undoubtedly attains Moksha ultimately.]

Tapasvibhyo 'Dhiko Yogi Jñānibhyo 'Pi Mato 'Dhikaḥ

Karmibhyaśh Chādhiko Yogi Tasmād Yogī Bhavārjuna II 46 II

Yoginām Api Sarveṣhāṁ Mad-Gatenāntar-Ātmanā

Śhraddhāvān Bhajate Yo Māṁ Sa Me Yuktatamo Mataḥ II 47 II

(46) (Karma) Yogis are considered to be superior to Tapasvi (austere), Dnyāni (knowledgeable) and Karmi (ritualistic). Therefore, O Arjun, you should become a (Karma) Yogi.

[This verse is very critical in understanding the message of Gitā. Through the word Tapasvi, Gitā mentions the Hatha Yogis who dwell in forests and perform austerities straining their body. Through the word Dnyāni, it mentions Sānkhya Yogi who follow path of Sānkhya or Sanyās (renunciation). Through the word Karmi, it mentions the ritualistic Mimāmsaks who perform all the rituals with an expectation in their mind. Gitā definitively states that a Karma Yogi is superior to all these three kinds of aspirants. This is reiteration of the same point made in 3rd Adhyāya (Karma is better than Akarma 3.8) and 5th Adhyāya (Karmayog is better than Karma Sanyās 5.2). The word Tasmāt (therefore) in the 46th verse aptly proves this and indicates the definitive principle of Gitā.]

(47) However, even in (Karma) Yogis, I consider that to be the supreme Yogi who focuses their mind on me and worships me devotedly.

[For a Karmayogi, addition of Bhakti (devotion) is like an icing on the cake. However, some infer from this verse that Bhakti is considered superior than Karmayog in Gitā. It is however an incorrect interpretation. In the 12th Adhyāya, it's mentioned that abandoning of expectation and attachment is superior to (devotional) meditation. It's one thing to show preference to Karmayog adorned with Bhakti and it's another to claim preference to Bhakti over Karmayog. It is the former here and not the latter but communalists have twisted this to favor their own sect. Anyway, this concludes the description of tools from Pātanjal Yog that help in attaining Samabuddhi (universal view) of Karma Yog. 7th Adhyāya begins description of the other tools Bhakti (devotion) and Dnyān (knowledge).]

This concludes the sixth Adhyāya **Dhyānayog** from the dialogue between Shri Krishna and Arjun on Yog Shāstra (Karmayog Shāstra) within Brahmavidyā (knowledge of Brahman) in the Upanishad sung (narrated) by Shri Bhagwān (Shri Krishna).

Saptamodhyāyah (Seventh Adhyāya)

Śhrī Bhagavān Uvācha

Mayyāsakta-Manāḥ Pārtha Yogaṁ Yuñjan Mad-Āśhrayaḥ

Asanśhayaṁ Samagraṁ Māṁ Yathā Jñāsyasi Tach Chhṛiṇu II 1 II

Jñānaṁ Te 'Haṁ Sa-Vijñānam Idaṁ Vakṣhyāmyaśheṣhataḥ

Yaj Jñātvā Neha Bhūyo 'Nyaj Jñātavyam-Avaśhiṣhyate II 2 II

Saptamodhyāyah (Seventh Adhyāya)

[So far, Karma Yog has been shown to be as potent in attaining Moksha as Sānkhya Mārg yet independent and superior and it's told that even a bit of its practice doesn't go waste. We saw how one is advised how to achieve restraint of senses in order to achieve our goal in this path. While the restraint is necessary to overcome sins such as lust, anger etc. it alone doesn't achieve anything. This has to be associated with Dnyān (Spiritual knowledge) and Vidnyān (Special knowledge). Dnyān (Knowledge) is what makes you understand that all manifest substances have one single unmanifest element and Vidnyān (Science) is what explains how this single element gets transformed into a plethora of different substances. This is now explained in the following 11 Adhyāyas – 7 through 17. The 18th Adhyāya then summarizes the entire Karma Yog. The Adhyāyas now begin with Ksharāksharvichār (Discussion of impermanent and permanent) and then proceed to Kshetrakshetradnyavichār (Discussion of Body and Soul). It's no wonder then that it has taken 11 Adhyāyas to explain it all, with explanation of Bhakti (devotion) and Dnyān (knowledge) paths indulging in understanding the manifest and unmanifest forms of Parmeshwar (respectively). However, one must remember that these, along with the explanation of Pātanjalyog we saw in 6th Adhyāya, are all subsets of the broader explanation of Karma Yog. This is evident once we reach the 18th Adhyāya. However, ignoring this clear reference, many critics of Gitā make divisions of Gitā with first 6 Adhyāyas explaining Karma, next 6 explaining Bhakti and final 6 explaining Dnyān. No doubt these topics have been covered. However, they're not independently covered but as a subset of explaining Karma Yog as we've explained in Chapter 14. Now let's see how Bhagwān Shri Krishna begins with the 7th Adhyāya.]

Shri Bhagwān said – (1) O Arjun! Listen to the way in which you shall gain complete and indubitable knowledge about me while you focus your mind on me and practice (Karma) Yog while taking refuge in me. (2) (Now) I tell you the Dnyān (knowledge) along with Vidnyān (science) omitting nothing, after knowing which there's nothing else left in this world to be known.

Manuṣhyāṇāṁ Sahasreṣhu Kaśhchid Yatati Siddhaye

Yatatām Api Siddhānāṁ Kaśhchin Māṁ Vetti Tattvataḥ II 3 II

Bhūmir-Āpo 'Nalo Vāyuḥ Khaṁ Mano Buddhir Eva Cha

Ahankāra Itīyaṁ Me Bhinnā Prakṛitir Aṣhṭadhā II 4 II

Apareyam Itas Tvanyāṁ Prakṛitiṁ Viddhi Me Parām

Jīva-Bhūtāṁ Mahā-Bāho Yayedaṁ Dhāryate Jagat II 5 II

Etad-Yonīni Bhūtāni Sarvāṇītyupadhāraya

Ahaṁ Kṛitsnasya Jagataḥ Prabhavaḥ Pralayas Tathā II 6 II

Mattaḥ Parataraṁ Nānyat Kiñchid Asti Dhanañjaya

Mayi Sarvam Idaṁ Protaṁ Sūtre Maṇi-Gaṇā Iva II 7 II

Raso 'Ham Apsu Kaunteya Prabhāsmi Śhaśhi-Sūryayoḥ

Praṇavaḥ Sarva-Vedeṣhu Śhabdaḥ Khe Pauruṣhaṁ Nṛiṣhu II 8 II

Puṇyo Gandhaḥ Pṛithivyāṁ Cha Tejaśh Chāsmi Vibhāvasau

Jīvanaṁ Sarva-Bhūteṣhu Tapaśh Chāsmi Tapasviṣhu II 9 II

Bījaṁ Māṁ Sarva-Bhūtānāṁ Viddhi Pārtha Sanātanam

Buddhir Buddhimatām Asmi Tejas Tejasvinām Aham II 10 II

(3) Only one among thousands attempts to gain supreme knowledge and out of many such aspiring enlightened beings, only one ever gains true knowledge of me.

[Of the two parts of knowledge about Parmeshwar, Shri Krishna now starts with Ksharāksharvichār (Discussion of impermanent and permanent).]

(4) Earth, Water, Fire, Air, Space (the five elements), Man (Mind), Buddhi (Intellect) and Ahankār (Ego) together constitute my eight-fold Prakruti (Nature). (5) This is the inferior kind of Prakruti (nature). O Arjun! Understand that apart from this, there's superior kind of Prakruti (nature) of mine in the form of Jeev (soul) that supports this whole universe. (6) Remember that all living beings arise from these two. I am the origin and the deluge (end) of the entire universe.

(7) O Arjun! Beyond me there's nothing else. Like beads strung on a thread, everything is embedded in me.

[These four verses cover the entire essence of the discussion about impermanent and permanent. Subsequent verses elaborate this. While Sānkhya describe two separate primordial elements Purush and Prakruti, Gitā based on Advaita Vedānta doesn't agree with this duality and hence considers them to be the two forms of Parmeshwar from which the universe is formed. From these, the superior Prakruti (Jeev) is discussed in detail in 13th Adhyāya. What remains is the inanimate Prakruti which is called inferior. This is not considered separate but under the control of Parmeshwar. While Gitā doesn't consider this as a separate primordial element, it agrees with the subsequent manifestations of Prakruti as explained in Sānkhya philosophy. Please refer to Chapter 8 for a detailed explanation of both schools of thought and their elements.]

(8) O Arjun! I am the taste in water, I am the radiance of the Sun and the Moon, I am the Omkar in Vedas, I am the sound of space and I am the manhood among all men! (9) I am the fragrance of the earth and I am the energy in fire. I am the life among all living beings and I'm the austerity of ascetics. (10) O Arjun! Consider me to be the eternal seed of all living beings. I am the intelligence of the intelligent and the aura of the glorious.

Balaṁ Balavatāṁ Chāhaṁ Kāma-Rāga-Vivarjitam

Dharmāviruddho Bhūteṣhu Kāmo 'Smi Bharatarṣhabha II 11 II

Ye Chaiva Sāttvikā Bhāvā Rājasās Tāmasāśh Cha Ye

Matta Eveti Tān Viddhi Na Tvahaṁ Teṣhu Te Mayi II 12 II

Tribhir Guṇa-Mayair Bhāvair Ebhiḥ Sarvam Idaṁ Jagat

Mohitaṁ Nābhijānāti Māmebhyaḥ Param Avyayam II 13 II

Daivī Hyeṣhā Guṇa-Mayī Mama Māyā Duratyayā

Mām Eva Ye Prapadyante Māyām Etāṁ Taranti Te II 14 II

Na Māṁ Duṣhkṛitino Mūḍhāḥ Prapadyante Narādhamāḥ

Māyayāpahṛita-Jñānā Āsuraṁ Bhāvam Āśhritāḥ II 15 II

Chatur-Vidhā Bhajante Māṁ Janāḥ Sukṛitino 'Rjuna

Ārto Jijñāsur Arthārthī Jñānī Cha Bharatarṣhabha II 16 II

Teṣhāṁ Jñānī Nitya-Yukta Eka-Bhaktir Viśhiṣhyate

Priyo Hi Jñānino 'Tyartham Ahaṁ Sa Cha Mama Priyaḥ II 17 II

Udārāḥ Sarva Evaite Jñānī Tvātmaiva Me Matam

Āsthitaḥ Sa Hi Yuktātmā Mām Evānuttamāṁ Gatim II 18 II

(11) I am the strength of the mighty devoid of lust and passion. And O Arjun! I am the sexuality among all living beings that doesn't antagonize Dharma (loosely translated as righteousness).

(12) And understand that the Sāttvic, Rājas and Tāmas Gunas (attributes) are all from me. However, they're all in me, I'm not in them.

[The sentence 'They're all in me, I'm not in them' has a very deep meaning. While everything has arisen from the essence of Parmeshwar like the thread running through all beads; Parmeshwar isn't limited only to that but is everything beyond that as well. Naturally, it's imperative that one goes beyond the universe of Nāmroope (name-forms) to grasp the true form of Parmeshwar. This is now explained.]

(13) Being deluded by the three Gunas (attributes namely Sattva, Raja and Tama), the world doesn't recognize the imperishable me beyond these. (14) This divine Māyā (appearance) of mine based in attributes is difficult to overcome. Hence, those who surrender to me get across this Māyā.

[It's clear from this verse that Bhagwān calls the same Trigunātmak (governed by three attributes) Prakruti of Sānkhya as his Māyā. We've elaborated on the concept of Māyā in Chapters 9 and 10.]

(15) Those fools and wicked scoundrels whose knowledge has been destroyed by Māyā turn vile and don't surrender to me.

[After describing those who get destroyed by forgetting about Parmeshwar. Now Bhagwān explains about those who surrender to and worship Parmeshwar.]

(16) O Arjun! Four kinds of virtuous people worship me. Troubled, inquisitive (of knowledge), hopeful (of getting wealth, power etc.) and wise (those who have attained knowledge yet worship me without expectation as they're consummate with knowledge). (17) Of these, the wise is special who worships me exclusively and is always steadfast (without any expectations). I am the most favorite of the wise and they're my most favorite. (18) While all my devotees are generous, I feel the wise are equal to me; because while enriching themselves they've attained the supreme stage in everything, which is me.

Bahūnāṁ Janmanām Ante Jñānavān Māṁ Prapadyate

Vāsudevaḥ Sarvam Iti Sa Mahātmā Su-Durlabhaḥ II 19 II

Kāmais Tais Tair Hṛita-Jñānāḥ Prapadyante 'Nya-Devatāḥ

Taṁ Taṁ Niyamam Āsthāya Prakṛityā Niyatāḥ Svayā II 20 II

Yo Yo Yāṁ Yāṁ Tanuṁ Bhaktaḥ Śhraddhayārchitum Ichchhati

Tasya Tasyāchalāṁ Śhraddhāṁ Tām Eva Vidadhāmyaham II 21 II

Sa Tayā Śhraddhayā Yuktas Tasyārādhanam Īhate

Labhate Cha Tataḥ Kāmān Mayaiva Vihitān Hi Tān II 22 II

Antavat Tu Phalaṁ Teṣhāṁ Tad Bhavatyalpa-Medhasām

Devān Deva-Yajo Yānti Mad-Bhaktā Yānti Mām Api II 23 II

Avyaktaṁ Vyaktim Āpannaṁ Manyante Mām Abuddhayaḥ

Paraṁ Bhāvam Ajānanto Mamāvyayam Anuttamam II 24 II

(19) After many births, the ones endowed with wisdom attain my level by experiencing "Everything that there is, is Vasudev (Parmeshwar)". Such a great soul is extremely rare.

[After saying that Prakruti and Purush are nothing but two forms of him, Bhagwān says that he's occupied the entire universe in unity. Worship is a must, be it of the unmanifest or the manifest. As worshipping the manifest or Bhakti (devotion) is easier, it is described here. It's also mentioned that those worshipping for selfish motives are novices and an inferior category of devotees. The worship of the wise who do so without any motive for themselves is considered superior.]

(20) By following their nature, people possessed by their desires (to possess certain heavenly goals) follow the respective codes to worship other (varied) deities. (21) I establish the reverence of each devotee as per the reverence in which they wish to worship the respective deities. (22) Thereafter, they start to worship the deity reverentially and thereby attain the corresponding fruits.

(23) However, the fruits achieved by (these) dimwits are perishable (not like the everlasting Moksha or liberation). Worshippers of deities go to the deities and my devotees come to me.

[These verses beautifully explain how different people find solace in worshipping different deities. Bhagwān says that he (Parmeshwar) makes people worship those deities which they identify themselves to be aiming for, based on their inherent nature. While common people believe that they get the fruits bestowed upon them by these respective deities, it is actually the Parmeshwar who's bestowing everything as per their respective reverence. Bhagwān says that by worshipping different deities, one's mind matures and ultimately begins to pursue the single Almighty Parmeshwar. While we say it is Parmeshwar who makes people worship respective deities, it is actually based on the past Karma and hence Parmeshwar is actually not involved actively. We've discussed this in detail in 10th and 13th Chapter.]

(24) Unwise people, without knowing my supreme, superlative and unmanifest form, consider me manifest even though I'm unmanifest.

Nāhaṁ Prakāśhaḥ Sarvasya Yoga-Māyā-Samāvṛitaḥ

Mūḍho 'Yaṁ Nābhijānāti Loko Mām Ajam Avyayam II 25 II

Vedāhaṁ Samatītāni Vartamānāni Chārjuna

Bhavişhyāṇi Cha Bhūtāni Māṁ Tu Veda Na Kaśhchana II 26 II

Ichchhā-Dveṣha-Samutthena Dvandva-Mohena Bhārata

Sarva-Bhūtāni Sammohaṁ Sarge Yānti Parantapa II 27 II

Yeṣhāṁ Tvanta-Gataṁ Pāpaṁ Janānāṁ Puṇya-Karmaṇām

Te Dvandva-Moha-Nirmuktā Bhajante Māṁ Dṛiḍha-Vratāḥ II 28 II

Jarā-Maraṇa-Mokṣhāya Mām Āśhritya Yatanti Ye

Te Brahma Tadviduḥ Kṛitsnam Adhyātmaṁ Karma Chākhilam II 29 II

Sādhibhūtādhidaivaṁ Māṁ Sādhiyajñaṁ Cha Ye Viduḥ

Prayāṇa-Kāle 'Pi Cha Māṁ Te Vidur Yukta-Chetasaḥ II 30 II

(25) I am not visible to everyone clearly, as I'm enveloped by the Yogic Māyā. Fools don't know that I'm unborn and unchanging.

[The tact or idea (Yukti or Yog) of being expressed in manifest form from the original unmanifest one is called Māyā. As this Māyā is with name-forms, it is considered merely an appearance and true Parmeshwar is beyond it, according to Vedānta as well as Gitā. It tells us that only the unwise or fools worship the manifest deities instead of worshipping the ultimate Parmeshwar.]

(26) I know all the living beings from past, present and future. However, O Arjun! No one knows me. (27) Because, O Arjun! All living beings are deluded in this world due to the dualistic illusions (happiness and sorrow) of desire and aversion (of senses). (28) But the virtuous people whose sins have ended, free themselves of the dualistic illusion and worship me with resolve. (29) Those who, by taking shelter in me, take efforts to free themselves from the cycle of birth and death; they understand entire Brahman (absolute), Adhyātma (spirituality) and Karma (action). (30) And those who know me to be all of Adhibhoot (matter), Adhidaiva (deities of heaven) and Adhiyadnya (deities worshipped in rituals), know me even at the time of death because of having an enriched mind.

[We'll see explanation of Adhyātma, Adhibhoot, Adhidaiva and Adhiyadnya in the next Adhyāya. It's said in our scriptures and Upanishads that one attains the next birth as per the state of mind at the time of their death. The words 'even at the time of death' reiterate this in 30th verse. This verse acts as a preface of the detailed explanation on this topic covered in the next Adhyāya.]

This concludes the seventh Adhyāya **Dnyānvidnyānyog** from the dialogue between Shri Krishna and Arjun on Yog Shāstra (Karmayog Shāstra) within Brahmavidyā (knowledge of Brahman) in the Upanishad sung (narrated) by Shri Bhagwān (Shri Krishna).

Ashtamodhyāyah (Eighth Adhyāya)

Arjuna Uvācha

Kiṁ Tad Brahma Kim Adhyātmaṁ Kiṁ Karma Puruṣhottama

Adhibhūtaṁ Cha Kiṁ Proktam Adhidaivaṁ Kim Uchyate II 1 II

Adhiyajñaḥ Kathaṁ Ko 'Tra Dehe 'Smin Madhusūdana

Prayāṇa-Kāle Cha Kathaṁ Jñeyo 'Si Niyatātmabhiḥ II 2 II

Śhrī Bhagavān Uvācha

Akṣharaṁ Brahma Paramaṁ Svabhāvo 'Dhyātmam Uchyate

Bhūta-Bhāvodbhava-Karo Visargaḥ Karma-Sanjñitaḥ II 3 II

Ashtamodhyāyah (Eighth Adhyāya)

[The eighth Adhyāya continues with the explanation of Dnyān-Vidnyān. The different forms of Parmeshwar cited at the end of the last Adhyāya viz. Adhyātma, Karma, Adhibhoot, Adhidaiva and Adhiyadnya, are explained in this Adhyāya. However, it is given very briefly. Refer to the respective chapters to study these in detail. Arjun develops curiosity about these words and enquires about them at the beginning of the eighth Adhyāya.]

Arjun said – (1) O Krishna! What is that Brahman? What is Adhyātma? What's Karma? What's to be called Adhibhoot? And what is to be called Adhidaivat? (2) How is Adhiyadnya? And O Krishna, who's (the Adhideha) in this body? How do those who restrain their senses recognize you at the end? (Pray tell me)

[In addition to the other terms, Arjun adds a question about the Adhideha (one who resides in the body). Remembering this helps us understand the answer.]

Shri Bhagwān said – (3) Supreme undying principle is Brahman; the inherent nature of every object is Adhyātma. The process that generates all material entities (living and non-living beings, from Brahman) is Karma.

Adhibhūtaṁ Kşharo Bhāvaḥ Puruşhaśh Chādhidaivatam

Adhiyajño 'Ham Evātra Dehe Deha-Bhṛitāṁ Vara II 4 II

Anta-Kāle Cha Mām Eva Smaran Muktvā Kalevaram

Yaḥ Prayāti Sa Mad-Bhāvaṁ Yāti Nāstyatra Sanśhayaḥ II 5 II

Yaṁ Yaṁ Vāpi Smaran Bhāvaṁ Tyajatyante Kalevaram

Taṁ Tam Evaiti Kaunteya Sadā Tad-Bhāva-Bhāvitaḥ II 6 II

(4) (From all the entities made) mortal entity (with name-forms) is Adhibhoot, and the conscious being (within them) is Adhidaivat; the Adhiyadnya (the worshipped deity of all rituals) is me who is, O great one, the one within the body (Adhideha).

[The adjective 'Supreme' in 3rd verse is used for undying and not for Brahman. Sānkhya call Prakruti Akshar (undying). However, Vedānti consider Brahman to be beyond the unmanifest, undying Prakruti. Hence, an additional adjective 'Param' (Supreme) is added to denote Brahman and avoid confusion with Sānkhya Prakruti. The word Swabhāv is taken as inherent nature of any substance. By calling himself as the Adhiyadnya (deity worshipped in all rituals) and the one that resides within the body, Bhagwān denotes that Adhidaiva, Adhiyadnya and Adhideha in a human body are all him. Sānkhya believe in numerous Purush (souls) whereas Vedānti disagree and affirm that there's one universal soul that resides within everybody, which is indicated in this verse. Thus, in summary, when Bhagwān says that he's the one, he means it for all the terms described in the two verses – Brahman, Karma, Adhyātma etc. By first enlisting different perceived worshipped forms and then declaring all of those to be himself, Bhagwān unifies everything; debunking the multiplicity and asserting the universal nature of Parmeshwar. Now he continues to answer Arjun's question about recognizing it –]

(5) And the one who leaves the body while remembering me at the end, undoubtedly goes on to become one with me.

(6) Otherwise, O Arjun, whatever one spends their life being engrossed in and remembering at the time of their death, becomes one with that.

[5th verse explains why one must remember Parmeshwar while 6th verse describes how one would naturally remember that what they've been holding to be true all along. Thus, the significance of remembering Parmeshwar throughout the life as well as at the end is explained and what's also explained is how those thinking of Parmeshwar unite with it while those thinking of deities unite with them.]

Tasmāt Sarveşhu Kāleşhu Mām Anusmara Yudhya Cha

Mayyarpita-Mano-Buddhir Mām Evaişhyasyasanśhayam II 7 II

Abhyāsa-Yoga-Yuktena Chetasā Nānya-Gāminā

Paramaṁ Puruşhaṁ Divyaṁ Yāti Pārthānuchintayan II 8 II

Kaviṁ Purāṇam Anuśhāsitāram Aṇor Aṇīyānsam Anusmared Yaḥ

Sarvasya Dhātāram Achintya-Rūpam Āditya-Varṇaṁ Tamasaḥ Parastāt II 9 II

Prayāṇa-Kāle Manasāchalena Bhaktyā Yukto Yoga-Balena Chaiva

Bhruvor Madhye Prāṇam Āveśhya Samyak Sa Taṁ Paraṁ Puruşham Upaiti Divyam II 10 II

Yad Akşharaṁ Veda-Vido Vadanti Viśhanti Yad Yatayo Vīta-Rāgāḥ

Yad Ichchhanto Brahmacharyaṁ Charanti Tat Te Padaṁ Saṅgraheṇa Pravakşhye II 11 II

Sarva-Dvārāṇi Sanyamya Mano Hṛidi Nirudhya Cha

Mūrdhnyādhāyātmanaḥ Prāṇam Āsthito Yoga-Dhāraṇām II 12 II

Oṁ Ityekākşharaṁ Brahma Vyāharan Mām Anusmaran

Yaḥ Prayāti Tyajan Dehaṁ Sa Yāti Paramāṁ Gatim II 13 II

Ananya-Chetāḥ Satataṁ Yo Māṁ Smarati Nityaśhaḥ

Tasyāhaṁ Sulabhaḥ Pārtha Nitya-Yuktasya Yoginaḥ II 14 II

Mām Upetya Punar Janma Duḥkhālayam Aśhāśhvatam

Nāpnuvanti Mahātmānaḥ Sansiddhiṁ Paramāṁ Gatāḥ II 15 II

(7) Therefore, remember me all the time and go to war. Once you dedicate your Man (mind) and Buddhi (intellect) to me, it is beyond doubt that you'd become one with me (despite going to war). (8) O Arjun! When one meditates on the Divine, Supreme Being; without letting their mind waver; they undoubtedly reach there.

[7th verse is a glorious reminder to those claiming Bhagavad Gitā to favor Bhakti (devotion) without focusing on material life. Bhagwān clearly states that Moksha (liberation) is attained through knowledge and remembrance of Parmeshwar even at the end of one's life. While practice is essential throughout life, one doesn't have to quit Karma (action). Rather, he reiterates that one must perform all their duties without expectations.]

(9) One who remembers the poet (omniscient), ancient controller, one smaller than the smallest particle (most subtle), everyone's support, unthinkable form and glorious like the Sun beyond darkness, (10) by focusing their mind with Yogic might, with devotion and fixing Prāna (life energy) between their eyebrows properly; certainly attains the Divine, Supreme Being. (11) Let me now briefly tell you that concept (Omkar Brahman) which scholars of Vedas call 'Akshar' (undying), what ascetics enter by quitting all desire and attachment, aiming which they practice celibacy. (12) One who brings Prāna (life energy) to their head by restraining all (sensory) doors and restricting mind to their heart (13) and leaves their body while chanting the single syllable 'Om' which represents undying Brahman and while remembering me; attains the ultimate destiny.

[The description of Parmeshwar given in the verses 9-11 is from Upanishads. Om is one of the syllables from the Devanagari alphabet and is considered symbolic of the supreme.]

(14) O Arjun! The perpetually enriched Yogi who remembers me absolutely all the time, attains me easily. (15) After becoming one with me, the enlightened being is not bestowed with reincarnation which is impermanent and the house of sorrow.

Ā-Brahma-Bhuvanāl Lokāḥ Punar Āvartino 'Rjuna

Mām Upetya Tu Kaunteya Punar Janma Na Vidyate II 16 II

Sahasra-Yuga-Paryantam Ahar Yad Brahmaṇo Viduḥ

Rātriṁ Yuga-Sahasrāntāṁ Te 'Ho-Rātra-Vido Janāḥ II 17 II

Avyaktād Vyaktayaḥ Sarvāḥ Prabhavantyahar-Āgame

Rātryāgame Pralīyante Tatraivāvyakta-Sanjñake II 18 II

Bhūta-Grāmaḥ Sa Evāyaṁ Bhūtvā Bhūtvā Pralīyate

Rātryāgame 'Vaśhaḥ Pārtha Prabhavatyahar-Āgame II 19 II

Paras Tasmāt Tu Bhāvo 'Nyo 'Vyakto 'Vyaktāt Sanātanaḥ

Yaḥ Sa Sarveṣhu Bhūteṣhu Naśhyatsu Na Vinaśhyati II 20 II

Avyakto 'Kṣhara Ityuktas Tam Āhuḥ Paramāṁ Gatim

Yaṁ Prāpya Na Nivartante Tad Dhāma Paramaṁ Mama II 21 II

Puruṣhaḥ Sa Paraḥ Pārtha Bhaktyā Labhyas Tvananyayā

Yasyāntaḥ-Sthāni Bhūtāni Yena Sarvam Idaṁ Tatam II 22 II

(16) Even those who are in heaven are bound to return to be born on earth sometime. However, O Arjun, once they become one with me, there's no rebirth.

[The verses show how attaining a place in different heavens is also not permanent and one must return or be reborn on the earth once they exhaust their earned goodness. Hence, those destinies are considered inferior. However, Moksha (liberation) through knowledge of Parmeshwar is everlasting as it destroys any chance of rebirth and thus considered superior.]

(17) Those who understand (the meaning of) day and night know a day to be consisting of a thousand (Maha) Yug (eons) of Brahmadev and the night to be of a thousand (Maha) Yug (as well).

[This verse mentions the concepts of Mahāyug and Day-Night without explaining the terminology and hence we must refer to the same given elsewhere. It's given in both Mahābhārat (of which Gitā is a part) and Manusmriti. There are four Yug (eons) viz. Krut, Treta, Dwāpar and Kali. These four Yug together constitute a Mahāyug. This Mahāyug is considered to be one day of Brahma and the same time corresponds to one night as well. The word Avyakta (unmanifest) in the next verse points to unmanifest Prakruti of Sānkhya and not Brahman. We've discussed this and many other related concepts in detail in the 8th chapter.]

(18) Once this day (of Brahma) starts, all manifest (substances) arises from the unmanifest; and once the night starts, they all converge into the same unmanifest. (19) The same group of living beings take birth again and again involuntarily, obscure once the night starts, and are reborn once the day begins. (20) However, the unmanifest substance which is beyond the unmanifest stated above, which doesn't get obscured even when all living beings do; (21) the unmanifest which is called Akshar (undying), is said to be the Supreme (superlative) or ultimate destiny; attaining which there's no return, which is my ultimate abode, too.

(22) The Supreme Being within whom all living beings lie and who inhabits all this, is attainable only through absolute devotion.

[The word Avyakta (unmanifest) is first used to denote the Prakruti of Sānkhya and later to denote the Brahman. However, 20th and 21st

Yatra Kāle Tvanāvṛittim Āvṛittiṁ Chaiva Yoginaḥ

Prayātā Yānti Taṁ Kālaṁ Vakṣhyāmi Bharatarṣhabha II 23 II

Agnir Jyotir Ahaḥ Śhuklaḥ Ṣhaṇ-Māsā Uttarāyaṇam

Tatra Prayātā Gachchhanti Brahma Brahma-Vido Janāḥ II 24 II

Dhūmo Rātris Tathā Kṛiṣhṇaḥ Ṣhaṇ-Māsā Dakṣhiṇāyanam

Tatra Chāndramasaṁ Jyotir Yogī Prāpya Nivartate II 25 II

Śhukla-Kṛiṣhṇe Gatī Hyete Jagataḥ Śhāśhvate Mate

Ekayā Yātyanāvṛittim Anyayāvartate Punaḥ II 26 II

Naite Sṛitī Pārtha Jānan Yogī Muhyati Kaśhchana

Tasmāt Sarveṣhu Kāleṣhu Yoga-Yukto Bhavārjuna II 27 II

Vedeṣhu Yajñeṣhu Tapaḥsu Chaiva Dāneṣhu Yat Puṇya-Phalaṁ Pradiṣhṭam

Atyeti Tat Sarvam Idaṁ Viditvā Yogī Paraṁ Sthānam Upaiti Chādyam II 28 II

verses explain how the Parabrahma or Parmeshwar is Akshar (undying) and the ultimate principle. The words 'Avyakta' and 'Akshar' are both thus used in Gitā to denote Sānkhya Prakruti once and Parabrahma or Parmeshwar in another instance. We need to read the context to understand which one is denoted when. Bhagwān now explains about fate of those who have to return from heaven to take rebirth.]

(23) Now, O Arjun, I shall tell you the period when a (Karma) Yogi dies never to take birth again and the period when they do. (24) Those with knowledge of Brahman who pass away through fire, flame, day, waxing moon or during the (6 months indicating) northward movement of the sun attain Parabrahma after death (don't return).

(25) Yogis who pass away through (fire), smoke, night, waning moon and during the (6 months indicating) southward movement of the sun reach the Chandralok (House of the moonshine) and (subsequently) return. (26) Thus, Waxing and waning (meaning illumined and dark) are considered as two permanent paths of the world. Following the former, one doesn't return while following the latter one does.

[These two paths Shukla (waxing moon) and Krishna (waning moon) are also called Devayān and Pitruyān or Archirādi and Dhumrādi paths in Upanishads and are also mentioned in Rig Veda. Both these paths begin once a corpse is cremated after one's death and hence both begin with fire. Hence, one must consider the first step in 25th verse to be implicit as fire. Detailed discussion about this is done in 10th chapter.]

(27) O Arjun! No (Karma) Yogi knowing these two paths gets deluded. Therefore, O Arjun, you remain enriched in Yog all the time.

(28) Knowing this (principle), a (Karma) Yogi surpasses the fruits of Vedas, Yadnya (sacrificial fire), Tapa (austerities) and Dāna (charity) to attain the Superlative place beyond.

This concludes the eighth Adhyāya **Aksharbrahmayog** from the dialogue between Shri Krishna and Arjun on Yog Shāstra (Karmayog Shāstra) within Brahmavidyā (knowledge of Brahman) in the Upanishad sung (narrated) by Shri Bhagwān (Shri Krishna).

Navamodhyāyah (Ninth Adhyāya)

Śhrī Bhagavān Uvācha

Idaṁ Tu Te Guhyatamaṁ Pravakṣhyāmyanasūyave

Jñānaṁ Vijñāna-Sahitaṁ Yaj Jñātvā Mokṣhyase 'Śhubhāt II 1 II

Rāja-Vidyā Rāja-Guhyaṁ Pavitram Idam Uttamam

Pratyakṣhāvagamaṁ Dharmyaṁ Su-Sukhaṁ Kartum Avyayam II 2 II

Aśhraddadhānāḥ Puruṣhā Dharmasyāsya Parantapa

Aprāpya Māṁ Nivartante Mṛityu-Samsāra-Vartmani II 3 II

Mayā Tatam Idaṁ Sarvaṁ Jagad Avyakta-Mūrtinā

Mat-Sthāni Sarva-Bhūtāni Na Chāhaṁ Teṣhvavasthitaḥ II 4 II

Na Cha Mat-Sthāni Bhūtāni Paśhya Me Yogam Aiśhwaram

Bhūta-Bhṛin Na Cha Bhūta-Stho Mamātmā Bhūta-Bhāvanaḥ II 5 II

Yathākāśha-Sthito Nityaṁ Vāyuḥ Sarvatra-Go Mahān

Tathā Sarvāṇi Bhūtāni Mat-Sthānītyupadhāraya II 6 II

Navamodhyāyah (Ninth Adhyāya)

[In order to show how a Karmayogi attains complete knowledge of Parmeshwar to attain Moksha (liberation) and everlasting peace, we began with the explanation of Dnyān-Vidnyān in 7th Adhyāya. We also saw path to attain Samādhi (meditative transcendence) through chanting of Omkar. However, these paths are so arduous that knowledge of Parmeshwar would never be accessible for common people if these were the only ways. Thus, Bhagwān now begins with description of an easier path where one can understand the form of Parmeshwar through love and devotion in a direct way. This path is now explained in Adhyāyas 9 through 12. However, one must remember that this path is not separate but a part of the explanation of Dnyān-Vidnyān which has begun since 7th Adhyāya for practicing Karmayog.]

Shri Bhagwān said – (1) As you're free of envy, let me now reveal to you the most confidential knowledge along with the science; knowing which you shall be free of sins. (2) This knowledge is supreme among secrets, best among sciences, holy, superlative, directly comprehensible, undiminishing and righteous. (3) O Arjun! The ones not believing in this Dharma (righteous knowledge) return to the path of mortal Samsāra (cycle of birth and death) without becoming one with me (do not attain Moksha).

(4) I've occupied the whole world with my unmanifest form. All living beings are in me; I'm not in them. (5) And yet, all living beings are not in me. Behold my divine Yogic might! My soul who creates all living beings is not among them despite sustaining them!

(6) Just as the great gas (air) occupies the space, understand that all living beings exist within me.

[This apparent paradox is created because of the Saguna-Nirguna (with form and formless) nature of Parmeshwar. After piquing the curiosity of Arjun through such words, Bhagwān now reiterates the description of how universe is formed, albeit in a slightly different way. This Yog (tact or capability) of becoming manifest from the original unmanifest form is 'Māyā'. As this Yog (ability) is easily accessible to Parmeshwar (rather, it's owned by Parmeshwar), Parmeshwar is also called Yogeshwar (God of Yog).]

Sarva-Bhūtāni Kaunteya Prakṛitiṁ Yānti Māmikām

Kalpa-Kṣhaye Punas Tāni Kalpādau Visṛijāmyaham II 7 II

Prakṛitiṁ Svām Avaṣhṭabhya Visṛijāmi Punaḥ Punaḥ

Bhūta-Grāmam Imaṁ Kṛitsnam Avaśhaṁ Prakṛiter Vaśhāt II 8 II

Na Cha Māṁ Tāni Karmāṇi Nibadhnanti Dhanañjaya

Udāsīna-Vad Āsīnam Asaktaṁ Teṣhu Karmasu II 9 II

Mayādhyakṣheṇa Prakṛitiḥ Sūyate Sa-Charācharam

Hetunānena Kaunteya Jagad Viparivartate II 10 II

Avajānanti Māṁ Mūḍhā Mānuṣhīṁ Tanum Āśhritam

Paraṁ Bhāvam Ajānanto Mama Bhūta-Maheśhvaram II 11 II

Moghāśhā Mogha-Karmāṇo Mogha-Jñānā Vichetasaḥ

Rākṣhasīm Āsurīṁ Chaiva Prakṛitiṁ Mohinīṁ Śhritāḥ II 12 II

Mahātmānas Tu Māṁ Pārtha Daivīṁ Prakṛitim Āśhritāḥ

Bhajantyananya-Manaso Jñātvā Bhūtādim Avyayam II 13 II

Satataṁ Kīrtayanto Māṁ Yatantaśh Cha Dṛiḍha-Vratāḥ

Namasyantaśh Cha Māṁ Bhaktyā Nitya-Yuktā Upāsate II 14 II

Jñāna-Yajñena Chāpyanye Yajanto Mām Upāsate

Ekatvena Pṛithaktvena Bahudhā Viśhvato-Mukham II 15 II

(7) O Arjun! At the end of Kalpa (a unit of time explained earlier), all living beings converge into my Prakruti (unmanifest form) and at the beginning of Kalpa (new day of Brahma), I create them again. (8) I join hands with my Prakruti to create, again and again, this plethora of living beings who are dependent on Prakruti because of being owned by it. (9) However, O Arjun! As I'm not involved in (attached to) these actions and I'm inert throughout, these actions are not binding on me.

(10) I chair the process of creation of universe through Prakruti. For this reason, O Arjun! The cycle of the world is going on.

[While the process of creation of manifest from the unmanifest is explained earlier in 8th Adhyāya, above verses additionally mention how Parmeshwar creates everything as per their previous Karma (actions) and is thus detached from the process of creation. While a scientific analysis would entail all of this together, the style of Gitā is conversational thus explaining a few concepts here and a few there as and when they come in the flow of answers.]

(11) The fools who don't recognize my ultimate form as the grand Ishwar (almighty) of all living beings insult me in the humanoid form (considering me to be human). (12) Their hopes go waste, actions become futile, knowledge becomes empty and mind becomes corrupted while they harbor delusional monstrosities and evil tendencies.

(13) However, O Arjun! The greats who harbor divine nature recognize me as the everlasting, primordial origin of all living beings and worship me. (14) And by being perseverant, determined and constantly enriched (with Yog), bow down to me and worship me.

(15) Yet others worship my cosmic version in single, dual or multiple forms through the sacrificial rituals of knowledge.

[These verses describe the different kinds of people of saintly and evil nature. The meaning of Dnyān Yadnya (sacrificial rituals of knowledge) is understanding of Parmeshwar through pure knowledge, as described earlier. Even this knowledge can be attained through monist, dualist or polytheist approaches. This shows how these concepts are ancient, even though the sects following these are relatively recent.]

Ahaṁ Kratur Ahaṁ Yajñaḥ Svadhāham Aham Auṣhadham

Mantro 'Ham Aham Evājyam Aham Agnir Ahaṁ Hutam II 16 II

Pitāham Asya Jagato Mātā Dhātā Pitāmahaḥ

Vedyaṁ Pavitram Oṁkāra Ṛik Sāma Yajur Eva Cha II 17 II

Gatir Bhartā Prabhuḥ Sākṣhī Nivāsaḥ Śharaṇaṁ Suhṛit

Prabhavaḥ Pralayaḥ Sthānaṁ Nidhānaṁ Bījam Avyayam II 18 II

Tapāmyaham Ahaṁ Varṣhaṁ Nigṛihṇāmyutsṛijāmi Cha

Amṛitaṁ Chaiva Mṛityuśh Cha Sad Asach Chāham Arjuna II 19 II

Trai-Vidyā Māṁ Soma-Pāḥ Pūta-Pāpā Yajñair Iṣhṭvā Svar-Gatiṁ Prārthayante

Te Puṇyam Āsādya Surendra-Lokam Aśhnanti Divyān Divi Deva-Bhogān II 20 II

Te Taṁ Bhuktvā Swarga-Lokaṁ Viśhālaṁ Kṣhīṇe Puṇye Martya-Lokaṁ Viśhanti

Evaṁ Trayī-Dharmam Anuprapannā Gatāgataṁ Kāma-Kāmā Labhante II 21 II

(16) I am Kratu (Sacrifices described in Shrutis). I am Yadnya (Sacrifices described in Smrutis). I am Svadhā (the food offered to the ancestors). I am Aushadh (the food prepared from plants). I am the chants (uttered while making the offerings during sacrifices). I am the Ghee (clarified butter). I am the (sacrificial) fire and I am the offerings (put in the sacrificial fire).

[While Kratu and Yadnya are synonymous, Kratu essentially means the ritualistic sacrifices mentioned in orthodox texts while Yadnya has a broader meaning covering all kinds of sacrifices and rituals. This is the interpretation in Shānkarbhāshya as well and the one we agree with.]

(17) I am the father, mother, supporter and grandsire. I am whatever is holy and to be known. I am Omkar, Rig Veda, Yajur Veda and Sāma Veda. (18) I am (everyone's) destiny, nurturer, lord, witness, shelter, surrender, mate, origin, dissolution, repository, resting place as well as the imperishable seed.

(19) I bring in the sunshine, I hold and cause rain. O Arjun, I am the immortality, death, Sat (truth) and Asat (untruth).

[While a similar description of Parmeshwar in also given in subsequent Adhyāyas (10, 11 and 12), here the role of Parmeshwar is described like a mother, father, friend etc. which is unique. Parmeshwar is also described as the one causing a favorable as well as unfavorable event (holding as well as causing rain).]

(20) Three different (performing actions from the three Vedas viz. Rig, Yajur and Sāma) Somapi (drinkers of Somras which is left after the sacrificial fire burns out) and sinless who worship me through Yadnya (ritualistic sacrifices) for attaining a place in heaven, reach the pious abode of Indra and enjoy many pleasures of celestial deities. (21) And after enjoying the pleasures of the grand heavenly abode and exhausting the fruits of their good deeds, take rebirth to appear on the earth. This way, followers of the rituals from the three Vedas and those aspiring for desirous pleasures make trips to (heaven) and fro.

[The fact that one has to return to the earth after enjoying the pleasures of heaven once they exhaust their quota is mentioned several times

Ananyāśh Chintayanto Māṁ Ye Janāḥ Paryupāsate

Teṣhāṁ Nityābhiyuktānāṁ Yoga-Kṣhemaṁ Vahāmyaham II 22 II

Ye 'Pyanya-Devatā-Bhaktā Yajante Śhraddhayānvitāḥ

Te 'Pi Mām Eva Kaunteya Yajantyavidhi-Pūrvakam II 23 II

Ahaṁ Hi Sarva-Yajñānāṁ Bhoktā Cha Prabhureva Cha

Na Tu Mām Abhijānanti Tattvenātaśh Chyavanti Te II 24 II

Yānti Deva-Vratā Devān Pitṝn Yānti Pitṛi-Vratāḥ

Bhūtāni Yānti Bhūtejyā Yānti Mad-Yājino 'Pi Mām II 25 II

Patraṁ Puṣhpaṁ Phalaṁ Toyaṁ Yo Me Bhaktyā Prayachchhati

Tadahaṁ Bhaktyupahṛitam Aśhnāmi Prayatātmanaḥ II 26 II

Yat Karoṣhi Yad Aśhnāsi Yaj Juhoṣhi Dadāsi Yat

Yat Tapasyasi Kaunteya Tat Kuruṣhva Mad-Arpaṇam II 27 II

earlier as well. One may doubt that if one gives up performing these prescribed rituals or worshipping of deities, how the cycle of universe would go on. The subsequent verses answer this question.]

(22) I ensure the survival of those enriched Yogis who are absolute devotees, remember me and worship me.

(23) O Arjun! Those that worship by being thoroughly reverent devotees of numerous deities, (in turn) worship me even though they don't follow prescribed rituals. (24) Because I am the consumer of all ritualistic offerings and their overlord. However, they slip because they don't have my knowledge principally.

[The key point being made in these two verses is that while different people worship different deities, they're indirectly worshipping one of the qualities of Parmeshwar; as each deity represents one or a few attributes of the Almighty. What's important is the devotion and not the deity.]

(25) Those worshipping the deities go to the deities. Those worshipping the ancestors go to the ancestors. Those worshipping different beings go to those beings. And those who worship me come to me.

[While Parmeshwar is one, the fruits of worship differ, based on the state of mind and the aim behind the worship, for different people. However, even the fruit is not awarded by the worshipped entity but Parmeshwar itself, based on the actions of the devotees as mentioned earlier (Gitā 7.20-23).

(26) Even if someone offers me a leaf, flower, fruit or just some water (as per their capacity) with devotion, I (happily) consume the devotional offering of the devotee having controlled mind.

[The principle of the intellect being more important than the action is substantiated here in the form of Bhakti Mārg (path of devotion). This is why it's said that Parmeshwar only demands true devotion. The object offered is immaterial.]

(27) O Arjun! Dedicate to me everything you do, eat, offer, and donate, so also the austerities you perform.

Śhubhāśhubha-Phalair Evaṁ Mokṣhyase Karma-Bandhanaiḥ

Sannyāsa-Yoga-Yuktātmā Vimukto Mām Upaiṣhyasi II 28 II

Samo 'Haṁ Sarva-Bhūteṣhu Na Me Dveṣhyo 'Sti Na Priyaḥ

Ye Bhajanti Tu Māṁ Bhaktyā Mayi Te Teṣhu Chāpyaham II 29 II

Api Chet Su-Durāchāro Bhajate Mām Ananya-Bhāk

Sādhur Eva Sa Mantavyaḥ Samyag Vyavasito Hi Saḥ II 30 II

Kṣhipraṁ Bhavati Dharmātmā Śhaśhvach-Chhāntiṁ Nigachchhati

Kaunteya Pratijānīhi Na Me Bhaktaḥ Praṇaśhyati II 31 II

Māṁ Hi Pārtha Vyapāśhritya Ye 'Pi Syuḥ Pāpa-Yonayaḥ

Striyo Vaiśhyās Tathā Śhūdrās Te 'Pi Yānti Parāṁ Gatim II 32 II

Kiṁ Punar Brāhmaṇāḥ Puṇyā Bhaktā Rājarṣhayas Tathā

Anityam Asukhaṁ Lokam Imaṁ Prāpya Bhajasva Mām II 33 II

(28) By doing so, you get free from the bindings of your Karma (actions) may they be good or bad fruits; and by following this Yog of renunciation (of the fruits of Karma), you shall become a free, enriched soul and reach me.

[This makes it clear that even a devotee must perform all actions, not quit them. The same principle which has been told in the context of Karmayog (path of Karma), Dnyānyog (path of knowledge) is now narrated in the context of Bhakti Yog (path of devotion). According to Gitā, this is the true renunciation (of attachment and expectations of fruits) and not of actual actions.]

(29) I am the same for all living beings. I neither favor nor dislike anyone. Those who worship me devotionally are with me and so am I with them. (30) Even a sinner is to be considered a sage if they're worshipping me absolutely, because their intellect has a strong resolve. (31) They soon become righteous and attain lasting peace. O Arjun! Know this definitely that my devotee never perishes.

[One mustn't misinterpret the 30th to mean that Bhagwān likes their devotees even if they're sinners. The point made there is that even if one is a sinner, they automatically stop the way of sins once they definitively start on the path of devotion to Parmeshwar and gradually become righteous and attain peace.]

(32) Because, O Arjun! By taking refuge in me, women, Vaishyas (traders), Shudras (craftsmen) or even sinners attain ultimate destiny. (33) What then to say about the pious Brāhmans, warriors and my devotees? As you're in this impermanent and unhappy world, you should worship me.

[Some critics categorize women, Vaishyas and Shudras to be under the term Pāpayoni (sinners). However, it's a wrong interpretation according to us. Women, Vaishyas and Shudras were not considered to be born so because of any sins. They're separately included here as earlier they were denied rights to hear or utter Vedas, indicating that even they're included in this path of devotion abolishing all discrimination.]

Man-Manā Bhava Mad-Bhakto Mad-Yājī Māṁ Namaskuru

Mām Evaiṣhyasi Yuktvaivam Ātmānaṁ Mat-Parāyaṇaḥ II 34 II

(34) Focus mind on me. Be my devotee. Worship me and bow to me. Once you dedicate so to me and continue with your Yog, you shall surely reach me.

[Beginning in the 33rd verse, the message of the world being impermanent and the Parabrahma being permanent continues in the 34th verse albeit not in the Adhyātmik language as stated earlier but in the language of devotion; by replacing the words Parabrahma or Parmātmā by describing them in 1st person like 'Worship me, Focus on me, Bow to me' etc. The final message is still the same – By dedicating yourself to me with devotion, you must continue performing your duties and actions. Doing so, you shall definitely become one with me. This is told first through the way of Adhyātma (spirituality) and now through the way of devotion (Bhakti).]

This concludes the ninth Adhyāya **Rājavidyārājaguhyayog** from the dialogue between Shri Krishna and Arjun on Yog Shāstra (Karmayog Shāstra) within Brahmavidyā (knowledge of Brahman) in the Upanishad sung (narrated) by Shri Bhagwān (Shri Krishna).

Dashamodhyāyah (Tenth Adhyāya)

Śhrī Bhagavān Uvācha

Bhūya Eva Mahā-Bāho Śhṛiṇu Me Paramaṁ Vachaḥ

Yatte 'Haṁ Prīyamāṇāya Vakṣhyāmi Hita-Kāmyayā II 1 II

Na Me Viduḥ Sura-Gaṇāḥ Prabhavaṁ Na Maharṣhayaḥ

Aham Ādir Hi Devānāṁ Maharṣhīṇāṁ Cha Sarvaśhaḥ II 2 II

Yo Māmajam Anādiṁ Cha Vetti Loka-Maheśhvaram

Asammūḍhaḥ Sa Martyeṣhu Sarva-Pāpaiḥ Pramuchyate II 3 II

Buddhir Jñānam Asammohaḥ Kṣhamā Satyaṁ Damaḥ Śhamaḥ

Sukhaṁ Duḥkhaṁ Bhavo 'Bhāvo Bhayaṁ Chābhayameva Cha II 4 II

Ahinsā Samatā Tuṣhṭis Tapo Dānaṁ Yaśho 'Yaśhaḥ

Bhavanti Bhāvā Bhūtānāṁ Matta Eva Pṛithag-Vidhāḥ II 5 II

Dashamodhyāyah (Tenth Adhyāya)

[After explaining the path of devotion of manifest form of Parmeshwar in the 9th Adhyāya, Bhagwān now explains the different forms of Parmeshwar while answering different questions of Arjun. Later in 11th Adhyāya Shri Krishna shows him his universal form making him feel complete.]

Shri Bhagwān said – (1) O Arjun! Listen from me yet another finest thing that I tell you, who feels delighted (by my words), for your own good. (2) Neither sages nor the people of heaven understand my evolution, as I'm the source from where all the deities and sages come. (3) The one who recognizes that I am the supreme lord devoid of birth or origin, gets rid of all delusions on this earth and gets freed of all sins.

(4) Intellect, knowledge, clarity of thought, forgiveness, truth, control of senses, control of mind, happiness, sorrow, origin, destruction, fear and courage; (5) non-violence, equanimity, contentment, austerity, charity, success and failure etc. are all different qualities of living beings that originate from me.

[Bhāv (qualities) is used as 'states' or 'tendencies' of the living. Sānkhya divide them as 'qualities of intellect' and 'qualities of body'. As Sānkhya consider Purush to be inert and intellect to be a manifestation of Prakruti, they consider these qualities of Linga Shareer (subtle body) to be the cause behind getting different births. However, Nāsadiya Sookta from Rig Veda says that an eternal principle exists beyond Prakruti and Purush which develops the desire of creating the universe and which results in its formation. This is the view shared by Vedānta and they claim all the substances with name-forms to be the attributes of the mind of Parabrahma.]

Maharşhayaḥ Sapta Pūrve Chatvāro Manavas Tathā

Mad-Bhāvā Mānasā Jātā Yeşhāṁ Loka Imāḥ Prajāḥ II 6 II

(6) Seven great sages, the earlier four and the Manus from whom all people have descended; are all born from my mind.

[There's a lot of debate and speculation around the words 'earlier' and 'four'. Seven great sages are famous. However, there are 14 Manvantar in each Kalpa of Brahmadev. Each Manvantar has a separate Manu, Dev (deity) and Saptarshi (Seven great sages). Some claim that by the word earlier, those Saptarshi are denoted that occurred before the current (Vaivaswat) Manvantar. However, it doesn't make any sense as why would Bhagwān mention the Saptarshi from earlier Manvantar? We feel that by Saptarshi, Gitā wants to name the seven great sages of the current Manvantar viz. Mareechi, Angiras, Atri, Pulastya, Pulaha, Kratu and Vasishtha. These seven names are also contested but it is of no consequence as long as they are from the current Manvantar.

Some others claim that the words 'earlier four' are used to describe the earlier Manus. In all there are 14 Manus, in 2 groups of 7 each. Of these, first 7 are called Swāyambuvādi whereas the next 7 are called Sāvarni Manus. As Gitā is narrated in the current (7th) Manvantar, it doesn't make sense to mention 'earlier four' Manus. This makes us conclude that 'earlier four' is said about some other four people in older times. Some claim these four to be the four sons of Brahmadev viz. Sanak, Sanand, Sanātan and Sanatkumar. However, the objection to this is that these four were ascetics and hence the sentence 'from whom all people have descended' is contradictory. The question now remains as to who are the 'earlier four'? We feel that these four are Vāsudev (Ātmā or soul), Sankarshan (Jeev or life), Pradyumna (Man or mind) and Aniruddha (Ahankār or eg0). As per Bhāgwat Purāna (whose predecessor Bhāgwat or Nārāyaneeya Dharma is followed in Gitā), before the Saptarshi, there were these four entities. From the fourth one (Aniruddha), the seven great sages were born. While one sect from Bhāgwat Dharma considers that these four were separate and some consider two or three; Gitā disagrees with this concept and goes on to state that a single Parmeshwar led to everything. This is why it's stated that these four, along with Saptarshi and Manus, are different Bhāv (qualities) of one all-pervasive Vāsudev (Parmeshwar). This way, the verse makes perfect sense which is why we've interpreted it so.]

Etāṁ Vibhūtiṁ Yogaṁ Cha Mama Yo Vetti Tattvataḥ

So 'Vikampena Yogena Yujyate Nātra Sanśhayaḥ II 7 II

Ahaṁ Sarvasya Prabhavo Mattaḥ Sarvaṁ Pravartate

Iti Matvā Bhajante Māṁ Budhā Bhāva-Samanvitāḥ II 8 II

Mach-Chittā Mad-Gata-Prāṇā Bodhayantaḥ Parasparam

Kathayantaśh Cha Māṁ Nityaṁ Tuṣhyanti Cha Ramanti Cha II 9 II

Teṣhāṁ Satata-Yuktānāṁ Bhajatāṁ Prīti-Pūrvakam

Dadāmi Buddhi-Yogaṁ Taṁ Yena Mām Upayānti Te II 10 II

Teṣhām Evānukampārtham Aham Ajñāna-Jaṁ Tamaḥ

Nāśhayāmyātma-Bhāva-Stho Jñāna-Dīpena Bhāsvatā II 11 II

Arjuna Uvācha

Paraṁ Brahma Paraṁ Dhāma Pavitraṁ Paramaṁ Bhavān

Puruṣhaṁ Śhāśhvataṁ Divyam Ādi-Devam Ajaṁ Vibhum II 12 II

Āhus Tvām Ṛiṣhayaḥ Sarve Devarṣhir Nāradas Tathā

Asito Devalo Vyāsaḥ Svayaṁ Chaiva Bravīṣhi Me II 13 II

Sarvam Etad Ṛitaṁ Manye Yan Māṁ Vadasi Keśhava

Na Hi Te Bhagavan Vyaktiṁ Vidur Devā Na Dānavāḥ II 14 II

Swayam Evātmanātmānaṁ Vettha Tvaṁ Puruṣhottama

Bhūta-Bhāvana Bhūteśha Deva-Deva Jagat-Pate II 15 II

Vaktum Arhasyaśheṣheṇa Divyā Hyātma-Vibhūtayaḥ

Yābhir Vibhūtibhir Lokān Imāṁs Tvaṁ Vyāpya Tiṣhṭhasi II 16 II

Kathaṁ Vidyām Ahaṁ Yogins Tvāṁ Sadā Parichintayan

Keṣhu Keṣhu Cha Bhāveṣhu Chintyo 'Si Bhagavan Mayā II 17 II

Vistareṇātmano Yogaṁ Vibhūtiṁ Cha Janārdana

Bhūyaḥ Kathaya Tṛiptir Hi Śhṛiṇvato Nāsti Me 'Mṛitam II 18 II

(7) One who understands the principle behind this extension of mine and the Yog (capacity) behind this extension, obtains stable (Karma) Yog undoubtedly. (8) Wise people worship me reverentially, understanding that I'm the origin of everyone and everything has evolved from me. (9) They're always content and immersed in focusing their mind on me, devoting themselves to me and educating each other through my stories. (10) I grant the Yog (idea) of (equanimous) intellect of reaching me to those who thus worship me by being content, loving. (11) And for blessing them, I enter their mind and dispel the darkness of ignorance within through the lamp of knowledge.

[Just as it's stated in 6th Adhyāya that once a person develops curiosity for Karmayog, it is certain that they'd be enlightened (Gitā 6.44), the statement in 10th Adhyāya about Parmeshwar facilitating the equanimous intellect of the devotees is synonymous, albeit in the context of Bhakti Mārg (path of devotion).]

Arjun said – (12) You are Parabrahma (absolute), supreme place and ultimate holy object; divine and eternal persona, primordial deity, unborn, all-pervasive.

(13) You're regarded so by all sages, celestial sages Nārad, Asit, Deval and Vyās; while you tell me the same yourself. (14) O Krishna! I consider whatever you're saying to be true. Bhagwān, neither deities nor demons know your true self (origin). (15) O supreme lord, the creator of all living beings! God of all gods and master of the universe! O best among humans! You alone know yourself! (16) Therefore, pray tell me about the divine extensions through which you've occupied the whole universe! (17) O Yogi! How do I recognize you while continuously thinking of you? And O Bhagwān! In what all entities should I think of you?

(18) O Krishna! Please explain me in detail your extensions and Yog (capabilities), as I can't get enough of this nectar (of your speech).

[Yog here means the capacity of Parmeshwar to manifest itself as varied entities while Vibhuti means the different extensions. It's critical to note that Arjun asks about the different extensions not to worship them

Śhrī Bhagavān Uvācha

Hanta Te Kathayiṣhyāmi Divyā Hyātma-Vibhūtayaḥ

Prādhānyataḥ Kuru-Śhreṣhṭha Nāstyanto Vistarasya Me II 19 II

Aham Ātmā Guḍākeśha Sarva-Bhūtāśhaya-Sthitaḥ

Aham Ādiśh Cha Madhyaṁ Cha Bhūtānām Anta Eva Cha II 20 II

Ādityānām Ahaṁ Viṣhṇur Jyotiṣhāṁ Ravir Anśhumān

Marīchir Marutām Asmi Nakṣhatrāṇām Ahaṁ Śhaśhī II 21 II

Vedānāṁ Sāma-Vedo 'Smi Devānām Asmi Vāsavaḥ

Indriyāṇāṁ Manaśh Chāsmi Bhūtānām Asmi Chetanā II 22 II

Rudrāṇāṁ Śhaṅkaraśh Chāsmi Vitteśho Yakṣha-Rakṣhasām

Vasūnāṁ Pāvakaśh Chāsmi Meruḥ Śhikhariṇām Aham II 23 II

Purodhasāṁ Cha Mukhyaṁ Māṁ Viddhi Pārtha Bṛihaspatim

Senānīnām Ahaṁ Skandaḥ Sarasām Asmi Sāgaraḥ II 24 II

Maharṣhīṇāṁ Bhṛigur Ahaṁ Girām Asmyekam Akṣharam

Yajñānāṁ Japa-Yajño 'Smi Sthāvarāṇāṁ Himālayaḥ II 25 II

Aśhvatthaḥ Sarva-Vṛikṣhāṇāṁ Devarṣhīṇāṁ Cha Nāradaḥ

Gandharvāṇāṁ Chitrarathaḥ Siddhānāṁ Kapilo Muniḥ II 26 II

separately as respective deities. Rather, he asks that to know in which different entities he must see Parmeshwar manifested (note 17th verse).]

Shri Bhagwān said – (19) Alright, O Arjun! Now I shall tell you about the select significant few among my divine extensions, as there's no end to my expansion. (20) O Arjun! I am the soul at the core of all living beings. I'm the beginning, middle and end of all living beings. (21) I'm the Vishnu among the (twelve) Āditya. I'm the radiant sun among all luminous objects. I'm the Marichi among (7 or 49) Marut. I'm the moon among constellations.

(22) Among the Vedas I'm Sāma Veda. I'm Indra among the gods; and mind among the senses. Among all living beings, I'm the consciousness.

[While there's a lot of debate around the statement – 'Among the Vedas, I', Sām Veda', we believe the answer is pretty straightforward. As songs of praise about Parmeshwar are given importance over rituals and procedures in Bhaktiyog (path of devotion), Sāma Veda is deemed superior in this verse which is in an Adhyāya describing Bhaktiyog.]

(23) And I'm Shankar among the (eleven) Rudra. I'm Kuber among Yaksha (demi gods) and Rākshasas (demons). I'm Pāvak (fire) among (seven) Vasu. Among the (seven) mountains, I'm Meru. (24) O Arjun! Among the Purohit (priests), consider that I'm Bruhaspati. Among military generals, I'm Skanda (Kārtikeya). Among water bodies, I'm the sea. (25) I'm Bhrugu among the great sages. I'm 'Om' among all syllables. I'm the chant of Parmeshwar among all ritualistic sacrifices. Among the immovable objects, I'm Himālaya.

[The sentence 'I'm the chant of Parmeshwar among all ritualistic sacrifices' is important. While sacrificial activities and rituals are given importance in some other paths, Bhakti Mārg gives importance to remembrance and chanting of the name of Parmeshwar]

(26) Among all the trees, I'm Aśhvattha (sacred fig tree) and Nārad among all celestial sages. I'm Chitrarath among Gandharva (celestial singers), sage Kapil among accomplished beings.

Uchchaiḥśhravasam Aśhvānāṁ Viddhi Mām Amṛitodbhavam

Airāvataṁ Gajendrāṇāṁ Narāṇāṁ Cha Narādhipam II 27 II

Āyudhānām Ahaṁ Vajraṁ Dhenūnām Asmi Kāmadhuk

Prajanaśh Chāsmi Kandarpaḥ Sarpāṇām Asmi Vāsukiḥ II 28 II

Anantaśh Chāsmi Nāgānāṁ Varuṇo Yādasām Aham

Pitṝīṇām Aryamā Chāsmi Yamaḥ Sanyamatām Aham II 29 II

Prahlādaśh Chāsmi Daityānāṁ Kālaḥ Kalayatām Aham

Mṛigāṇāṁ Cha Mṛigendro 'Haṁ Vainateyaśh Cha Pakṣhiṇām II 30 II

Pavanaḥ Pavatām Asmi Rāmaḥ Śhastra-Bhṛitām Aham

Jhaṣhāṇāṁ Makaraśh Chāsmi Srotasām Asmi Jāhnavī II 31 II

Sargāṇām Ādir Antaśh Cha Madhyaṁ Chaivāham Arjuna

Adhyātma-Vidyā Vidyānāṁ Vādaḥ Pravadatām Aham II 32 II

Akṣharāṇām A-Kāro 'Smi Dvandvaḥ Sāmāsikasya Cha

Aham Evākṣhayaḥ Kālo Dhātāhaṁ Viśhvato-Mukhaḥ II 33 II

Mṛityuḥ Sarva-Haraśh Chāham Udbhavaśh Cha Bhaviṣhyatām

Kīrtiḥ Śhrīr Vāk Cha Nārīṇāṁ Smṛitir Medhā Dhṛitiḥ Kṣhamā II 34 II

Bṛihat-Sāma Tathā Sāmnāṁ Gāyatrī Chhandasām Aham

Māsānāṁ Mārga-Śhīrṣho 'Ham Ṛitūnāṁ Kusumākaraḥ II 35 II

(27) Among horses, I'm Ucchaihshrava (the horse) found during churning of the ocean for Amrut (nectar of immortality). I'm Airāvat among the royal elephants and king among humans. (28) Among the weapons I'm Vajra (thunderbolt of Indra). I'm Kāmdhenu (wish-fulfilling cow) among cows; and I'm cupid among the forces of procreation. I'm Vāsuki among the serpents.

(29) And I'm Anant among the Cobras. I'm Varun among aquatic beings. Among the ancestors I'm Aryamā; and I'm Yama (God of death) among the facilitators of law.

(30) Among the demons, I'm Pralhād. Among all governing principles, I'm Time. I'm Lion among the animals and Eagle among the birds. (31) Among the speedy ones, I'm the Wind. I'm Rām among the armed warriors; and Nakra among the fish. I'm Bhāgirathi among all rivers. (32) O Arjun! I'm the beginning, middle and the end of all creation. I'm Adhyātma (spirituality) among all disciplines. I'm the debate among all debaters.

[The difference between 20th verse and 32nd is that while in the former Parmeshwar is said to be the beginning, middle and end of all living beings while in the 32nd it's said about everything that there is in the universe.]

(33) I'm 'A' among all letters; and Dwandwa (duality) among all Samās (grammatical compounds). I'm the perpetual time and Brahmadev having mouths in all directions.

(34) I'm the death that concludes everything; and I'm the origin of everything being born. Among feminine qualities, I'm fame, prosperity, speech, memory, intelligence, courage and forgiveness. (35) Similarly, I'm Bruhatsāma among Sāma (the sung Vedic hymns) and Gāyatri among poetic meters. Among the months I'm Māragasheersha and I'm Spring among the seasons.

[In the erstwhile times, Māragasheersha was the first month from which the year began.]

Dyūtaṁ Chhalayatām Asmi Tejas Tejasvinām Aham

Jayo 'Smi Vyavasāyo 'Smi Sattvaṁ Sattvavatām Aham II 36 II

Vṛiṣhṇīnāṁ Vāsudevo 'Smi Pāṇḍavānāṁ Dhanañjayaḥ

Munīnām Apyahaṁ Vyāsaḥ Kavīnām Uśhanā Kaviḥ II 37II

Daṇḍo Damayatām Asmi Nītir Asmi Jigīṣhatām

Maunaṁ Chaivāsmi Guhyānāṁ Jñānaṁ Jñānavatām Aham II 38 II

Yach Chāpi Sarva-Bhūtānāṁ Bījaṁ Tad Aham Arjuna

Na Tad Asti Vinā Yat Syān Mayā Bhūtaṁ Charācharam II 39 II

Nānto 'Sti Mama Divyānāṁ Vibhūtīnāṁ Parantapa

Eṣha Tūddeśhataḥ Prokto Vibhūter Vistaro Mayā II 40 II

Yad Yad Vibhūtimat Sattvaṁ Śhrīmad Ūrjitam Eva Vā

Tat Tad Evāvagachchha Tvaṁ Mama Tejo 'Nśha-Sambhavam II 41 II

Atha Vā Bahunaitena Kiṁ Jñātena Tavārjuna

Viṣhṭabhyāham Idaṁ Kṛitsnam Ekānśhena Sthito Jagat II 42 II

(36) Among the cheaters, I'm Dyoot (game of gamble). I'm the radiance of the radiant. I'm the victory (of victors). I'm the resolve (of the resolute). I'm truthfulness of the truthful. (37) I'm Vāsudev among the descendants of Vrushnis (Yadav) and Arjun among Pāndav. Among the sages I'm Vyās; and Shukrāchārya among poets. (38) I'm the punishment of the punishers. I'm the Diplomacy of those aspiring to be victorious; and among all the secrets I'm Silence. I'm the wisdom of the wise. (39) Moreover, O Arjun! I'm the seed of all living beings. There's nothing living or non-living without me.

(40) O Arjun! There's no end to my divine extensions. I've only told the expansion of my extensions as a directive.

[After enlisting the key extensions, now Bhagwān concludes the chapter]

(41) Consider everything endowed with prosperity, wealth and radiance to have born from the essence of my radiant self.

(42) Otherwise, O Arjun! What have you got to do with knowing this expansion of mine? (In short), I've occupied the whole universe through a fraction of my essence.

[The word 'a fraction' indicates that just through a fraction of it, Parmeshwar has occupied every ounce of the universe. Thus, it's clear that Parmeshwar in its entirety is definitely even more majestic than this.]

This concludes the tenth Adhyāya **Vibhutiyog** from the dialogue between Shri Krishna and Arjun on Yog Shāstra (Karmayog Shāstra) within Brahmavidyā (knowledge of Brahman) in the Upanishad sung (narrated) by Shri Bhagwān (Shri Krishna).

Ekādashodhyāyah (Eleventh Adhyāya)

Arjuna Uvācha

Mad-Anugrahāya Paramaṁ Guhyam Adhyātma-Sanjñitam

Yat Tvayoktaṁ Vachas Tena Moho 'Yaṁ Vigato Mama II 1 II

Bhavāpyayau Hi Bhūtānāṁ Śhrutau Vistaraśho Mayā

Tvattaḥ Kamala-Patrākṣha Māhātmyam Api Chāvyayam II 2 II

Evam Etad Yathāttha Tvam Ātmānaṁ Parameśhvara

Draṣhṭum Ichchhāmi Te Rūpam Aiśhwaraṁ Puruṣhottama II 3 II

Manyase Yadi Tach Chhakyaṁ Mayā Draṣhṭum Iti Prabho

Yogeśhvara Tato Me Tvaṁ Darśhayātmānam Avyayam II 4 II

Śhrī-Bhagavān Uvācha

Paśhya Me Pārtha Rūpāṇi Śhataśho 'Tha Sahasraśhaḥ

Nānā-Vidhāni Divyāni Nānā-Varṇākṛitīni Cha II 5 II

Paśhyādityān Vasūn Rudrān Aśhvinau Marutas Tathā

Bahūny Adṛiṣhṭa-Pūrvāṇi Paśhyāśhcharyāṇi Bhārata II 6 II

Ihaika-Sthaṁ Jagat Kṛitsnaṁ Paśhyādya Sa-Charācharam

Mama Dehe Guḍākeśha Yach Chānyad Draṣhṭum Ichchhasi II 7 II

Na Tu Māṁ Śhakyase Draṣhṭum Anenaiva Sva-Chakṣhuṣhā

Divyaṁ Dadāmi Te Chakṣhuḥ Paśhya Me Yogam Aiśhwaram II 8 II

Sañjaya Uvācha

Evam Uktvā Tato Rājan Mahā-Yogeśhvaro Hariḥ

Darśhayām Āsa Pārthāya Paramaṁ Rūpam Aiśhwaram II 9 II

Ekādashodhyāyah (Eleventh Adhyāya)

[After hearing about the different extensions of Bhagwān, Arjun expresses his wish to see the cosmic form of Parmeshwar. This Adhyāya has the description of this cosmic form shown to Arjun by Bhagwān. This description is so splendid that it's considered one of the best sections of Gitā and most other versions of Gitā have copied it as it is.]

Arjun said – (1) My delusion has disappeared by listening to the ultimate secret which speaks about Adhyātma (spirituality), that you shared with me as a blessing. (2) Moreover, O Krishna! I listened in detail from you the ceaseless saga of evolution and dissolution of living beings. (3) O Parmeshwar! Just as you described yourself, I'd wish to see your divine form, O great one! (4) O Almighty! If you feel that I'm capable of watching you in that form; show me your eternal form, O Krishna!

[What Arjun has called Adhyātma is the knowledge and science of the eternal and unmanifest form of Parmeshwar shared in 7th and 8th Adhyāyas along with the extensions in manifest form described in 9th and 10th Adhyāyas. By 'evolution and dissolution of living beings' Arjun, acknowledges understanding the explanation of evolution and dissolution of universe, described in 7th, 8th and 9th Adhyāyas. By asserting in the first half of the 3rd verse that he's understood what Bhagwān explained to him till now, he expresses in the second half his wish to see the divine form with his own eyes.]

Shri Bhagwān said – (5) O Arjun! Behold my hundreds and thousands of divine forms with numerous colors and shapes. (6) See, (twelve) Āditya, (eight) Vasu, (eleven) Rudra, (two) Ashwinikumār and (forty-nine) Marudgan! O Arjun! Behold the unforeseen miracles! (7) O Arjun! Witness the entire universe assembled here within my body along with anything else that you wish to! (8) However, you won't be able to watch me with your existing vision. Let me grant you divine vision with which, behold my divine Yogic might!

Sanjay said – (9) After saying so, O Dhrutarāshtra! Bhagwān Shri Krishna displayed his supreme divine form (cosmic form) to Arjun!

Aneka-Vaktra-Nayanam Anekādbhuta-Darśhanam

Aneka-Divyābharaṇaṁ Divyānekodyatāyudham II 10 II

Divya-Mālyāmbara-Dharaṁ Divya-Gandhānulepanam

Sarvāśhcharya-Mayaṁ Devam Anantaṁ Viśhvato-Mukham II 11 II

Divi Sūrya-Sahasrasya Bhaved Yugapad Utthitā

Yadi Bhāḥ Sadṛiśhī Sā Syād Bhāsas Tasya Mahātmanaḥ II 12 II

Tatraika-Sthaṁ Jagat Kṛitsnaṁ Pravibhaktam Anekadhā

Apaśhyad Deva-Devasya Śharīre Pāṇḍavas Tadā II 13 II

Tataḥ Sa Vismayāviṣhṭo Hṛiṣhṭa-Romā Dhanañjayaḥ

Praṇamya Śhirasā Devaṁ Kṛitāñjalir Abhāṣhata II 14 II

Arjuna Uvācha

Paśhyāmi Devāns Tava Deva Dehe Sarvāns Tathā Bhūta-Viśheṣha-Saṅghān

Brahmāṇam Īśhaṁ Kamalāsana-Stham Ṛiṣhīnśh Cha Sarvān Uragānśh Cha Divyān II 15 II

Aneka-Bāhūdara-Vaktra-Netraṁ Paśhyāmi Tvāṁ Sarvato 'Nanta-Rūpam

Nāntaṁ Na Madhyaṁ Na Punas Tavādiṁ Paśhyāmi Viśhveśhvara Viśhva-Rūpa II 16 II

Kirīṭinaṁ Gadinaṁ Chakriṇaṁ Cha Tejo-Rāśhiṁ Sarvato Dīptimantam

Paśhyāmi Tvāṁ Durnirīkṣhyaṁ Samantād Dīptānalārka-Dyutim Aprameyam II 17 II

Tvam Akṣharaṁ Paramaṁ Veditavyaṁ Tvam Asya Viśhvasya Paraṁ Nidhānam

Tvam Avyayaḥ Śhāśhvata-Dharma-Goptā Sanātanas Tvaṁ Puruṣho Mato Me II 18 II

Anādi-Madhyāntam Ananta-Vīryam Ananta-Bāhuṁ Śhaśhi-Sūrya-Netram

Paśhyāmi Tvāṁ Dīpta-Hutāśha-Vaktraṁ Sva-Tejasā Viśhvam Idaṁ Tapantam II 19 II

(10) It had many mouths and eyes, and it displayed different amazing scenes. It bore many divine ornaments and different divine weapons shone bright in it.

(11) The Almighty in its timeless, omniscient form full of wonders bore divine fragrance and it wore divine flowers and clothes. (12) If a thousand suns burn bright in the sky, it would somewhat resemble the skin of the Almighty!

(13) Arjun then witnessed the universe (which is otherwise divided in different types) in its entirety within the body of the god of gods. (14) His hair stood on its end in bewilderment and Arjun bowed down reverentially with folded hands and said to Parmeshwar –

Arjun said – (15) O Bhagwān! I can see all gods, group of varied living creatures, lord Brahmadev seated on lotus, all sages and all divine serpents. (16) I see you with countless hands, bellies, mouths and eyes. However, O cosmic Parmeshwar! I don't see your beginning, middle or the end anywhere.

(17) I see you adorned with crown, mace and disc, radiating in all directions, glorious, scorching, bright like flaming sun, impossible to look at and limitless; everywhere I look. (18) You are the eternal ultimate to be known. You're the final darkness of the universe. You're ceaseless and the protector of Dharma (loosely righteousness and morals) and eternal being, according to me.

(19) I see you having no beginning, middle or end, with countless hands, with the sun, the moon and inferno as your mouth; and I see you warming the entire universe with all your power!

Dyāv Ā-Pṛithivyor Idam Antaraṁ Hi Vyāptaṁ Tvayaikena Diśhaśh Cha Sarvāḥ

Dṛiṣhṭvādbhutaṁ Rūpam Ugraṁ Tavedaṁ Loka-Trayaṁ Pravyathitaṁ Mahātman II 20 II

Amī Hi Tvāṁ Sura-Saṅghā Viśhanti Kechid Bhītāḥ Prāñjalayo Gṛiṇanti

Svastīty Uktvā Maharṣhi-Siddha-Saṅghāḥ Stuvanti Tvāṁ Stutibhiḥ Puṣhkalābhiḥ II 21 II

Rudrādityā Vasavo Ye Cha Sādhyā Viśhve 'Śhvinau Marutaśh Choṣhmapāśh Cha

Gandharva-Yakṣhāsura-Siddha-Saṅghā Vīkṣhante Tvāṁ Vismitāśh Chaiva Sarve II 22 II

Rūpaṁ Mahat Te Bahu-Vaktra-Netraṁ Mahā-Bāho Bahu-Bāhūru-Pādam

Bahūdaraṁ Bahu-Danṣhṭrā-Karālaṁ Dṛiṣhṭvā Lokāḥ Pravyathitās Tathāham II 23 II

Nabhaḥ-Spṛiśhaṁ Dīptam Aneka-Varṇaṁ Vyāttānanaṁ Dīpta-Viśhāla-Netram

Dṛiṣhṭvā Hi Tvāṁ Pravyathitāntar-Ātmā Dhṛitiṁ Na Vindāmi Śhamaṁ Cha Viṣhṇo II 24 II

Danṣhṭrā-Karālāni Cha Te Mukhāni Dṛiṣhṭvaiva Kālānala-Sannibhāni

Diśho Na Jāne Na Labhe Cha Śharma Prasīda Deveśha Jagan-Nivāsa II 25 II

Amī Cha Tvāṁ Dhṛitarāśhtrasya Putrāḥ Sarve Sahaivāvani-Pāla-Saṅghaiḥ

Bhīṣhmo Droṇaḥ Sūta-Putras Tathāsau Sahāsmadīyair Api Yodha-Mukhyaiḥ II 26 II

Vaktrāṇi Te Tvaramāṇā Viśhanti Danṣhṭrā-Karālāni Bhayānakāni

Kechid Vilagnā Daśhanāntareṣhu Sandṛiśhyante Chūrṇitair Uttamāṅgaiḥ II 27 II

Yathā Nadīnāṁ Bahavo 'Mbu-Vegāḥ Samudram Evābhimukhā Dravanti

Tathā Tavāmī Nara-Loka-Vīrā Viśhanti Vaktrāṇy Abhivijvalanti II 28 II

Yathā Pradīptaṁ Jvalanaṁ Pataṅgā Viśhanti Nāśhāya Samṛiddha-Vegāḥ

Tathaiva Nāśhāya Viśhanti Lokās Tavāpi Vaktrāṇi Samṛiddha-Vegāḥ II 29 II

(20) As you've pervaded the entire distance between the earth and the space, O great one! Looking at this mesmerizing and terrible form, I see all three worlds trembling with fear. (21) Look, celestial beings are entering your form and some are praying in fear with folded hands. Great sages and realized beings are chanting 'Swasti, Swasti' and pronouncing different hymns in your praise. (22) Moreover, Rudra, Āditya, Vasu, Sādhya, Vishwadev, (both) Ashwinikumārs, Marudgan, ancestors, Gandharva (celestial singers), Yaksha (demigods), Rākshasa (demons) and realized beings are all looking at you being mesmerized.

(23) O Krishna! I, along wiih the whole world, am scared of looking at your terrible form with many mouths, eyes, arms, thighs, legs, bellies and teeth. (24) O Vishnu! Looking at your radiant, colorful form touching the sky with widespread jaws and huge, fiery eyes I have lost courage and peace of mind as I'm distraught with fear.

(25) And looking at your mouths bearing scary teeth and resembling the inferno at the time of total destruction, I have lost sense of direction and I'm unable to feel relieved. O lord of lords, resort of the universe! Bless me! (26) Behold! The assembly of kings along with all the sons of Dhrutarāshtra, Bheeshma, Drona, Sootaputra (Karna) along with other key warriors from our side (27) are rushing into your many mouths with terrifying teeth while heads of some of them appear to be crushed under the teeth. (28) Just as several streams of rivers enter the sea, these human heroes are entering your several fiery mouths.

(29) Just as moths vigorously jump into the fire to die, (these) people are entering your many jaws to perish. (30) O Vishnu! You're devouring all worlds in your flaming mouths with licking tongues and you're pervading entire universe with your glory while your effulgence is radiating in all directions.

Lelihyase Grasamānaḥ Samantāl Lokān Samagrān Vadanair Jvaladbhiḥ

Tejobhir Āpūrya Jagat Samagraṁ Bhāsas Tavogrāḥ Pratapanti Viṣhṇo II 30 II

Ākhyāhi Me Ko Bhavān Ugra-Rūpo Namo 'Stu Te Deva-Vara Prasīda

Vijñātum Ichchhāmi Bhavantam Ādyaṁ Na Hi Prajānāmi Tava Pravṛittim II 31 II

Śhrī-Bhagavān Uvācha

Kālo 'Smi Loka-Kṣhaya-Kṛit Pravṛiddho Lokān Samāhartum Iha Pravṛittaḥ

Ṛite 'Pi Tvāṁ Na Bhaviṣhyanti Sarve Ye 'Vasthitāḥ Pratyanīkeṣhu Yodhāḥ II 32 II

Tasmāt Tvam Uttiṣhṭha Yaśho Labhasva Jitvā Śhatrūn Bhuṅkṣhva Rājyaṁ Samṛiddham

Mayaivaite Nihatāḥ Pūrvam Eva Nimitta-Mātraṁ Bhava Savya-Sāchin II 33 II

Droṇaṁ Cha Bhīṣhmaṁ Cha Jayadrathaṁ Cha Karṇaṁ Tathānyān Api Yodha-Vīrān

Mayā Hatāṁs Tvaṁ Jahi Mā Vyathiṣhṭhā Yudhyasva Jetāsi Raṇe Sapatnān II 34 II

Sañjaya Uvācha

Etach Chhrutvā Vachanaṁ Keśhavasya Kṛitāñjalir Vepamānaḥ Kirīṭī

Namaskṛitvā Bhūya Evāha Kṛiṣhṇaṁ Sa-Gadgadaṁ Bhīta-Bhītaḥ Praṇamya II 35 II

Arjuna Uvācha

Sthāne Hṛiṣhīkeśha Tava Prakīrtyā Jagat Prahṛiṣhyaty Anurajyate Cha

Rakṣhānsi Bhītāni Diśho Dravanti Sarve Namasyanti Cha Siddha-Saṅghāḥ II 36 II

Kasmāch Cha Te Na Nameran Mahātman Garīyase Brahmaṇo 'Py Ādi-Kartre

Ananta Deveśha Jagan-Nivāsa Tvam Akṣharaṁ Sad-Asat Tat Paraṁ Yat II 37 II

(31) Pray tell me who you are with this fierce appearance. O greatest of gods, I bow down to you! Bless me! I want to know your identity as the primordial being, as I'm entirely unable to comprehend your deeds.

Shri Bhagwān said – (32) I am the time that destroys worlds and have grown big. And I've started off for annihilation of the worlds. Even without you, all these warriors standing in the opposing armies are going to disappear (be killed). (33) Therefore, get up, achieve success and enjoy the prosperous kingdom by conquering your enemies. I've already killed them earlier. (Therefore) O Arjun! You merely be the cause!

(34) I've already killed the brave warriors Drona, Bheeshma, Jayadrath, Karna and others. You kill them! Don't be afraid! Fight! You're going to be victorious over your enemies in battle.

[As evil people die due to their own Karma (actions) as per Karmavipāk principle, the person killing them is not at fault. They're merely a cause or an instrument. This is what Shri Krishna is trying to explain to Arjun.]

Sanjay said – (35) After listening to these words of Krishna, a frightened Arjun bowed down to Krishna with trembling hands with a lump in his throat and again said – Arjun said –

(36) O Krishna! Entire universe is happy singing your praise and is engrossed in it. Demons run amok being scared of you and groups of realized beings bow to you. It's all truly fitting. (37) O Krishna! You're the predecessor of Brahmadev and greater than him. Why wouldn't he bow down to you? O eternal one! O lord of lords! O refuge of the universe! You're both Truth and Untruth and also the imperishable beyond them!

[The words Sat and Asat here denote manifest and unmanifest or perishable and imperishable respectively. The principle beyond Sat and Asat is Parabrahma. As discussed earlier, Gitā uses the word Akshar (imperishable) sometimes as Prakruti and sometimes as Parabrahma.]

Tvam Ādi-Devaḥ Puruṣhaḥ Purāṇas Tvam Asya Viśhvasya Paraṁ Nidhānam

Vettāsi Vedyaṁ Cha Paraṁ Cha Dhāma Tvayā Tataṁ Viśhvam Ananta-Rūpa II 38 II

Vāyur Yamo 'Gnir Varuṇaḥ Śhaśhāṅkaḥ Prajāpatis Tvaṁ Prapitāmahaśh Cha

Namo Namas Te 'Stu Sahasra-Kṛitvaḥ Punaśh Cha Bhūyo 'Pi Namo Namas Te II 39 II

Namaḥ Purastād Atha Pṛiṣhṭhatas Te Namo 'Stu Te Sarvata Eva Sarva

Ananta-Vīryāmita-Vikramas Tvaṁ Sarvaṁ Samāpnoṣhi Tato 'Si Sarvaḥ II 40 II

Sakheti Matvā Prasabhaṁ Yad Uktaṁ He Kṛiṣhṇa He Yādava He Sakheti

Ajānatā Mahimānaṁ Tavedaṁ Mayā Pramādāt Praṇayena Vāpi II 41 II

Yach Chāvahāsārtham Asat-Kṛito 'Si Vihāra-Śhayyāsana-Bhojaneṣhu

Eko 'Tha Vāpy Achyuta Tat-Samakṣhaṁ Tat Kṣhāmaye Tvām Aham Aprameyam II 42 II

Pitāsi Lokasya Charācharasya Tvam Asya Pūjyaśh Cha Gurur Garīyān

Na Tvat-Samo 'Sty Abhyadhikaḥ Kuto 'Nyo Loka-Traye 'Py Apratima-Prabhāva II 43 II

Tasmāt Praṇamya Praṇidhāya Kāyaṁ Prasādaye Tvām Aham Īśham Īḍyam

Piteva Putrasya Sakheva Sakhyuḥ Priyaḥ Priyāyārhasi Deva Soḍhum II 44 II

Adṛiṣhṭa-Pūrvaṁ Hṛiṣhito 'Smi Dṛiṣhṭvā Bhayena Cha Pravyathitaṁ Mano Me

Tad Eva Me Darśhaya Deva Rūpaṁ Prasīda Deveśha Jagan-Nivāsa II 45 II

Kirīṭinaṁ Gadinaṁ Chakra-Hastam Ichchhāmi Tvāṁ Draṣhṭum Ahaṁ Tathaiva

Tenaiva Rūpeṇa Chatur-Bhujena Sahasra-Bāho Bhava Viśhva-Mūrte II 46 II

Śhrī-Bhagavān Uvācha

Mayā Prasannena Tavārjunedaṁ Rūpaṁ Paraṁ Darśhitam Ātma-Yogāt

Tejo-Mayaṁ Viśhvam Anantam Ādyaṁ Yan Me Tvad Anyena Na Dṛiṣhṭa-Pūrvam II 47 II

(38) You're the primordial deity. You're the ancient being. You alone are the ultimate support of this universe. You're the knower and to be known. You're the supreme place. And O great one with infinite forms! You alone have expanded and pervaded the universe. (39) You are Vāyu (air), Yama (God of death), Agni (fire), Varun (God of water), Chandra (moon), Prajāpati (the creator or Brahmadev) and great grandfather. Bow to you a thousand times! And bow to you once again! (40) Bow to you from the front and from the back! Bow to you from all directions! Your valor is limitless and your bravery is unparalleled. As you pervade everything, you are everything!

(41) Unaware of your majesty, I may have regarded you as my friend and called you as 'O Krishna', 'O Yadav' or 'O dear' by mistake. I may have spoken crossing all limits.

(42) O unshakeable! If I've ever insulted you by mistake while eating, playing, sleeping, sitting, alone or in front of anyone; I request you O Infinite, to forgive me! (43) You're the father of this universe – both living and non-living! You're worthy of worship and the master of masters! There's no one comparable to you in all three worlds! Then O incomparable! How can there be anyone greater?

(44) For this, I bow down with my entire body with folded hands and pray for your blessing, O praiseworthy and supremely capable. As father forgives the mistakes of his son or a friend forgives his friend; similarly O God! Pardon all mistakes of your loved one (i.e. me)!

(45) I'm overjoyed by witnessing the unforeseen and yet my mind is terrified with fear. O refuge of the universe, lord of lords! Bless me! And O Almighty! Show me your earlier form! (46) I want to see you in your older form adorning crown, mace and disc. Hence, O embodiment of all creation, O thousand-armed! Appear in your four-limbed form!

Shri Bhagwān said – (47) O Arjun! Being pleased with you, I showed you my radiant, infinite, primordial and ultimate cosmic form which no one has seen before you; using my Yogic power.

Na Veda-Yajñādhyayanair Na Dānair Na Cha Kriyābhir Na Tapobhir Ugraiḥ

Evaṁ-Rūpaḥ Śhakya Ahaṁ Nṛi-Loke Draṣhṭuṁ Tvad Anyena Kuru-Pravīra II 48 II

Mā Te Vyathā Mā Cha Vimūḍha-Bhāvo Dṛiṣhṭvā Rūpaṁ Ghoram Īdṛiṅ Mamedam

Vyapeta-Bhīḥ Prīta-Manāḥ Punas Tvaṁ Tad Eva Me Rūpam Idaṁ Prapaśhya II 49 II

Sañjaya Uvācha

Ity Arjunaṁ Vāsudevas Tathoktvā Svakaṁ Rūpaṁ Darśhayām Āsa Bhūyaḥ

Āśhvāsayām Āsa Cha Bhītam Enaṁ Bhūtvā Punaḥ Saumya-Vapur Mahatma II 50 II

Arjuna Uvācha

Dṛiṣhṭvedaṁ Mānuṣhaṁ Rūpaṁ Tava Saumyaṁ Janārdana

Idānīm Asmi Saṁvṛittaḥ Sa-Chetāḥ Prakṛitiṁ Gataḥ II 51 II

Śhrī-Bhagavān Uvācha

Su-Durdarśham Idaṁ Rūpaṁ Dṛiṣhṭavān Asi Yan Mama

Devā Apy Asya Rūpasya Nityaṁ Darśhana-Kāṅkṣhiṇaḥ II 52 II

Nāhaṁ Vedair Na Tapasā Na Dānena Na Chejyayā

Śhakya Evaṁ-Vidho Draṣhṭuṁ Dṛiṣhṭavān Asi Māṁ Yathā II 53 II

Bhaktyā Tv Ananyayā Śhakya Aham Evaṁ-Vidho 'Rjuna

Jñātuṁ Draṣhṭuṁ Cha Tattvena Praveṣhṭuṁ Cha Parantapa II 54 II

Mat-Karma-Kṛin Mat-Paramo Mad-Bhaktaḥ Saṅga-Varjitaḥ

Nirvairaḥ Sarva-Bhūteṣhu Yaḥ Sa Mām Eti Pāṇḍava II 55 II

(48) O Arjun! None other than you on this earth can get to witness my form like this by studying Vedas, performing Yadnya (ritualistic sacrifices), practice, charity, Karma (action) or through severe austerities. (49) Don't let your mind get sad by looking at this gruesome form of mine. Don't be dazed by it, either. Quit your fear and look at this form of mine again, with content mind. Sanjay said –

(50) Saying so, Shri Krishna showed Arjun his earlier form again and after assuming a mild form, the great one reassured Arjun. Arjun said – (51) O Krishna! After looking at this milder and humanoid form, I have come to my senses and become alert as earlier.

[The 36 verses of Vishwaroopdarshan and a few other verses from other Adhyāyas are from a different poetic meter than other similar meters from the period of Kālidās et al. This meter is based on the verses from Vedas, which further strengthens the argument about ancient origin of Gitā.]

Shri Bhagwān said – (52) Getting to see my form which you saw is extremely difficult to witness. Even gods always wish to see this form. (53) No one can see me like you did, even with study of Vedas, performing austerities, charity or ritualistic sacrifices.

(54) O Arjun! Only with absolute devotion is it possible to know me, see me and enter my being principally, O Arjun!

[With devotion, first the devotee has knowledge of Parmeshwar and then becomes one with it. This is what is described above, and also earlier in 4.29 as well as later in 18.55. We've discussed this in detail in 13th chapter. Now Bhagwān tells Arjun the essence of entire Gitā –]

(55) O Arjun! My devotee, who has non-enmity towards all living beings, is dedicated to me, is free from attachment and performs all actions considering them to be mine; reaches me.

This concludes the eleventh Adhyāya **Vishwaroopdarshanyog** from the dialogue between Shri Krishna and Arjun on Yog Shāstra (Karmayog Shāstra) within Brahmavidyā (knowledge of Brahman) in the Upanishad sung (narrated) by Shri Bhagwān (Shri Krishna).

Dwādashodhyāyah (Twelfth Adhyāya)

Arjuna Uvācha

Evaṁ Satata-Yuktā Ye Bhaktās Tvāṁ Paryupāsate

Ye Chāpy Akṣharam Avyaktaṁ Teṣhāṁ Ke Yoga-Vittamāḥ II 1 II

Śhrī-Bhagavān Uvācha

Mayy Āveśhya Mano Ye Māṁ Nitya-Yuktā Upāsate

Śhraddhayā Parayopetās Te Me Yuktatamā Matāḥ II 2 II

Ye Tv Akṣharam Anirdeśhyam Avyaktaṁ Paryupāsate

Sarvatra-Gam Achintyañcha Kūṭa-Stham Achalandhruvam II 3 II

Sanniyamyendriya-Grāmaṁ Sarvatra Sama-Buddhayaḥ

Te Prāpnuvanti Mām Eva Sarva-Bhūta-Hite Ratāḥ II 4 II

Kleśho 'Dhikataras Teṣhām Avyaktāsakta-Chetasām

Avyaktā Hi Gatir Duḥkhaṁ Dehavadbhir Avāpyate II 5 II

Ye Tu Sarvāṇi Karmāṇi Mayi Sannyasya Mat-Paraḥ

Ananyenaiva Yogena Māṁ Dhyāyanta Upāsate II 6 II

Teṣhām Ahaṁ Samuddhartā Mṛityu-Saṁsāra-Sāgarāt

Bhavāmi Na Chirāt Pārtha Mayy Āveśhita-Chetasām II 7 II

Mayy Eva Mana Ādhatsva Mayi Buddhiṁ Niveśhaya

Nivasiṣhyasi Mayy Eva Ata Ūrdhvaṁ Na Sanśhayaḥ II 8 II

Dwādashodhyāyah (Twelfth Adhyāya)

The explanation of knowledge and science began in 7th Adhyāya with 8th Adhyāya describing the imperishable, unmanifest form of Brahman, 9th Adhyāya initiating description of Bhakti Mārg (path of devotion), 10th Adhyāya describing different extensions while 11th Adhyāya showing Arjun the cosmic form of Parmeshwar. While 7th and 8th Adhyāya told Arjun that the unmanifest form is the greatest while 9th Adhyāya said that the path of devotion of manifest Parmeshwar is supreme. Arjun now asks Shri Krishna which path is superior. One must note here that even if different people worship different symbolic deities, it's the worship of single all-pervasive Parmeshwar that is implicit in this Adhyāya.

Arjun said – (1) Between the devotees who worship you while being engrossed in Yog and those that worship the unmanifest, imperishable Brahman; who are the best (Karma) Yogis?

Shri Bhagwān said – (2) According to me, those who focus their mind on me, remain engrossed and worship me with supreme reverence are the best, steadfast Yogis. (3) However, those who worship the indescribable, unmanifest, all-pervasive, unthinkable, fundamental, immovable, perpetual and imperishable Parabrahma (4) with restrained senses and equanimous intellect; these people engrossed in universal welfare reach me as well. (5) However, as their mind is attached to the unmanifest, they face more difficulties; because the path of worshipping the unmanifest is arduous. (6) However, those who dedicate all the actions to me, dedicate themselves to me and worship while meditating on me absolutely;

(7) O Arjun! I deliver these people engrossed in me, from the ocean (never-ending cycle) of birth and death without any delay. (8) (Therefore) focus your mind on me and steady your intellect on me, so that you would undoubtedly reside in me going forward.

[These verses elucidate the significance of Bhakti Yog (path of devotion). While Bhagwān mentions that Bhakti Yog is the greatest path, he also emphasizes that those worshipping his unmanifest form also reach

Atha Chittaṁ Samādhātuṁ Na Śhaknoṣhi Mayi Sthiram

Abhyāsa-Yogena Tato Mām Ichchhāptuṁ Dhanañjaya II 9 II

Abhyāse 'Py Asamartho 'Si Mat-Karma-Paramo Bhava

Mad-Artham Api Karmāṇi Kurvan Siddhim Avāpsyasi II 10 II

Athaitad Apy Aśhakto 'Si Kartuṁ Mad-Yogam Āśhritaḥ

Sarva-Karma-Phala-Tyāgaṁ Tataḥ Kuru Yatātmavān II 11 II

Śhreyo Hi Jñānam Abhyāsāj Jñānād Dhyānaṁ Viśhiṣhyate

Dhyānāt Karma-Phala-Tyāgas Tyāgāch Chhāntir Anantaram II 12 II

him, albeit with great difficulty. We've discussed the path of devotion in detail in 13th chapter. In a nutshell, worshippers of both manifest as well as unmanifest attain same Moksha through different paths. In doing so, both shall continue to perform actions but dedicating them to Parmeshwar, without getting attached to the outcomes.]

(9) O Arjun! If you're not able to focus your mind on me this way properly, practice persistently and aspire to attain me. (10) If you're unable to even practice, then continue to perform actions dedicated to me (meditation, hymns, study etc.). Even by continuing to perform these actions, you shall accomplish enlightenment. (11) However, if you're unable to do this as well, take shelter in my Yog (Karmayog). Continue to take efforts (gradually restraining mind) and later quit attachment to the fruits of all actions.

(12) Because, Dnyān (knowledge) is superior to Abhyas (practice), Dhyāna (meditation) is superior to Dnyān, sacrifice of fruits of action is superior to Dhyāna and this sacrifice further leads to peace.

[These verses are extremely important from the point of view of Karmayog. It mentions knowledge, meditation etc. while practicing Karmayog with Bhakti and finally emphasizes on importance of freeing oneself of attachment to fruits of one's Karma. This is not the first time in Gitā that Karmayog without attachment is praised. Other instances have been in third (3.8), fifth (5.2) and sixth (6.46) Adhyāyas earlier and Arjun has been insisted on following the same. As Nishkām Karmayog (Path of action without attachment) is shown as the superlative path, naturally sects exclusively insisting on superiority of knowledge (Dnyān Yog), meditation (Pātanjal Yog) and devotion without action (exclusive Bhakti Yog) feel offended by these verses and have tried their best at misquoting them. They've tried to derive an incorrect meaning forcefully. Ironically, followers of Bhaktiyukta Karmayog (Path of action enriched with devotion) were almost extinct, providing little contest against these communalistic interpretations. This was one of the reasons why we started out writing this bhāshya (commentary), attempting to show the true meaning intended in Gitā, as it is.]

Adveṣhṭā Sarva-Bhūtānāṁ Maitraḥ Karuṇa Eva Cha

Nirmamo Nirahankāraḥ Sama-Duḥkha-Sukhaḥ Kṣhamī II 13 II

Santuṣhṭaḥ Satataṁ Yogī Yatātmā Dṛiḍha-Niśhchayaḥ

Mayy Arpita-Mano-Buddhir Yo Mad-Bhaktaḥ Sa Me Priyaḥ II 14 II

Yasmān Nodvijate Loko Lokān Nodvijate Cha Yaḥ

Harṣhāmarṣha-Bhayodvegair Mukto Yaḥ Sa Cha Me Priyaḥ II 15 II

Anapekṣhaḥ Śhuchir Dakṣha Udāsīno Gata-Vyathaḥ

Sarvārambha-Parityāgī Yo Mad-Bhaktaḥ Sa Me Priyaḥ II 16 II

Yo Na Hṛiṣhyati Na Dveṣhṭi Na Śhochati Na Kāṅkṣhati

Śhubhāśhubha-Parityāgī Bhaktimān Yaḥ Sa Me Priyaḥ II 17 II

Samaḥ Śhatrau Cha Mitre Cha Tathā Mānāpamānayoḥ

Śhītoṣhṇa-Sukha-Duḥkheṣhu Samaḥ Saṅga-Vivarjitaḥ II 18 II

Tulya-Nindā-Stutir Maunī Santuṣhṭo Yena Kenachit

Aniketaḥ Sthira-Matir Bhaktimān Me Priyo Naraḥ II 19 II

(13) One who doesn't hate anyone, behaves friendly with all living beings, who's compassionate, is free of ego and pride, who considers happiness and sorrow equal, and who's forgiving, (14) ever content, composed, resolute, and who has dedicated their mind and intellect to me – such a (Karma) Yogi devotee is my favorite.

(15) One who is not troubled by people, who doesn't trouble people, who's detached from joy, anger, fear and regret – is my favorite. (16) One who's unconditional, pure, alert, indifferent (about outcomes), who can't be influenced, who's quit beginning all actions (with expectations of their fruits) – is my favorite. (17) One who neither loves nor hates, neither mourns nor desires, who's quit the holy and unholy (fruits of Karma) – such a devotional person is my favorite. (18) One who considers enemies and friends, respect and insult, hot and cold or happiness and sorrow as same, who's not attached to anything,

(19) who considers praise and criticism as same, who's brief in speech, happy with what they get, whose mind is stable and who has no home (in the form of attachment to fruits) – such a devotional person is my favorite.

[Aniket (who has no home) is a word often used to describe ascetics who leave their home and stay in forests and even literally means 'homeless'. This along with some other words are focused by proponents of asceticism and they emphatically point out these to try and prove that Gitā promotes asceticism. However, they forget that quitting, renunciation, giving up are all words used in Gitā only about the fruits of actions and not literally for actions. Once they ignore this central idea, they indulge enthusiastically in twisting straightforward meanings and derive forced interpretations. Here, Gitā implies by the word homeless, a person who's not attached to whatever they do. A normal person is firmly attached to where their home is. This is why this simile is used to indicate detachment, to fruits and not the actions themselves. Same is the case with the 16th verse where it's implied that a Karmayogi doesn't initiate any activity with an intention or desire for its fruits. Gitā insists that one shouldn't get indulged or involved in any activities that may bring them sorrow. This detached state of mind is described in above verses. While the words used may also find

Ye Tu Dharmyāmṛitam Idaṁ Yathoktaṁ Paryupāsate

Śhraddadhānā Mat-Paramā Bhaktās Te 'Tīva Me Priyāḥ II 20 II

mention in descriptions of ascetics elsewhere, in Gitā it is intended for attachment alone, as Gitā definitively insists on continuing actions without attachment often during its course and also conclusively.]

(20) Those who follow this nectar of wisdom stated above, dedicating to me reverentially – those devotees are my most favorite.

[On the one hand Gitā praises the wise devotee, calling them as favorite in the above verse, just as earlier in sixth (6.47) and seventh (7.18) Adhyāyas. On the other, it also mentions Bhagwān saying he considers all as same, having no favorites. Prima facie, it appears contradictory. However, once we see that while the former anecdotes are given explaining worship of manifest, the latter is mentioned during explanation of spirituality; we see that there's no contradiction. Please read the concluding section of 13th chapter where we've discussed this elaborately.]

This concludes the twelfth Adhyāya **Bhaktiyog** from the dialogue between Shri Krishna and Arjun on Yog Shāstra (Karmayog Shāstra) within Brahmavidyā (knowledge of Brahman) in the Upanishad sung (narrated) by Shri Bhagwān (Shri Krishna).

Trayodashodhyāyah (Thirteenth Adhyāya)

Śhrī-Bhagavān Uvācha

Idaṁ Śharīraṁ Kaunteya Kṣhetram Ity Abhidhīyate

Etad Yo Vetti Taṁ Prāhuḥ Kṣhetra-Jña Iti Tad-Vidaḥ II 1 II

Kṣhetra-Jñaṁ Chāpi Māṁ Viddhi Sarva-Kṣhetreṣhu Bhārata

Kṣhetra-Kṣhetrajñayor Jñānaṁ Yat Taj Jñānaṁ Mataṁ Mama II 2 II

Trayodashodhyāyah (Thirteenth Adhyāya)

[While it's true that focusing mentally on the indescribable and unmanifest Parmeshwar yields Moksha, we saw in last few Adhyāyas that the same Moksha can also be attained in a simpler way by reverentially devoting to manifest symbol of Parmeshwar and continuing to perform actions dedicated to it. However, the knowledge and science that we began to explain in 7th Adhyāya isn't over yet. To understand Parmeshwar truly, one must also learn about the human body and soul. In other words, Kshetrakshetradnyavichār (Discussion of body and soul) forms an integral part of this learning. We shall now begin with this in the 13th Adhyāya, discuss three Gunas in detail in the subsequent four Adhyāyas and summarize the whole discussion in the 18th Adhyāya. Unlike it is made to believe by many commentators, these 6 Adhyāyas do not form separate group but are a continuation of the same explanation that we began in 7th Adhyāya, about the Dnyān-Vidnyān (knowledge and science) for attaining true Karmayog.]

Shri Bhagwān said – (1) O Arjun! This body is called Kshetra (field). One who understands this (body) is called Kshetradnya (knower of the field) by knowledgeable people.

(2) O Arjun! Consider me to be the Kshetradnya in all Kshetra (bodies) as well. The knowledge of Kshetra and Kshetradnya is considered knowledge of me (Parmeshwar).

[The term 'chāpi' or 'as well' in the second verse is to denote that both Kshetra and Kshetradnya are nothing but Parmeshwar. While the controller soul in the body is a form of Parmeshwar, the body which is made up of five elements, is also in turn made of Prakruti, and in turn Parmeshwar. Thus, Kshetra (body) becomes a part of Kshar (impermanent) from Ksharāksharvichār (study of impermanent and permanent). Kshetradnya means Parmeshwar. Thus, Kshetrakshetradnyavichār (discussion of body and soul) becomes the discussion about Parmeshwar and this is what's implied in the last sentence of 2nd verse.]

Tat Kṣhetraṁ Yach Cha Yādṛik Cha Yad-Vikāri Yataśh Cha Yat

Sa Cha Yo Yat-Prabhāvaśh Cha Tat Samāsena Me Śhṛiṇu II 3 II

Ṛiṣhibhir Bahudhā Gītaṁ Chhandobhir Vividhaiḥ Pṛithak

Brahma-Sūtra-Padaiśh Chaiva Hetumadbhir Viniśhchitaiḥ II 4 II

Mahā-Bhūtāny Ahankāro Buddhir Avyaktam Eva Cha

Indriyāṇi Daśhaikaṁ Cha Pañcha Chendriya-Gocharāḥ II 5 II

Ichchhā Dveṣhaḥ Sukhaṁ Duḥkhaṁ Saṅghātaśh Chetanā Dhṛitiḥ

Etat Kṣhetraṁ Samāsena Sa-Vikāram Udāhṛitam II 6 II

Amānitvam Adambhitvam Ahinsā Kṣhāntir Ārjavam

Āchāryopāsanaṁ Śhauchaṁ Sthairyam Ātma-Vinigrahaḥ II 7 II

Indriyārtheṣhu Vairāgyam Anahankāra Eva Cha

Janma-Mṛityu-Jarā-Vyādhi-Duḥkha-Doṣhānudarśhanam II 8 II

Asaktir Anabhiṣhvaṅgaḥ Putra-Dāra-Gṛihādiṣhu

Nityaṁ Cha Sama-Chittatvam Iṣhṭāniṣhṭopapattiṣhu II 9 II

(3) Listen to me as I briefly tell you – what Kshetra means, how many types are there of it, and what evolves from what (in it); also, who it (Kshetradnya) is and what is its impact. (4) This (topic) has been sung in different ways, in different meters, by many sages and in carefully drafted verses of Brahma Sutras.

[The mention of Brahma Sutras (which are same as Vedānta Sutras) in Gitā and its origin is discussed in the Appendix chapter earlier. Upanishads are numerous accounts of philosophy expressed by different sages in different periods, thus creating apparent contradictions if studied in isolation. Brahma Sutras by Bādarāyan succinctly summarize all Upanishads and unify them into a common central meaning. Hence, this verse mentions both Upanishads and Brahma Sutras.]

(5) (Five) Elements, Ahankār (ego), Buddhi (intellect), Avyakta (Prakruti), Ten (subtle) senses, one Man (mind) and five subjects (sound, touch, form, taste and smell) of (five) senses, (6) desire, hatred, happiness, sorrow, the aggregate (whole body), life force and courage are collectively called Kshetra (body).

[These verses describe Body and its manifestations. 5th verse describes 24 out of the 25 elements of Sānkhya (except Purush). While Mind is included in these 24, the seven different emotions of the mind appear redundant in the 6th verse. However, some affiliate these emotions to the soul and in order to clarify the inclusion of these emotions within the bodily elements they are mentioned distinctly. While the word Chetanā (life force) is sometimes also used interchangeably as Chaitanya (consciousness), it is not the case here. Here, it only means the life force that brings about the operations of different elements of the body. The consciousness that causes these is separate and included in Kshetradnya (soul) as mentioned in 2nd verse.

(7) Having humility, having no arrogance, non-violence, compassion, straightforwardness, service to Guru, purity, stability, mental resolve; (8) Absence of passion for sensory objects, having no ego, intelligence of considering birth, death, old age, disease and sorrow to be the flaws stuck with us; (9) Detachment (about Karma), lack of over-involvement in wife, kids, home etc., tendency of mind to be stoic in favorable as

Mayi Chānanya-Yogena Bhaktir Avyabhichāriṇī

Vivikta-Deśha-Sevitvam Aratir Jana-Sansadi II 10 II

Adhyātma-Jñāna-Nityatvaṁ Tattva-Jñānārtha-Darśhanam

Etaj Jñānam Iti Proktam Ajñānaṁ Yad Ato 'Nyathā II 11 II

Jñeyaṁ Yat Tat Pravakṣhyāmi Yaj Jñātvāmṛitam Aśhnute

Anādi Mat-Paraṁ Brahma Na Sat Tan Nāsad Uchyate II 12 II

Sarvataḥ Pāṇi-Pādaṁ Tat Sarvato 'Kṣhi-Śhiro-Mukham

Sarvataḥ Śhrutimal Loke Sarvam Āvṛitya Tiṣhṭhati II 13 II

Sarvendriya-Guṇābhāsaṁ Sarvendriya-Vivarjitam

Asaktaṁ Sarva-Bhṛich Chaiva Nirguṇaṁ Guṇa-Bhoktṛi Cha II 14 II

Bahir Antaśh Cha Bhūtānām Acharaṁ Charam Eva Cha

Sūkṣhmatvāt Tad Avijñeyaṁ Dūra-Sthaṁ Chāntike Cha Tat II 15 II

Avibhaktaṁ Cha Bhūteṣhu Vibhaktam Iva Cha Sthitam

Bhūta-Bhartṛi Cha Taj Jñeyaṁ Grasiṣhṇu Prabhaviṣhṇu Cha II 16 II

Jyotiṣhām Api Taj Jyotis Tamasaḥ Param Uchyate

Jñānaṁ Jñeyaṁ Jñāna-Gamyaṁ Hṛidi Sarvasya Viṣhṭhitam II 17 II

well as unfavorable situations, (10) unshakeable, absolute devotion to me, staying in selected solitary places, aversion to common gatherings, (11) awareness of timelessness of spirituality and pursuit of principles of philosophy – is called Dnyān (Knowledge). Rest is ignorance.

[While it's important to know the different constituents of body and soul, it alone isn't sufficient. Before attaining Moksha, one must also inculcate everything in one's being, e.g. Non-violence, equanimity etc. Hence, these attributes are mentioned as a part of knowledge in the above verses. Some try to hint at the two attributes mentioned in 9th and 10th verse – lack of over-involvement with wife, kids, home etc. and staying in selected solitary places. They say that with these, Gitā is advocating ascetic life. While it's not debatable that Gitā includes these aspects as part of knowledge, what's important is what Gitā recommends after one gains knowledge. While Sānkhya or Sanyās claims one should quit everything and go live away alone in a forest, Gitā states that after attaining knowledge, one must stay within the society but live dispassionately or in a detached way, continue to perform all actions without attachment to fruits and strive for universal welfare.]

(12) Let me tell you that (thing), knowing which one attains immortality (Moksha or liberation). It's primordial Brahman beyond (everything). It's neither called Sat nor Asat (truth or untruth). (13) It has hands and legs on all sides. It has eyes, heads and mouths all over. It has ears on all sides and it has pervaded everything in this world. (14) There's an illusion of all senses in it whereas it is devoid of any sensory organ. It enjoys all qualities despite being detached from them. (15) It is inside as well as outside all living beings. It's mobile as well as immobile. It's unfathomable because it's subtle; and it is far yet near.

(16) Although it's indivisible, it is as if it's divided and present in all living beings; and (we) must consider it to support, pervade and generate all living beings. (17) It is also called radiance of the radiant and one beyond darkness. It is Dnyān (knowledge), Dnyeya (to be known) and Dnyānagamya (perceivable through knowledge) too. It is located in everyone's heart.

Iti Kṣhetraṁ Tathā Jñānaṁ Jñeyaṁ Choktaṁ Samāsataḥ

Mad-Bhakta Etad Vijñāya Mad-Bhāvāyopapadyate II 18 II

Prakṛitiṁ Puruṣhaṁ Chaiva Viddhy Anādī Ubhāv Api

Vikārānśh Cha Guṇānśh Chaiva Viddhi Prakṛiti-Sambhavān II 19 II

Kārya-Kāraṇa-Kartṛitve Hetuḥ Prakṛitir Uchyate

Puruṣhaḥ Sukha-Duḥkhānāṁ Bhoktṛitve Hetur Uchyate II 20 II

[The description of Kshetradnya or Parabrahma in the above verses is directly borrowed from various Upanishads viz. Shwetāshwatar, Ishāvāsya, Bruhadāranyak etc. It also borrows from Rig Veda when it says that it's neither Sat nor Asat. We have discussed this one in detail in chapter 9.]

(18) I thus explained briefly what is Kshetra, Dnyān and Dnyeya. By knowing this, my devotee attains my form.

[We discussed what is Kshetra, Dnyān and Dnyeya as per Adhyātma or Vedānta. As this Kshetrakshetradnyavichār (discussion of body and soul) covers the knowledge of Parmeshwar, it definitely leads to Moksha; which is stated in the 18th verse. This concludes the Kshetrakshetradnyavichār from Vedānta philosophy. Prakruti (from Sānkhya) leads to five elements and the manifest universe, and Adhyātma calls 'Ātmā' (soul) what Sānkhya call 'Purush'. Thus, Kshetrakshetradnyavichār can be termed as discussion of Prakruti and Purush. However, Gitā doesn't consider Prakruti and Purush as two separate originals and considers them to be the two forms of the same Parmeshwar – inferior and superior respectively; and hence this discussion is called discussion of Parmeshwar. Now Gitā describes the same knowledge through the language of Sānkhya, albeit without accepting the dualistic approach.]

(19) Consider Prakruti and Purush both to be primordial. Know that Vikār (manifestations) and Gunas (attributes) all arise from Prakruti.

[Sānkhya consider Prakruti not just to be primordial but also to be independent and original (self-manifested). Vedānti consider it to have arisen from Parmeshwar and thus neither independent nor self-manifested. However, as we can't figure out when Prakruti and Purush arose from Parmeshwar, they're both considered Anādi (Primordial). Chapter 7 deals with these concepts in detail.]

(20) Prakruti is considered to be the cause (responsible) for the creation of Kārya (effect, which here means body) and Kāran (cause, which here means senses); and Purush (Kshetradnya) is considered to be the cause (responsible) for enjoying happiness and sorrow (even though it is not the doer).

Puruşhaḥ Prakṛiti-Stho Hi Bhuṅkte Prakṛiti-Jān Guṇān

Kāraṇaṁ Guṇa-Saṅgo 'Sya Sad-Asad-Yoni-Janmasu II 21 II

Upadraşhṭānumantā Cha Bhartā Bhoktā Maheśhvaraḥ

Paramātmeti Chāpy Ukto Dehe 'Smin Puruşhaḥ Paraḥ II 22 II

Ya Evaṁ Vetti Puruşhaṁ Prakṛitiṁ Cha Guṇaiḥ Saha

Sarvathā Vartamāno 'Pi Na Sa Bhūyo 'Bhijāyate II 23 II

Dhyānenātmani Paśhyanti Kechid Ātmānam Ātmanā

Anye Sānkhyena Yogena Karma-Yogena Chāpare II 24 II

Anye Tv Evam Ajānantaḥ Śhrutvānyebhya Upāsate

Te 'Pi Chātitaranty Eva Mṛityuṁ Śhruti-Parāyaṇāḥ II 25 II

(21) Because once Purush becomes engaged with Prakruti, it enjoys the Gunas (attributes) of Prakruti and this entanglement with Gunas becomes the cause for its birth in superior or inferior Yoni (wombs). (22) Close witness, approver, contributor (to Prakruti's Gunas) and consumer is called the ultimate Purush within the body, Maheshwar (Supreme Lord) and Parmātmā (supreme soul).

(23) One who understands Purush (to be Nirguna or without attributes) and Prakruti (alone) to be present with all Gunas (attributes), never takes rebirth, however they may behave.

[Once Purush is declared to be the soul within the body in 22nd verse, the same inertness of Sānkhya Purush is equated with the soul of Vedānti and this unifies the explanation of Sānkhya and Vedānta. Unlike many who consider Sānkhya to be enemies of Vedānta, Gitā accepts Sānkhya philosophy with open arms and explains the Kshetrakshetradnyavichār both ways – once with pure Vedānta philosophy (in earlier verses) and once with the help of Sānkhya philosophy, albeit maintaining the Advaiti (monist) stand. This proves the equanimity of Gitā, as opposed to Upanishads. While Gitā denies the duality of Sānkhya, it nevertheless accepts whatever's plausible in their explanation.]

(24) Some people witness the soul within them through meditation, by themselves. Some others through Sānkhya Yog while some others through Karmayog. (25) However, many others who don't attain knowledge this way worship (Parmeshwar) by listening to others. Even these obedient people who follow the received advice cross the ocean of death and go beyond.

[These verses mention different paths of spiritual knowledge – Meditation as per Pātanjal Yog, Renunciation post knowledge as per Sānkhya, Dedication to Parmeshwar and continuation of action without attachment as per Karmayog and Devotion by listening to others in absence of knowledge as per Bhaktiyog. Whatever path you take, ultimately Moksha is certain through knowledge of Parmeshwar.]

Yāvat Sañjāyate Kiñchit Sattvaṁ Sthāvara-Jaṅgamam

Kṣhetra-Kṣhetrajña-Sanyogāt Tad Viddhi Bharatarṣhabha II 26 II

Samaṁ Sarveṣhu Bhūteṣhu Tiṣhṭhantaṁ Parameśhvaram

Vinaśhyatsv Avinaśhyantaṁ Yaḥ Paśhyati Sa Paśhyati II 27 II

Samaṁ Paśhyan Hi Sarvatra Samavasthitam Īśhvaram

Na Hinasty Ātmanātmānaṁ Tato Yāti Parāṁ Gatim II 28 II

Prakṛityaiva Cha Karmāṇi Kriyamāṇāni Sarvaśhaḥ

Yaḥ Paśhyati Tathātmānam Akartāraṁ Sa Paśhyati II 29 II

Yadā Bhūta-Pṛithag-Bhāvam Eka-Stham Anupaśhyati

Tata Eva Cha Vistāraṁ Brahma Sampadyate Tadā II 30 II

Anāditvān Nirguṇatvāt Paramātmāyam Avyayaḥ

Śharīra-Stho 'Pi Kaunteya Na Karoti Na Lipyate II 31 II

Yathā Sarva-Gataṁ Saukṣhmyād Ākāśhaṁ Nopalipyate

Sarvatrāvasthito Dehe Tathātmā Nopalipyate II 32 II

Yathā Prakāśhayaty Ekaḥ Kṛitsnaṁ Lokam Imaṁ Raviḥ

Kṣhetraṁ Kṣhetrī Tathā Kṛitsnaṁ Prakāśhayati Bhārata II 33 II

(26) O Arjun! Remember that whichever object gets created, mobile or immobile, does so through the union of Kshetra (body) and Kshetradnya (soul). (27) One, who sees Parmeshwar as someone who's within all living beings equally and someone who doesn't get destroyed even if all living beings disappear, is said to have understood (the true principle). (28) One who understands that almighty is present everywhere equally and who doesn't harm themselves (starts on a righteous path themselves) attains ultimate goal.

(29) Actions of all kinds are performed by Prakruti while Ātmā (soul) is inert. One who understands this, is said to have understood (the true principle). (30) When one starts perceiving the diversity in all living beings as unity and see that this unity has expanded into everything, one attains Brahman. (31) O Arjun! Being primordial and without attributes, this imperishable supreme soul doesn't do anything and is not stained (bound by any action), despite being present inside the body. (32) Just as despite being all pervasive, space is not stained by anything as it is subtle; similarly, this soul is not stained by anything even though it pervades the entire body.

(33) O Arjun! Just as the sun illuminates the whole world alone, Kshetradnya (knower of the field or soul) enlightens the entire Kshetra (field or whole body).

Kşhetra-Kşhetrajñayor Evam Antaraṁ Jñāna-Chakşhuşhā

Bhūta-Prakŗiti-Mokşhaṁ Cha Ye Vidur Yānti Te Param II 34 II

(34) Those who thus perceive the distinction between Kshetra (body) and Kshetradnya (soul) through eyes of knowledge and understand liberation of (elemental) Prakruti of all living beings; attain Parabrahma (the absolute).

[The last verse summarizes the entire chapter. We've interpreted the word 'Bhootaprakrutimoksha' from Sānkhya point of view. Attaining or not attaining liberation isn't the function of a soul as it's perpetually inert and detached. However, once it's aware that all qualities are of Prakruti and that they don't belong to itself, the attached Prakruti attains Moksha (is liberated) and stops dancing in front of Purush (soul). Thus, binding as well as liberation are functions of Prakruti according to Sānkhya; and we've stuck to this. However, many interpret this also as liberation of soul from Māyā (appearance) or Prakruti and five elements. We saw that this distinction between Kshetra and Kshetradnya is perceivable through eyes of knowledge (Gitā 13.34), Rāj Vidyā is perceivable through actual or physical eyes (Gitā 9.2) while Vishwaroopdarshan or witnessing of cosmic form is perceivable by a devotee only through divine eyes (Gitā 11.8). This distinction between the analysis of knowledge and science given in 9th, 11th and 13th Adhyāyas is worth noting.

This concludes the thirteenth Adhyāya **Kshetrakshetradnyavibhāgyog** from the dialogue between Shri Krishna and Arjun on Yog Shāstra (Karmayog Shāstra) within Brahmavidyā (knowledge of Brahman) in the Upanishad sung (narrated) by Shri Bhagwān (Shri Krishna).

Chaturdashodhyāyah (Fourteenth Adhyāya)

Śhrī-Bhagavān Uvācha

Paraṁ Bhūyaḥ Pravakṣhyāmi Jñānānāṁ Jñānam Uttamam

Yaj Jñātvā Munayaḥ Sarve Parāṁ Siddhim Ito Gatāḥ II 1 II

Idaṁ Jñānam Upāśhritya Mama Sādharmyam Āgatāḥ

Sarge 'Pi Nopajāyante Pralaye Na Vyathanti Cha II 2 II

Mama Yonir Mahad Brahma Tasmin Garbhaṁ Dadhāmy Aham

Sambhavaḥ Sarva-Bhūtānāṁ Tato Bhavati Bhārata II 3 II

Sarva-Yoniṣhu Kaunteya Mūrtayaḥ Sambhavanti Yāḥ

Tāsāṁ Brahma Mahad Yonir Ahaṁ Bīja-Pradaḥ Pitā II 4 II

Sattvaṁ Rajas Tama Iti Guṇāḥ Prakṛiti-Sambhavāḥ

Nibadhnanti Mahā-Bāho Dehe Dehinam Avyayam II 5 II

Tatra Sattvaṁ Nirmalatvāt Prakāśhakam Anāmayam

Sukha-Saṅgena Badhnāti Jñāna-Saṅgena Chānagha II 6 II

Rajo Rāgātmakaṁ Viddhi Tṛiṣhṇā-Saṅga-Samudbhavam

Tan Nibadhnāti Kaunteya Karma-Saṅgena Dehinam II 7 II

Tamas Tv Ajñāna-Jaṁ Viddhi Mohanaṁ Sarva-Dehinām

Pramādālasya-Nidrābhis Tan Nibadhnāti Bhārata II 8 II

Chaturdashodhyāyah (Fourteenth Adhyāya)

[After explaining Kshetrakshetradnyavichār (discussion of body and soul) in the 13th Adhyāya, once through Vedānta and once through Sānkhya philosophy, we now move on to the evolution of the universe from Prakruti. We've discussed this in detail in the 8th chapter. Bhagwān starts by saying that he shall now reiterate the supreme knowledge, wherein he begins explaining the process of evolution of everything we perceive.]

Shri Bhagwān said – (1) Additionally, let me tell you the best knowledge among all knowledge, knowing which all sages have had the ultimate accomplishment from these worlds. (2) With the support of this knowledge, those who have become one with me are neither born with birth of this universe nor annihilated at the time of (its) dissolution. (They are entirely liberated from the cycle of birth and death).

[This is the introduction. Now by saying that Prakruti is his form, Bhagwān removes the duality of Sānkhya and continues with the explanation of three Gunas (attributes) of Prakruti viz. Sattva, Raja and Tama without any contradiction with Vedānta].

(3) O Arjun! Mahadbrahma (meaning Prakruti) is my womb where I place the embryo. Subsequently, all living beings begin evolving from it. (4) O Arjun! Of all the entities that take birth as species (of living beings), Mahadbrahma (Prakruti) is the womb and I am the father who sows the seed.

(5) O Arjun! Sattva, Raja and Tama, the Gunas (attributes) that arise from Prakruti, bind the imperishable staying within the body (the unblemished soul) with the body. (6) Of them, O sinless Arjun! Sattva Guna which is radiant and flawless by virtue of being spotless, binds one with attachment to happiness and knowledge. (7) Rājas Guna is of passionate nature and understand that it leads to generation of desires and attachment. O Arjun! It binds one with attachment to perform Karma (actions). (8) However, Tāmas Guna is born of ignorance and understand that it deludes all living beings. It binds (them)

Sattvaṁ Sukhe Sañjayati Rajaḥ Karmaṇi Bhārata

Jñānam Āvṛitya Tu Tamaḥ Pramāde Sañjayaty Uta II 9 II

Rajas Tamaśh Chābhibhūya Sattvaṁ Bhavati Bhārata

Rajaḥ Sattvaṁ Tamaśh Chaiva Tamaḥ Sattvaṁ Rajas Tathā II 10 II

Sarva-Dvāreṣhu Dehe 'Smin Prakāśha Upajāyate

Jñānaṁ Yadā Tadā Vidyād Vivṛiddhaṁ Sattvam Ity Uta II 11 II

Lobhaḥ Pravṛittir Ārambhaḥ Karmaṇām Aśhamaḥ Spṛihā

Rajasy Etāni Jāyante Vivṛiddhe Bharatarṣhabha II 12 II

Aprakāśho 'Pravṛittiśh Cha Pramādo Moha Eva Cha

Tamasy Etāni Jāyante Vivṛiddhe Kuru-Nandana II 13 II

Yadā Sattve Pravṛiddhe Tu Pralayaṁ Yāti Deha-Bhṛit

Tadottama-Vidāṁ Lokān Amalān Pratipadyate II 14 II

Rajasi Pralayaṁ Gatvā Karma-Saṅgiṣhu Jāyate

Tathā Pralīnas Tamasi Mūḍha-Yoniṣhu Jāyate II 15 II

Karmaṇaḥ Sukṛitasyāhuḥ Sāttvikaṁ Nirmalaṁ Phalam

Rajasas Tu Phalaṁ Duḥkham Ajñānaṁ Tamasaḥ Phalam II 16 II

Sattvāt Sañjāyate Jñānaṁ Rajaso Lobha Eva Cha

Pramāda-Mohau Tamaso Bhavato 'Jñānam Eva Cha II 17 II

Ūrdhvaṁ Gachchhanti Sattva-Sthā Madhye Tiṣhṭhanti Rājasāḥ

Jaghanya-Guṇa-Vṛitti-Sthā Adho Gachchhanti Tāmasāḥ II 18 II

Nānyaṁ Guṇebhyaḥ Kartāraṁ Yadā Draṣhṭānupaśhyati

Guṇebhyaśh Cha Paraṁ Vetti Mad-Bhāvaṁ So 'Dhigachchhati II 19 II

with negligence, laziness and sleep. (9) O Arjun! Sattva Guna creates attachment with happiness while Rājas Guna with action. However, O Arjun! Tāmas Guna indeed creates attachment to negligence by clouding wisdom.

[While we learnt the individual qualities of the three Gunas viz. Sattva, Rājas and Tāmas, these three Gunas never occur in isolation but always in a combination of all three. E.g. Even though the motivation for a good deed is a virtue of Sattva Guna, activity is a virtue of Rājas Guna that enables one to perform this good deed. Thus, Sattva Guna needs Rājas Guna always. Different combinations of these three Gunas bring about generation of different substances in this universe.]

(10) Sattva dominates by defeating Rājas and Tāmas. Similarly, Rājas (dominates) by defeating Sattva and Tāmas while Tāmas (dominates) by defeating Sattva and Rājas. (11) When light, meaning spotless knowledge, radiates from all doors of this body, understand that Sattva Guna has increased.

(12) O Arjun! When Rājas Guna increases, greed, tendency to act, action, dissatisfaction and desire develop. (13) And O Arjun! When Tāmas Guna increases, darkness, inactivity, negligence and delusion too develop.

(14) If one dies when Sattva Guna has progressed, they attain pure world of the learned (like heaven). (15) If one dies when Rājas Guna has progressed, they take birth among those attached to Karma (action) and if one dies in (predominance of) Tāmas Guna, they take birth in the womb of fools (as animals, birds etc.). (16) It is said that the fruit of good Karma is spotless and Sāttvic but the fruit of Rājas Karma is sorrow and the fruit of Tāmas Karma is ignorance. (17) Sattva Guna leads to knowledge, Rājas Guna leads to greed while Tāmas Guna leads not only to negligence and delusion but also to ignorance. (18) Sāttvic people go upwards (heavenly abode). Rājas people stay in the middle (on earth). Those Tāmas people with inferior qualities go downwards.

(19) When a visionary (a person with stoic attitude) sees that there's no doer other than the (three) Gunas (of Prakruti) and sees (the principle) beyond (the three) Gunas, they reach my form.

Guṇān Etān Atītya Trīn Dehī Deha-Samudbhavān

Janma-Mṛityu-Jarā-Duḥkhair Vimukto 'Mṛitam Aśhnute II 20 II

Arjuna Uvācha

Kair Liṅgais Trīn Guṇān Etān Atīto Bhavati Prabho

Kim Āchāraḥ Kathaṁ Chaitāns Trīn Guṇān Ativartate II 21 II

Śhrī-Bhagavān Uvācha

Prakāśhaṁ Cha Pravṛittiṁ Cha Moham Eva Cha Pāṇḍava

Na Dveṣhṭi Sampravṛittāni Na Nivṛittāni Kāṅkṣhati II 22 II

Udāsīna-Vad Āsīno Guṇair Yo Na Vichālyate

Guṇā Vartanta Ity Evaṁ Yo 'Vatiṣhṭhati Neṅgate II 23 II

Sama-Duḥkha-Sukhaḥ Sva-Sthaḥ Sama-Loṣhṭāśhma-Kāñchanaḥ

Tulya-Priyāpriyo Dhīras Tulya-Nindātma-Sanstutiḥ II 24 II

Mānāpamānayos Tulyas Tulyo Mitrāri-Pakṣhayoḥ

Sarvārambha-Parityāgī Guṇātītaḥ Sa Uchyate II 25 II

(20) An embodied person goes beyond the three Gunas responsible for development of the body, frees themselves of the sorrow of birth, old age and death; and experiences immortality (Moksha).

[Vedānti call it Māyā while Sānkhya call it Trigunātmak (made of three Gunas) Prakruti. Thus, going beyond three Gunas is same as freedom from Māyā and understanding Parabrahma (the absolute). This is called Brāhmi state or state of being established in Brahman. Being intrigued by this description of Trigunāteet (someone who's gone beyond three Gunas), Arjun now asks Shri Krishna about a Sthitapradnya (someone firm in wisdom or with stoic calm) just like in 2nd Adhyāya.]

Arjun said – (21) O Bhagwān! With which qualities does one go beyond the three Gunas? How does one behave and how does one go beyond the three Gunas? (Pray tell me).

Shri Bhagwān said – (22) O Arjun! One who neither hates attainment of light, action and delusion (meaning the fruits of Sāttvic, Rājas and Tāmas actions respectively) nor yearns their attainment if not attained; (23) Who remains inert (to the fruits of Karma), who's not perturbed by (three) Gunas, remains stable considering that Gunas are performing (their respective) tasks, is unmoved and unblemished; (24) Who considers happiness and sorrow to be equal, is firm, considers soil, rock and gold to be equal; is equanimous towards pleasant and unpleasant or criticism or praise, is always courageous;

(25) For whom respect or disrespect and friend or foe are equal, and (by knowing that Prakruti does everything) who has quit all (desirous) actions; is called Gunāteet (beyond Gunas).

[These verses answer with the qualities and behavior of a Trigunāteet (beyond three Gunas). These closely resemble the description of a Sthitapradnya (firm in wisdom) in 2nd Adhyāya and supreme devotee in 12th Adhyāya. Even many adjectives used are common. Thus, it is clear that whichever path one takes, behavior and qualities of a realized person are the same. However, one must remember that as emphasized earlier in the 3rd, 4th and 5th Adhyāyas, these Sthitapradnya, Supreme devotee or Trigunāteet persons are from the path of Karmayog and must continue to perform actions without attachment. Even here,

Māṁ Cha Yo 'Vyabhichāreṇa Bhakti-Yogena Sevate

Sa Guṇān Samatītyaitān Brahma-Bhūyāya Kalpate II 26 II

Brahmaṇo Hi Pratiṣhṭhāham Amṛitasyāvyayasya Cha

Śhāśhvatasya Cha Dharmasya Sukhasyaikāntikasya Cha II 27 II

the followers of asceticism claim that Gitā recommends renunciation from all actions. However, we've often explained how this claim is communalistic and opposed to the spirit of the core essence of Gitā.]

(26) And who serves me with unadulterated devotion, goes beyond these three Gunas and becomes capable of attaining the level of Brahman (the absolute).

(27) Because, I'm the ultimate destination of immortal and imperishable Brahman, eternal Dharma and ultimate, perpetual bliss.

[This verse means that once we quit the duality of Sānkhya and accept universal nature of Parmeshwar, the same Trigunāteet (beyond three Gunas) state is also attained through its devotion. While Gitā says that path of Bhakti (devotion) is the simplest, it doesn't consider other paths inferior. All communalistic claims are post-facto. The central theme of Gitā is completely different from the comparison of these paths. It deals with what one should do after gaining the knowledge of Parmeshwar – whether one continues to perform actions for universal welfare or take renunciation and adopt ascetic life. It's already established clearly that the answer of Gitā to the aforementioned question is Karmayog.]

This concludes the fourteenth Adhyāya **Gunatrayavibhāgyog** from the dialogue between Shri Krishna and Arjun on Yog Shāstra (Karmayog Shāstra) within Brahmavidyā (knowledge of Brahman) in the Upanishad sung (narrated) by Shri Bhagwān (Shri Krishna).

Panchdashodhyāyah (Fifteenth Adhyāya)

Śhrī-Bhagavān Uvācha

Ūrdhva-Mūlam Adhaḥ-Śhākham Aśhvatthaṁ Prāhur Avyayam

Chhandānsi Yasya Parṇāni Yas Taṁ Veda Sa Veda-Vit II 1 II

Adhaśh Chordhvaṁ Prasṛitās Tasya Śhākhā Guṇa-Pravṛiddhā Viṣhaya-Pravālāḥ

Adhaśh Cha Mūlāny Anusantatāni Karmānubandhīni Manuṣhya-Loke II 2 II

Panchdashodhyāyah (Fifteenth Adhyāya)

[After Kshetrakshetradnyavichār (discussion of body and soul), we saw in the 13th Adhyāya the differential explanation of Purush and Prakruti as per Sānkhya philosophy. In the 14th Adhyāya we saw how combinations of three Gunas (attributes) of Prakruti result in diverse nature of human beings and how one can attain a stage beyond the influence of these Gunas and be realized. We maintained the Advaita (monist) idea throughout. Now in this Adhyāya we explore the description of the whole expanse of universe in the metaphor of a tree or a forest.]

Shri Bhagwān said – (1) An imperishable tree with its roots facing up, many branches downward and with Chhanda (Vedas) as its leaves. One who knows this Ashwattha tree thus described is (truly) the knower of Vedas.

[This is the description of the tree of universe. Just as a tiny seed leads to a skyscraper tree, unmanifest Parmeshwar has led to this gigantic universe. This metaphor of a tree is also found in ancient scriptures elsewhere. There's some debate about which tree it refers to, Vat (Banyan), Pipal (Ficus Religiosa) or Audumbar (Cluster Fig). However, upon investigating carefully, we understand that it's Pipal tree.]

(2) The branches, nourished by three Gunas, and from where the objects (of senses namely voice, touch, form, taste and smell) have sprouted, spread below and above as well. The roots, which ultimately take the form of Karma (action), have grown long downwards in human world as well.

[The second verse adds more aspects stating that branches (governed by three Gunas) have grown above as well while the roots have grown to the human world in the form of Karma. As Gitā follows Vedānta and thus shows that entire universe has been manifested from a single Parmeshwar, unlike Sānkhya who propose that Purush and Prakruti are the two primordial originals. Now we begin the way of freeing ourselves from this vast, expansive universe to attain Moksha.]

Na Rūpam Asyeha Tathopalabhyate Nānto Na Chādir Na Cha Sampratiṣhṭhā

Aśhvattham Enaṁ Su-Virūḍha-Mūlam Asaṅga-Śhastreṇa Dṛiḍhena Chhittvā II 3 II

Tataḥ Padaṁ Tat Parimārgitavyaṁ Yasmin Gatā Na Nivartanti Bhūyaḥ

Tam Eva Chādyaṁ Puruṣhaṁ Prapadye Yataḥ Pravṛittiḥ Prasṛitā Purāṇī II 4 II

Nirmāna-Mohā Jita-Saṅga-Doṣhā Adhyātma-Nityā Vinivṛitta-Kāmāḥ

Dvandvair Vimuktāḥ Sukha-Duḥkha-Sanjñair Gachchhanty Amūḍhāḥ Padam Avyayaṁ Tat II 5 II

Na Tad Bhāsayate Sūryo Na Śhaśhāṅko Na Pāvakaḥ

Yad Gatvā Na Nivartante Tad Dhāma Paramaṁ Mama II 6 II

Mamaivānśho Jīva-Loke Jīva-Bhūtaḥ Sanātanaḥ

Manaḥ-Ṣhaṣhṭhānīndriyāṇi Prakṛiti-Sthāni Karṣhati II 7 II

Śharīraṁ Yad Avāpnoti Yach Chāpy Utkrāmatīśhvaraḥ

Gṛihītvaitāni Sanyāti Vāyur Gandhān Ivāśhayāt II 8 II

(3) However, the form (of this tree) is not accessible in our world. We don't find its origin, end or support. After cutting through this Ashwattha (tree), whose roots have grown very deep, using the sword of detachment; (4) we must later find the place from where there's no return – (by deciding – "I'm going to the primordial Purush from whom the ancient Pravrutti (activity) has originated".)

[The expanse of the universe is Karma (actions) with Nāmroope (name-forms) and this Karma is primordial. The only way to get rid of it, is by adopting detachment. Only by not attaching oneself to the actions and their fruits can one escape the binding of Karma, as Karma is primordial and eternal.]

(5) Those wise people who are free from ego and delusion, who have won over attachment, who are stable in knowledge of spirituality, who are free from desire and who are free from the duality of happiness and sorrow reach the imperishable place. (6) It is my ultimate place, going where, they don't return. It is not illuminated by the Sun, the Moon or fire.

[As Sun, Moon or fire are all under the purview of objects with Nāmroope (name-forms), it's mentioned that the place is not illuminated by these. The place is Parabrahma and hence it's self-effulgent. In fact, the radiance of Sun, Moon or fire comes from Parabrahma. Becoming one with this Parabrahma is Moksha.]

(7) My eternal essence becomes Jeev (individual self or soul) in the mortal world and attracts six (subtle) senses including mind (This is called Linga shareer or subtle body).

(8) When this Ishwar (self) obtains a gross body and when it exits a gross body, then it (self) takes the aforementioned (mind and five senses) with it, just as air takes fragrance from a substance (like flower).

Śhrotraṁ Chakṣhuḥ Sparśhanaṁ Cha Rasanaṁ Ghrāṇam Eva Cha

Adhiṣhṭhāya Manaśh Chāyaṁ Viṣhayān Upasevate II 9 II

Utkrāmantaṁ Sthitaṁ Vāpi Bhuñjānaṁ Vā Guṇānvitam

Vimūḍhā Nānupaśhyanti Paśhyanti Jñāna-Chakṣhuṣhaḥ II 10 II

Yatanto Yoginaśh Chainaṁ Paśhyanty Ātmany Avasthitam

Yatanto 'Py Akṛitātmāno Nainaṁ Paśhyanty Achetasaḥ II 11 II

Yad Āditya-Gataṁ Tejo Jagad Bhāsayate 'Khilam

Yach Chandramasi Yach Chāgnau Tat Tejo Viddhi Māmakam II 12 II

Gām Āviśhya Cha Bhūtāni Dhārayāmy Aham Ojasā

Puṣhṇāmi Chauṣhadhīḥ Sarvāḥ Somo Bhūtvā Rasātmakaḥ II 13 II

Ahaṁ Vaiśhvānaro Bhūtvā Prāṇināṁ Deham Āśhritaḥ

Prāṇāpāna-Samāyuktaḥ Pachāmy Annaṁ Chatur-Vidham II 14 II

Sarvasya Chāhaṁ Hṛidi Sanniviṣhṭo Mattaḥ Smṛitir Jñānam Apohanaṁ Cha

Vedaiśh Cha Sarvair Aham Eva Vedyo Vedānta-Kṛid Veda-Vid Eva Chāham II 15 II

Dvāv Imau Puruṣhau Loke Kṣharaśh Chākṣhara Eva Cha

Kṣharaḥ Sarvāṇi Bhūtāni Kūṭa-Stho 'Kṣhara Uchyate II 16 II

Uttamaḥ Puruṣhas Tv Anyaḥ Paramātmety Udāhṛitaḥ

Yo Loka-Trayam Āviśhya Bibharty Avyaya Īśhvaraḥ II 17 II

(9) By establishing itself in ears, eyes, skin, tongue, nose and mind it (self) consumes the objects of the senses.

[These verses explain what a subtle body is and also explains how it enters a gross body and enjoys material things. It shows how soul doesn't originate from Parmeshwar every time a birth happens but it merely moves from bodies with every birth and death. We've deliberately used the word 'essence' and not a 'fragment or a part' as soul is not different from Parmeshwar in its properties but is a complete representative of it; just as air inside a pot is not different from air outside in any way other than being enclosed within.]

(10) Fools don't perceive the one (soul) leaving the body or the one that consumes by being enriched with Gunas (attributes). People seeing through eyes of knowledge recognize it. (11) Moreover, the striving Yogis, recognize the soul residing within their body. But those ignorant people whose soul is not purified don't recognize despite striving for it.

(12) Know that the effulgence of the Sun that brightens the whole world, the radiance of the moon and that of the fire are mine. (13) Moreover, I sustain all living beings with my radiance by entering the earth, and nourish all plants by becoming the juicy moon.

(14) I reside within the bodies of living beings by becoming the fire of digestion and being enriched with incoming and outgoing breaths, digest food of four kinds (chewed, sucked, licked and drunk). (15) And I am present in everyone's heart. Memory, knowledge and amnesia arise from me. I am all the knowledge in Vedas, author of Vedānta and also knower of the Vedas.

[The second line of the 15th verse is borrowed from Kaivalya Upanishad with a slight variation. The word Vedānta also appears in Mundak and Shwetāshwatar Upanishads thus proving its prevalence in the erstwhile period of Gitā.]

(16) In this world, there are two types of beings, Kshar (perishable) and Akshar (imperishable). Kshar are all living beings while the one at their root (the unmanifest principle called Prakruti) is called Akshar. (17) However, the supreme Purush (being) is different (from these two). It's called Parmātmā. That imperishable Ishwar pervades all three worlds and nourishes them.

Yasmāt Kṣharam Atīto 'Ham Akṣharād Api Chottamaḥ

Ato 'Smi Loke Vede Cha Prathitaḥ Puruṣhottamaḥ II 18 II

Yo Mām Evam Asammūḍho Jānāti Puruṣhottamam

Sa Sarva-Vid Bhajati Māṁ Sarva-Bhāvena Bhārata II 19 II

Iti Guhyatamaṁ Śhāstram Idam Uktaṁ Mayānagha

Etad Buddhvā Buddhimān Syāt Kṛita-Kṛityaśh Cha Bhārata II 20 II

(18) As I'm beyond Kshar and superior than Akshar, I'm famous in common parlance and in Vedas by the name of Purushottam (Supreme Being).

[In the 16th verse, the words Kshar and Akshar are used to denote manifest and unmanifest Prakruti respectively. Of these, Kshar is easily identifiable as the perishable five elements. However, some get confused as the word Akshar is often used for denoting Parabrahma as well. However, in the above verses it's not the meaning intended and to clarify it the 16th verse clearly mentions the meaning. Purushottam and Parabrahma are the same. 13th Adhyāya explained how this Parmātmā occupies the body in the form of Kshetradnya. Collectively, we see the unity between Ātman and Brahman (individual and universal soul). The Dnyān Vidnyān (knowledge and science) of Gitā says that one who understands this attains Parmeshwar while practicing Karmayog. While one can attain Moksha by worshipping without indulging in actions, the intention behind the Dnyān-Vidnyān of Gitā is not to advocate that but to explain how a person enlightened by knowledge or devotion must continue to perform actions without attachment and attain Moksha while doing so.]

(19) O Arjun! Thus, one who understands without delusion that I am the Supreme Being, worships me while knowing everything and with their whole being. (20) O sinless Arjun! I told you the secret of secret sciences. Understanding this, one becomes intelligent (enlightened) and attains everything that is to be attained.

[This verse uses the word Buddhimān (intelligent) as Buddha (enlightened)]

This concludes the fifteenth Adhyāya **Purushottamyog** from the dialogue between Shri Krishna and Arjun on Yog Shāstra (Karmayog Shāstra) within Brahmavidyā (knowledge of Brahman) in the Upanishad sung (narrated) by Shri Bhagwān (Shri Krishna).

Shodashodhyāyah (Sixteenth Adhyāya)

Śhrī-Bhagavān Uvācha

Abhayaṁ Sattva-Sanśhuddhir Jñāna-Yoga-Vyavasthitiḥ

Dānaṁ Damaśh Cha Yajñaśh Cha Svādhyāyas Tapa Ārjavam II 1 II

Ahinsā Satyam Akrodhas Tyāgaḥ Śhāntir Apaiśhunam

Dayā Bhūteṣhv Aloluptvaṁ Mārdavaṁ Hrīr Achāpalam II 2 II

Tejaḥ Kṣhamā Dhṛitiḥ Śhaucham Adroho Nāti-Mānitā

Bhavanti Sampadaṁ Daivīm Abhijātasya Bhārata II 3 II

Dambho Darpo 'Bhimānaśh Cha Krodhaḥ Pāruṣhyam Eva Cha

Ajñānaṁ Chābhijātasya Pārtha Sampadam Āsurīm II 4 II

Daivī Sampad Vimokṣhāya Nibandhāyāsurī Matā

Mā Śhuchaḥ Sampadaṁ Daivīm Abhijāto 'Si Pāṇḍava II 5 II

Dvau Bhūta-Sargau Loke 'Smin Daiva Āsura Eva Cha

Daivo Vistaraśhaḥ Prokta Āsuraṁ Pārtha Me Śhṛiṇu II 6 II

Pravṛittiṁ Cha Nivṛittiṁ Cha Janā Na Vidur Āsurāḥ

Na Śhauchaṁ Nāpi Chāchāro Na Satyaṁ Teṣhu Vidyate II 7 II

Shodashodhyāyah (Sixteenth Adhyāya)

[Purushottamyog is the epitome of Ksharākshar Dnyān (knowledge of perishable and imperishable). As a matter of fact, the Dnyān Vidnyān (knowledge and science) that began in 7th Adhyāya has to be concluded and summarized now. However, Bhagwān said in 9th Adhyāya how demonic people don't recognize the true and superior form of Parmeshwar. This Adhyāya deals with explaining this form.]

Shri Bhagwān said – (1) Fearlessness, Pure Sāttvic tendency, appropriate moderation of Dnyān (path of knowledge) and Yog (path of Karma), generosity, control, sacrifice, practice, austerity, straightforwardness, (2) Non-violence, truthfulness, absence of anger, renunciation (of fruits of action), peacefulness, broad-mindedness, compassion towards all living beings, absence of greed, gentleness, modesty, absence of fickleness, (3) Radiance, forgiveness, courage, purity, absence of enmity, absence of vanity. O Arjun! Those people who are born with divine wealth possess these (qualities).

[These 26 qualities are the same as the 20 signs of knowledge mentioned in the 13th Adhyāya. There may even be some overlap among these 26 qualities. However, that's not really the point. Many could argue derivatives of each of these qualities merging with derivatives of some other. The point is to convey the indication of Sāttvic nature of divine wealth. Now Bhagwān describes the demonic qualities.]

(4) O Arjun! Those born with demonic wealth possess following qualities – Hypocrisy, arrogance, vanity, anger, ruthlessness and ignorance.

(5) Divine wealth is considered to endow Moksha (liberation) while demonic wealth (endows) bondage. O Arjun, fear not for you're born in divine wealth.

(6) In this world, there are two kinds of people that take birth – one divine and other demonic. I explained the divine (qualities) in detail. O Arjun, hear the description of demonic (qualities) which I tell you. (7) Demonic people don't understand what to do and what not to do. And they possess neither purity, nor (good) behavior and not even truthfulness.

Asatyam Apratiṣhṭhaṁ Te Jagad Āhur Anīśhvaram

Aparaspara-Sambhūtaṁ Kim Anyat Kāma-Haitukam II 8 II

Etāṁ Dṛiṣhṭim Avaṣhṭabhya Naṣhṭātmāno 'Lpa-Buddhayaḥ

Prabhavanty Ugra-Karmāṇaḥ Kṣhayāya Jagato 'Hitāḥ II 9 II

Kāmam Āśhritya Duṣhpūraṁ Dambha-Māna-Madānvitāḥ

Mohād Gṛihītvāsad-Grāhān Pravartante 'Śhuchi-Vratāḥ II 10 II

Chintām Aparimeyāṁ Cha Pralayāntām Upāśhritāḥ

Kāmopabhoga-Paramā Etāvad Iti Niśhchitāḥ II 11 II

Āśhā-Pāśha-Śhatair Baddhāḥ Kāma-Krodha-Parāyaṇāḥ

Īhante Kāma-Bhogārtham Anyāyenārtha-Sañchayān II 12 II

Idam Adya Mayā Labdham Imaṁ Prāpsye Manoratham

Idam Astīdam Api Me Bhaviṣhyati Punar Dhanam II 13 II

Asau Mayā Hataḥ Śhatrur Haniṣhye Chāparān Api

Īśhvaro 'Ham Ahaṁ Bhogī Siddho 'Haṁ Balavān Sukhī II 14 II

(8) They say, 'Entire world is without truth, baseless, without Parmeshwar and not created through causality. (Hence) what other purpose would it have other than lust?'

[There's a lot of debate about the meaning of the 8th verse, especially the last part. According to us, the verse describes the view of atheists like Chārvāk who deny the principles of universe as envisaged by Sānkhya or Vedānta, thus using terms antonymous to those used by them. E.g. while Vedānti consider that the visible world is Māyā and the principle behind it is the truth, demonic people consider the whole world to be untrue and also baseless, without any Parmeshwar. Once they don't accept any principle to be behind the existence, they automatically deny any prevalence of causality which is why the term 'Aparāsparasambhootam' is used which means without any causality or cause and effect. Many other club the word with the next word 'Kim anyat' meaning 'what else' and translate it as 'There's nothing else but products of sexual intercourse between male and female'. They then translate the next term as 'Thus the purpose of the world is nothing but sexual gratification.' However, we don't feel that is the implied meaning. We feel the meaning is to deny causality as otherwise demonic people would have to agree with the whole chain going all the way back to Prakruti and Purush and ultimately to Parmeshwar. Thus, the meaning we've mentioned is the most apt according to us.]

(9) By assuming such view, these dimwit, misdirected souls and evil people, while performing cruel actions, rise to cause destruction of the world.

(10) By resorting to endless lust, being occupied with hypocrisy, ego and arrogance they (demonic people) follow false tenets with delusion and tend to perform abominable acts. (11) Moreover, people occupied with countless lifelong worries, immersed in lustful enjoyment and resolutely considering it to be everything, (12) bound by hundreds of bonds of hope, are greedy of earning ample wealth for material enjoyment through injustice, while being controlled by lust and anger. (13) I earned this today, shall complete that desire (tomorrow), (I) have this wealth, and again that would be mine too; (14) Killed this enemy, and shall kill others too, I'm Almighty, I'm the enjoyer (too),

Āḍhyo 'Bhijanavān Asmi Ko 'Nyo 'Sti Sadṛiśho Mayā

Yakṣhye Dāsyāmi Modiṣhya Ity Ajñāna-Vimohitāḥ II 15 II

Aneka-Chitta-Vibhrāntā Moha-Jāla-Samāvṛitāḥ

Prasaktāḥ Kāma-Bhogeṣhu Patanti Narake 'Śhuchau II 16 II

Ātma-Sambhāvitāḥ Stabdhā Dhana-Māna-Madānvitāḥ

Yajante Nāma-Yajñais Te Dambhenāvidhi-Pūrvakam II 17 II

Ahankāraṁ Balaṁ Darpaṁ Kāmaṁ Krodhaṁ Cha Sanśhritāḥ

Mām Ātma-Para-Deheṣhu Pradviṣhanto 'Bhyasūyakāḥ II 18 II

Tān Ahaṁ Dviṣhataḥ Krūrān Sansāreṣhu Narādhamān

Kṣhipāmy Ajasram Aśhubhān Āsurīṣhv Eva Yoniṣhu II 19 II

Āsurīṁ Yonim Āpannā Mūḍhā Janmani Janmani

Mām Aprāpyaiva Kaunteya Tato Yānty Adhamāṁ Gatim II 20 II

Tri-Vidhaṁ Narakasyedaṁ Dvāraṁ Nāśhanam Ātmanaḥ

Kāmaḥ Krodhas Tathā Lobhas Tasmād Etat Trayaṁ Tyajet II 21 II

Etair Vimuktaḥ Kaunteya Tamo-Dvārais Tribhir Naraḥ

Ācharaty Ātmanaḥ Śhreyas Tato Yāti Parāṁ Gatim II 22 II

Yaḥ Śhāstra-Vidhim Utsṛijya Vartate Kāma-Kārataḥ

Na Sa Siddhim Avāpnoti Na Sukhaṁ Na Parāṁ Gatim II 23 II

I'm accomplished, might and happy; (15) I'm endowed and of noble birth, who else is like me? I shall perform Yadnya (sacrifice), I shall do charity, I shall indulge – They're thus deluded by ignorance;

(16) Led astray by various imaginations, trapped in the web of delusion and addicted to material pleasures, (these demonic people) fall in abominable hell. (17) Conceited, stiff and with arrogance of wealth and pride, they ostentatiously perform namesake Yadnya (sacrifices) without following rituals given in scriptures.

(18) Swollen with ego, power, arrogance, lust and anger, (they) despise and disapprove me who's present within their own body and in those of others. (19) I always throw these sinful, hateful, cruel and vile people in demonic wombs in Samsāra (this cycle of death and rebirth). (20) O Arjun! These fools, while getting demonic womb birth after birth, never come to me and finally reach abysmal lows.

(21) Lust, anger and greed are the three types of doors to hell and are self-destructive. Therefore, one must quit all three.

(22) O Arjun! Once free from these three dark doors, one starts practicing that which is for their own welfare and later attains supreme goal.

[It's obvious that one would attain Moksha once they quit the three doors of hell. However, now Bhagwān explains the practice through which one should get rid of them.]

(23) One who strays from scriptural rituals and starts following their own whims doesn't get accomplished, become happy or attain supreme goal.

Tasmāch Chhāstraṁ Pramāṇaṁ Te Kāryākārya-Vyavasthitau

Jñātvā Śhāstra-Vidhānoktaṁ Karma Kartum Ihārhasi II 24 II

(24) Therefore, to decide what's to be done and what's not to be done, you must consider scriptures to be the authority; and it is appropriate for you to understand the scriptures and perform Karma (actions) accordingly.

[Through the words Kāryākāryavyavasthiti (what's to be done and what's not to be done), it indicates that Gitā is composed to explain and decode ethics. This is called Karmayogshāstra as explained in Chapter 3.]

This concludes the sixteenth Adhyāya **Daivāsurasampadvibhāgyog** from the dialogue between Shri Krishna and Arjun on Yog Shāstra (Karmayog Shāstra) within Brahmavidyā (knowledge of Brahman) in the Upanishad sung (narrated) by Shri Bhagwān (Shri Krishna).

Saptadashodhyāyah (Seventeenth Adhyāya)

Arjuna Uvācha

Ye Śhāstra-Vidhim Utsṛijya Yajante Śhraddhayānvitāḥ

Teṣhāṁ Niṣhṭhā Tu Kā Kṛiṣhṇa Sattvam Āho Rajas Tamaḥ II 1 II

Śhrī-Bhagavān Uvācha

Tri-Vidhā Bhavati Śhraddhā Dehināṁ Sā Svabhāva-Jā

Sāttvikī Rājasī Chaiva Tāmasī Cheti Tāṁ Śhṛiṇu II 2 II

Sattvānurūpā Sarvasya Śhraddhā Bhavati Bhārata

Śhraddhā-Mayo 'Yaṁ Puruṣho Yo Yach-Chhraddhaḥ Sa Eva Saḥ II 3 II

Saptadashodhyāyah (Seventeenth Adhyāya)

[After understanding the nature of people who perpetuate the processes of the world and later that of people that bring about its destruction, the natural question that comes to mind is why do people of such different nature exist? The simple answer is told in 7th Adhyāya – to each their own, or due to everyone's nature. However, as Three Gunas (attributes) and their impact was not explained then, we couldn't distinguish nature of different people based on these. Thus, after learning about the three Gunas and their manifestation in the 14th Adhyāya, we now conclude the explanation of Dnyān-Vidnyān (Knowledge and Science) with the explanation of faith and view of life as a whole according to these three Gunas. It also explains why there are different types of Bhakti (devotion) as studied in 9th Adhyāya.]

Arjun said – (1) O Krishna! What state (of mind) should be considered of those who worship without following rituals given in scriptures, despite being full of faith? Sāttvic, Rājas or Tāmas?

[Arjun has raised this doubt after listening to the explanation in the last Adhyāya that advised following of guidelines given in the scriptures. Some people are faithful but commit mistakes. They get hooked on to some deities instead of worshipping the almighty Parmeshwar. The query is about such people and not demonic people who disrespect the scriptures. Yet, Shri Krishna has also explained their characteristics contextually.]

Shri Bhagwān said – (2) People's faith is of three types according to nature – Sāttvic, Rājas and Tāmas. Listen to it (how).

(3) O Arjun! Faith of all people becomes as per their nature (tendency). Human is full of faith. Whatever one's faith, so do they (become).

[The word 'Sattva' is used as nature or tendency in these verses, as it is used in Kathopanishad or Shānkarbhāshya. Sānkhya and Vedānta both agree that nature or Prakruti is the most fundamental and from it manifest the intellect and mind subsequently. This verse is reiteration of the principles followed earlier in 'one becomes as per their faith' (Gitā

Yajante Sāttvikā Devān Yakṣha-Rakṣhānsi Rājasāḥ

Pretān Bhūta-Gaṇānśh Chānye Yajante Tāmasā Janāḥ II 4 II

Aśhāstra-Vihitaṁ Ghoraṁ Tapyante Ye Tapo Janāḥ

Dambhāhankāra-Sanyuktāḥ Kāma-Rāga-Balānvitāḥ II 5 II

Karṣhayantaḥ Śharīra-Sthaṁ Bhūta-Grāmam Achetasaḥ

Māṁ Chaivāntaḥ Śharīra-Sthaṁ Tān Viddhy Āsura-Niśhchayān II 6 II

Āhāras Tv Api Sarvasya Tri-Vidho Bhavati Priyaḥ

Yajñas Tapas Tathā Dānaṁ Teṣhāṁ Bhedam Imaṁ Śhṛiṇu II 7 II

7.20-23) and 'Worshippers of deities go to deities' (Gitā 9.25). The question that then arises is how to improve this Prakruti that leads to intellect and mind? The answer to this is discussed in the 10th chapter of this book. For now, we study how different types of faith manifest as per different nature governed by three Gunas (attributes).]

(4) Sāttvic people worship celestial deities, Rājas worship Yaksha (demigods) and Rākshasa (demons) while remaining Tāmas people worship Ghosts and spirits.

[While this explained the types of people as per their faith and what they worship, this covers people who believe in scriptures. Now Bhagwān speaks about a different type of people, those driven by lust and vanity. These people obviously have no belief in scriptures and are not Sāttvic. However, they can't be only Tāmas. While their tendency is to act against the scriptures, they're still active. Activity is an attribute of Rājas. Thus, they can't be categorized under Sāttvic, Rājas or Tāmas individually. Thus, a separate classification of Daivi (divine) and Āsuri (demonic) is done. The cruel, heinous people are classified as Asuras and are described in the next verses.]

(5) However, those people who perform severe austerities based on lust and attachment, being enriched with vanity and pride; (6) and trouble not only the group of five elements residing in the body but also me who lies within; consider them to be immoral and of demonic intellect.

[This covers the answers to Arjun's questions. What they essentially convey is this – while it is true that everyone's beliefs are as per their innate nature, Sāttvic, Rājas or Tāmas. They'd also perform karmas according to this nature and be destined for their fate accordingly. However, only this doesn't classify someone as Āsuri (demonic). Using the freedom of the soul, one could slowly improve their natural tendencies. Those that instead of doing so justify their nature with ego and behave against the scriptures are the ones termed as Āsuri.]

(7) Now, even the diet preferred by everyone is classified into three types and similar is the case with Yadnya (sacrifice), Tapa (austerity) and Dāna (charity). Hear, as I tell you the difference.

Āyuḥ-Sattva-Balārogya-Sukha-Prīti-Vivardhanāḥ

Rasyāḥ Snigdhāḥ Sthirā Hṛidyā Āhārāḥ Sāttvika-Priyāḥ II 8 II

Kaṭv-Amla-Lavaṇāty-Uṣhṇa- Tīkṣhṇa-Rūkṣha-Vidāhinaḥ

Āhārā Rājasasyeṣhṭā Duḥkha-Śhokāmaya-Pradāḥ II 9 II

Yāta-Yāmaṁ Gata-Rasaṁ Pūti Paryuṣhitaṁ Cha Yat

Uchchhiṣhṭam Api Chāmedhyaṁ Bhojanaṁ Tāmasa-Priyam II 10 II

Aphalākāṅkṣhibhir Yajño Vidhi-Driṣhṭo Ya Ijyate

Yaṣhṭavyam Eveti Manaḥ Samādhāya Sa Sāttvikaḥ II 11 II

Abhisandhāya Tu Phalaṁ Dambhārtham Api Chaiva Yat

Ijyate Bharata-Śhreṣhṭha Taṁ Yajñaṁ Viddhi Rājasam II 12 II

Vidhi-Hīnam Asṛiṣhṭānnaṁ Mantra-Hīnam Adakṣhiṇam

Śhraddhā-Virahitaṁ Yajñaṁ Tāmasaṁ Parichakṣhate II 13 II

Deva-Dwija-Guru-Prājña- Pūjanaṁ Śhaucham Ārjavam

Brahmacharyam Ahinsā Cha Śhārīraṁ Tapa Uchyate II 14 II

Anudvega-Karaṁ Vākyaṁ Satyaṁ Priya-Hitaṁ Cha Yat

Svādhyāyābhyasanaṁ Chaiva Vāṅ-Mayaṁ Tapa Uchyate II 15 II

Manaḥ-Prasādaḥ Saumyatvaṁ Maunam Ātma-Vinigrahaḥ

Bhāva-Sanśhuddhir Ity Etat Tapo Mānasam Uchyate II 16 II

Śhraddhayā Parayā Taptaṁ Tapas Tat Tri-Vidhaṁ Naraiḥ

Aphalākāṅkṣhibhir Yuktaiḥ Sāttvikaṁ Parichakṣhate II 17 II

Satkāra-Māna-Pūjārthaṁ Tapo Dambhena Chaiva Yat

Kriyate Tad Iha Proktaṁ Rājasaṁ Chalam Adhruvam II 18 II

Mūḍha-Grāheṇātmano Yat Pīḍayā Kriyate Tapaḥ

Parasyotsādanārthaṁ Vā Tat Tāmasam Udāhṛitam II 19 II

(8) The diet preferred by Sāttvic people amplifies longevity, Sāttvic character, strength, health, happiness and love; is juicy, moist, stays long by being ingrained in the body and pleasing to the mind. (9) The diet preferred by Rājas people is pungent, sour, very hot, spicy, dry and burning; causes sorrow, grief and causes disease.

(10) The diet preferred by Tāmas is stale, without essence, putrid, left over, pre-tasted and impure.

[Sāttvic, Rājas and Tāmas people respectively prefer Sāttvic, Rājas and Tāmas diet. In turn, consuming Sāttvic, Rājas and Tāmas diet also slowly changes your tendencies, because mind, intellect etc. are the manifestations of Prakruti. Now we learn the different types of Yadnya (sacrifice).]

(11) The Yadnya (sacrifice) performed without keeping any expectations of its fruits, by considering it to be one's duty, performed with a calm mind and as prescribed by scriptures is said to be Sāttvic. (12) However, O Arjun, the Yadnya performed with expectation of its fruits, vanity to show off one's opulence is to be considered Rājas. (13) The Yadnya performed without following scriptures, without distributing Prasād (food distributed after sacrifice), without mantra (hymns), without donation to priests and without faith is regarded Tāmas.

(14) Worshipping Devas (celestial deities), Brāhman (priests), Guru and wise; cleanliness, simplicity, celibacy and non-violence are termed as austerities of body. (15) A speech that doesn't hurt the mind, is true, lovable and beneficial; along with recitation of scriptures are called austerities of speech. (16) Serenity of mind, gentleness, silence, restraint of mind and purity of thought are called austerities of mind.

(17) When people perform these three kinds of austerities without expectation of their fruits, with supreme faith and with Yogic intellect, they're regarded as Sāttvic. (18) When wavering and unstable austerities are performed by people with ostentations to garner respect, honor or worship, such austerities are called Rājas in scriptures. (19) The austerities performed with foolish stubbornness, inflicting torture to themselves or to harm others are called Tāmas.

Dātavyam Iti Yad Dānaṁ Dīyate 'Nupakāriṇe

Deśhe Kāle Cha Pātre Cha Tad Dānaṁ Sāttvikaṁ Smṛitam II 20 II

Yat Tu Pratyupakārārthaṁ Phalam Uddiśhya Vā Punaḥ

Dīyate Cha Parikliṣhṭaṁ Tad Dānaṁ Rājasaṁ Smṛitam II 21 II

Adeśha-Kāle Yad Dānam Apātrebhyaśh Cha Dīyate

Asat-Kṛitam Avajñātaṁ Tat Tāmasam Udāhṛitam II 22 II

[These were the three types of austerities. Now we move to three kinds of charity.]

(20) Charity done considering it as one's duty and by looking at (appropriateness of) place, time & worth, and without any expectation of returns is called Sāttvic. (21) However, charity done in return of a favor, with expectation of a fruit in return and with difficulty is called Rājas.

(22) Charity done at inappropriate place or time or to unworthy person; without respect or with insult is called Tāmas.

[After describing three kinds of diet, sacrifice, austerity and charity, next verses describe the three kinds of Dnyān (knowledge), Karma (actions), Karta (doer), Buddhi (intellect), Dhruti (courage) and Sukh (happiness). This Adhyāya now describes, through a famous Sanskrit notion 'Om Tat Sat', the answer to any doubt raised as to question the relevance of any karma. One may say that if apparently every action is faulty and giver of sorrow, be it Sāttvic, Rājas or Tāmas; what is the point of performing any action? Gitā answers this by stating that while the different kinds of Karma viz. Sāttvic, Rājas and Tāmas are not out of the purview of Parabrahma (the absolute). The notion explaining the meaning of Parabrahma (i.e. Om Tat Sat) includes Sāttvic and good Karma. Thus, these actions are not renounceable even from spiritual point of view. Now from this three-word notion, 'Om' is a syllable which is used in many scriptures and described in many Upanishads. It's considered that this was present at the birth of the universe and thus it marked the onset of every action. 'Tat' meaning 'that' is used to describe the Karma beyond common actions or the Sāttvic karma performed without any expectations. 'Sat' denotes those actions which are performed with expectations of fruits but are pure and done in accordance to the scriptures. This proves that actions performed without expectations or the good deeds performed according to scriptures are Sāttvic and thus need not be renounced.]

Oṁ Tat Sad Iti Nirdeśho Brahmaṇas Tri-Vidhaḥ Smṛitaḥ

Brāhmaṇās Tena Vedāśh Cha Yajñāśh Cha Vihitāḥ Purā II 23 II

Tasmād Oṁ Ity Udāhṛitya Yajña-Dāna-Tapaḥ-Kriyāḥ

Pravartante Vidhānoktāḥ Satataṁ Brahma-Vādinām II 24 II

Tad Ity Anabhisandhāya Phalaṁ Yajña-Tapaḥ-Kriyāḥ

Dāna-Kriyāśh Cha Vividhāḥ Kriyante Mokṣha-Kāṅkṣhibhiḥ II 25 II

Sad-Bhāve Sādhu-Bhāve Cha Sad Ity Etat Prayujyate

Praśhaste Karmaṇi Tathā Sach-Chhabdaḥ Pārtha Yujyate II 26 II

Yajñe Tapasi Dāne Cha Sthitiḥ Sad Iti Chochyate

Karma Chaiva Tad-Arthīyaṁ Sad Ity Evābhidhīyate II 27 II

(23) Parabrahma is denoted (in scriptures) in three kinds (of words) as 'Om Tat Sat'. From this (denotation), Brāhman (priests), Vedas and Yadnya (sacrifices) have been created.

[It is mentioned in Gitā earlier (Gitā 3.10) that Brāhman, Vedas and Yadnya have been created at the beginning of the universe. However, the form of this Parabrahma from which everything was created, is described as 'Om Tat Sat'. This is explained in subsequent verses.]

(24) Therefore, Yadnya (sacrifice), Dāna (charity), Tapa (austerity) and other scriptural Karma are always initiated with the word 'Om', as the universe began with this notion. (25) With the word 'Tat', aspirants of Moksha (liberation) perform actions such as sacrifice, austerity, charity etc. without any expectations for their fruits. (26) The word 'Sat' is used as existence and goodness. And O Arjun! The word Sat is also used for denoting good deeds. (27) The state of being stable towards performing sacrifice, austerity and charity; and any actions performed towards these are also termed as 'Sat'.

[Sacrifice, Austerity and Charity are the chief Dhārmic deeds. The actions performed for these are called sacrificial actions by Mimāmsaks. These are classified under 'Sat', while those actions performed without any expectations fall under 'Tat'. As 'Om Tat Sat' is uttered at the beginning of every action, both the actions are in accordance with Parabrahma. Now what remains is 'Asat' which is described in the next verse.]

Aśhraddhayā Hutaṁ Dattaṁ Tapas Taptaṁ Kṛitaṁ Cha Yat

Asad Ity Uchyate Pārtha Na Cha Tat Pretya No Iha II 28 II

(28) The sacrifice, charity or austerity performed and any actions performed without faith are called 'Asat'. O Arjun! This (karma) doesn't (reward), either after death or here (in this world).

[This shows that the unanimous notion denoting Parabrahma includes actions performed as duty and without expectations, Sāttvic actions and good deeds performed according to scriptures. Rest actions are futile. As these actions are included in denotation of the absolute, have started along with Brahma and are impossible to quit, they're definitely not to be renounced. The intention behind describing the notion 'Om Tat Sat' here is as per Karmayog and hence precisely placed here along with types of actions. We've elaborated on original meaning of the notion 'Om Tat Sat' towards the end of 9th chapter.]

This concludes the seventeenth Adhyāya **Shraddhātrayavibhāgyog** from the dialogue between Shri Krishna and Arjun on Yog Shāstra (Karmayog Shāstra) within Brahmavidyā (knowledge of Brahman) in the Upanishad sung (narrated) by Shri Bhagwān (Shri Krishna).

Ashtādashodhyāyah (Eighteenth Adhyāya)

Arjuna Uvācha

Sannyāsasya Mahā-Bāho Tattvam Ichchhāmi Veditum

Tyāgasya Cha Hṛiṣhīkeśha Pṛithak Keśhi-Niṣhūdana II 1 II

Ashtādashodhyāyah (Eighteenth Adhyāya)

[Eighteenth Adhyāya is the epilogue of entire philosophy of Gitā. So, let's recap what we have seen till now. Arjun became perplexed and wanted to quit the war which he was duty bound to and wished to renounce and beg for alms. Gitā was told in order to convince Arjun to perform his duty. This is evident in the **First Adhyāya**. Arjun was skeptical that performing a karma which involved killing of his Guru, kith and kin would not be beneficial for his soul. Hence, Shri Krishna told the two paths of spending one's life adopted by enlightened people in the **Second Adhyāya** – One Sānkhya (Sanyās) and the other Yog (Karmayog). He said that both are equally potent for attaining Moksha, although Karmayog is better. In Karmayog, Buddhi (intellect) is considered superior. When Buddhi is stable and equanimous, Karma is not binding to you. Moreover, as quitting Karma is anyway impossible, one shouldn't even attempt quitting it. Instead, one should just quit expectation of fruits; as Karma is important for universal welfare, even though one may not want it for oneself. When intellect is in right place, knowledge and karma don't antagonize each other. If you observe history, the likes of Janak spent their lives like this. The above stated points are covered in **Third to Fifth Adhyāyas**. The next topic that logically follows is how one should earn this equanimity of intellect required for Karmayog and how this ultimately leads to Moksha. To achieve this equanimity, one must restrain their senses and thoroughly understand that there's one Parmeshwar within everyone. There's no other way. In the **Sixth Adhyāya**, we find the methods of achieving sensory restraint. After this, Adhyāyas Seventh through Seventeenth cover how one attains knowledge of Parmeshwar and also what this knowledge is all about. Of these, **Seventh and Eighth Adhyāyas** explain the knowledge of Ksharākshar (perishable and imperishable) or manifest and unmanifest. **Adhyāyas Ninth through Twelfth** explain that while the unmanifest form of Parmeshwar is supreme, it is the worship of manifest Parmeshwar which is direct and thus simple. **Thirteenth Adhyāya** covered Kshetrakshetradnyavichār (Discussion of body and soul). Later, **Fourteenth to Seventeenth Adhyāyas** covered

Śhrī-Bhagavān Uvācha

Kāmyānāṁ Karmaṇāṁ Nyāsaṁ Sannyāsaṁ Kavayo Viduḥ

Sarva-Karma-Phala-Tyāgaṁ Prāhus Tyāgaṁ Vichakşhaṇāḥ II 2 II

in detail how Gunas (attributes) of Prakruti result in people and objects of different nature. This completed the elucidation of Dnyān-Vidnyān (Knowledge and Science). Throughout these Adhyāyas, Bhagwān Shri Krishna has reiterated, how the path of performing all actions as duty while dedicating them to Parmeshwar, is the most superior one. After covering the entire explanation of Karmayog rooted in knowledge and full of devotion, Bhagwān has prompted Arjun to get ready for war in the **Eighteenth Adhyāya**. He did not ask Arjun to adopt the path of renunciation and become a Sanyāsi. Instead, Bhagwān Shri Krishna has proven how someone who follows such a path of Karmayog is a Sanyāsi in true sense of the word, without actually renunciating action.]

Arjun said – (1) O Krishna, I want to understand the principle in Sanyās (renunciation) and O Krishna, I separately want to understand the principle behind Tyāg (giving up or abandonment).

[This is not an enquiry into etymology of these two words. While Bhagwān has never asked to quit actions, he's asked Arjun to 'give up' or 'abandon' the desire or expectation of fruits. He's asked him to renounce all Karma in the name of Parmeshwar as well. Upanishads also tell how numerous great beings gave up Karma symbolically to attain Moksha. Arjun has thus asked for a clarification on these two words – Tyāg and Sanyās and their intended meaning.

Shri Bhagwān said – (2) Wise people consider giving up of desirous Karma as Sanyās while scholars call sacrifice of fruits of all Karma as Tyāg.

[This verse clearly mentions what is understood by Sanyās and Tyāg in Karmayog. However, commentators from the path of Sanyās don't find the clear-cut meaning of this verse conducive to them and hence attempt to twist it beyond imagination, simply to prove their point. Communalistic view has prompted such commentators to defy reason and attempt to prove how their path is the most superior and how it was the one suggested by Bhagwān Shri Krishna. Alas, subsequent verses communicate the true meaning intended by him too clearly which forces these commentators to claim that Bhagwān has offered false praise of Karmayog here. It is ironic to see how someone claims

Tyājyaṁ Doṣha-Vad Ity Eke Karma Prāhur Manīṣhiṇaḥ

Yajña-Dāna-Tapaḥ-Karma Na Tyājyam Iti Chāpare II 3 II

Niśhchayaṁ Śhṛiṇu Me Tatra Tyāge Bharata-Sattama

Tyāgo Hi Puruṣha-Vyāghra Tri-Vidhaḥ Samprakīrtitaḥ II 4 II

Yajña-Dāna-Tapaḥ-Karma Na Tyājyaṁ Kāryam Eva Tat

Yajño Dānaṁ Tapaśh Chaiva Pāvanāni Manīṣhiṇām II 5 II

Etāny Api Tu Karmāṇi Saṅgaṁ Tyaktvā Phalāni Cha

Kartavyānīti Me Pārtha Niśhchitaṁ Matam Uttamam II 6 II

Niyatasya Tu Sannyāsaḥ Karmaṇo Nopapadyate

Mohāt Tasya Parityāgas Tāmasaḥ Parikīrtitaḥ II 7 II

Duḥkham Ity Eva Yat Karma Kāya-Kleśha-Bhayāt Tyajet

Sa Kṛitvā Rājasaṁ Tyāgaṁ Naiva Tyāga-Phalaṁ Labhet II 8 II

Bhagwān Shri Krishna to commit such an act just because it proves their sect as superior. One must note here that with the word Kāmya, it's not the Mimāmsak classification of Karma (into Nitya, Naimittik, Kāmya and Nishiddha) which is intended. As per Karmayog, all Karma are divided into two types – Kāmya and Nishkām. Kāmya Karma are those performed with expectation for their fruits, while Nishkām Karma are those that are performed without having any expectation for their fruits. Be it Nitya (periodic), Naimittik (causal), Kāmya (desirous), Kāyik (bodily), Mānasik (mental) or any other. Once someone does any action without any expectation for its fruits, it is Nishkām (free of expectations). Karmayog advises performing all Karma as Nishkām. It doesn't insist on actual renunciation of actions at all as it lays emphasis on Buddhi (intellect) behind any act.]

(3) Many scholars say that Karma is riddled with faults and hence must be (completely) given up; and others say that one should never give up Yadnya (sacrifice), Dāna (charity), Tapa (austerity) and Karma (action). (4) Still, O Arjun! Hear my decision on Tyāg. O Arjun! Tyāg (abandonment) is said to be of three types. (5) Yadnya, Dāna, Tapa and Karma should not be abandoned. Those (actions) must be performed. Yadnya, Dāna and Tapa purify the mind of wise people (as well). (6) Therefore, these actions should also be performed without attachment and expectation for their fruits. O Arjun! This is my definite and supreme verdict!

[This is the conclusive interpretation of the central theme of Karmayog that Karma itself isn't binding but becomes binding because of the expectation in it for its fruits. Therefore, one must perform all Karma without any expectations. Gitā doesn't accept the opinion of Sanyās path of giving up Karma altogether. Gitā thus shows the path of performing the recommended actions of sacrifice, charity and austerity with Nishkām mindset (without expectations). Such actions are always purifying.]

(7) Renunciation of that Karma which is assigned to you is not appropriate for anyone. Abandoning these (actions) under delusion is said to be Tāmas.

Kāryam Ity Eva Yat Karma Niyataṁ Kriyate 'Rjuna

Saṅgaṁ Tyaktvā Phalaṁ Chaiva Sa Tyāgaḥ Sāttviko Mataḥ II 9 II

Na Dveşhṭy Akuśhalaṁ Karma Kuśhale Nānuşhajjate

Tyāgī Sattva-Samāvişhṭo Medhāvī Chhinna-Sanśhayaḥ II 10 II

Na Hi Deha-Bhṛitā Śhakyaṁ Tyaktuṁ Karmāṇy Aśheşhataḥ

Yas Tu Karma-Phala-Tyāgī Sa Tyāgīty Abhidhīyate II 11 II

Anişhṭam Işhṭaṁ Miśhraṁ Cha Tri-Vidhaṁ Karmaṇaḥ Phalam

Bhavaty Atyāgināṁ Pretya Na Tu Sannyāsināṁ Kvachit II 12 II

Pañchaitāni Mahā-Bāho Kāraṇāni Nibodha Me

Sānkhye Kṛitānte Proktāni Siddhaye Sarva-Karmaṇām II 13 II

Adhişhṭhānaṁ Tathā Kartā Karaṇaṁ Cha Pṛithag-Vidham

Vividhāśh Cha Pṛithak Cheşhṭā Daivaṁ Chaivātra Pañchamam II 14 II

Śharīra-Vāṅ-Manobhir Yat Karma Prārabhate Naraḥ

Nyāyyaṁ Vā Viparītaṁ Vā Pañchaite Tasya Hetavaḥ II 15 II

Tatraivaṁ Sati Kartāram Ātmānaṁ Kevalaṁ Tu Yaḥ

Paśhyaty Akṛita-Buddhitvān Na Sa Paśhyati Durmatiḥ II 16 II

(8) If someone abandons Karma fearing that it would be painful for the body, such abandonment becomes Rājas and they wouldn't get the fruits of Tyāg.

(9) O Arjun! When Karma is performed considering the assigned work as duty, quitting attachment and (expectation for) fruits, such a Tyāg is considered Sāttvic.

[One should not mistake the word 'Niyata' as 'Nitya' as some people do. Niyata means assigned or allocated. This word is also used with same meaning earlier (Gitā 3.8). Thus, Gitā regards that when you perform the work allocated to you by Dharma as duty and do so without attachment and expectations, such abandonment is Sāttvic. This is Tyāg or Sanyās in Karmayog.]

(10) The Sāttvic, intelligent people who have no doubt, who don't hate some Karma because it's not beneficial and don't seek some Karma because it's beneficial; are called Tyāgi (ascetic). (11) because, for anyone who has a body, it is impossible to absolutely give up actions. Hence, one who abandons fruits of actions is said to be (truly) ascetic. (12) For those who don't abandon (the attachment to fruits of their actions), there are three types of fruits of Karma accrued upon death – Pleasant, Unpleasant and mixed. However, for an ascetic (who performs actions without any expectation for fruits) they (the three types of fruits) don't exist.

[This thought about Tyāg, Tyāgi or Sanyāsi has been covered earlier as well (Gitā 3.4, 7.5, 6.1 etc.). It's summarized here in conclusion. Complete renunciation of action would never be supported by Gitā.]

(13) O Arjun! Listen to me as I tell you the five reasons stated in the doctrines of Sānkhya for all actions to happen. (14) The place, the doer, different types of tools, many different kinds of efforts and with it the fifth one, fate.

(15) Whatever actions a person initiates – through body, speech or mind; these five are the reasons.

(16) In spite of this fact, those who, due to uncultured intellect, think that they alone are the doers, are fools who don't understand anything.

Yasya Nāhankṛito Bhāvo Buddhir Yasya Na Lipyate

Hatvā 'Pi Sa Imāñl Lokān Na Hanti Na Nibadhyate II 17 II

Jñānaṁ Jñeyaṁ Parijñātā Tri-Vidhā Karma-Chodanā

Karaṇaṁ Karma Karteti Tri-Vidhaḥ Karma-Saṅgrahaḥ II 18 II

Jñānaṁ Karma Cha Kartā Cha Tridhaiva Guṇa-Bhedataḥ

Prochyate Guṇa-Saṅkhyāne Yathāvach Chhṛiṇu Tāny Api II 19 II

(17) For those who don't feel they're the doers and whose intellect is detached; even if they kill people, it's neither killing nor is it (Karma) binding.

[These verses tell us that while one may think they've done something, various factors are responsible for the outcome of any action. Those factors are enlisted here for us and explained. Someone who with their ego may consider only themselves to be the cause are sorely mistaken. For instance, in agriculture, even if a farmer tills the soil, sows the seeds and waters the plants; there are many other factors required for the crop to bear fruit – Rain, sunshine, wind, texture of soil, pests etc. While we try and anticipate as many factors as possible, there are factors beyond our control which affect the outcome nevertheless. They're referred to as Daiva (fate). Thus, not only is it foolish to feel that you're the only one responsible, but it's also imprudent to expect the outcome as you wish it to be. At the same time, one must remember that this doesn't mean you could get away with doing anything and it wouldn't affect the outcome or that you're free to commit sins and get away with it. Common people commit sins out of selfish motives. However, for someone who has lost all selfishness, greed or expectation of fruits, no sin is possible. This is because sin is in intellect or thought, not in action. Some action may appear sinful at the outset but must have originated out of a good intention if the person doing it is a true Karmayogi.]

(18) Dnyān, Dnyeya and Dnyāta (Knowledge, to be known and knower) are the three inspirations for Karma. While tools, action and doer are three different constituents of Karma. (19) It is said in Gunasankhyān (Kāpilsānkhya) scripture that Dnyān (Knowledge), Karma (action) and Karta (doer) are each of three different types according to difference in Gunas (attributes). Listen (as I narrate them) as they are.

[Karmachodanā and Karmasangraha are jargons that are used to denote the three internal and external factors behind an action respectively. Internal factors are mental or psychological while external factors are physical.]

Sarva-Bhūteşhu Yenaikaṁ Bhāvam Avyayam Īkşhate

Avibhaktaṁ Vibhakteşhu Taj Jñānaṁ Viddhi Sāttvikam II 20 II

Pṛithaktvena Tu Yaj Jñānaṁ Nānā-Bhāvān Pṛithag-Vidhān

Vetti Sarveşhu Bhūteşhu Taj Jñānaṁ Viddhi Rājasam II 21 II

Yat Tu Kṛitsna-Vad Ekasmin Kārye Saktam Ahaitukam

Atattvārtha-Vad Alpaṁ Cha Tat Tāmasam Udāhṛitam II 22 II

Niyataṁ Saṅga-Rahitam Arāga-Dveşhataḥ Kṛitam

Aphala-Prepsunā Karma Yat Tat Sāttvikam Uchyate II 23 II

Yat Tu Kāmepsunā Karma Sāhankārena Vā Punaḥ

Kriyate Bahulāyāsaṁ Tad Rājasam Udāhṛitam II 24 II

Anubandhaṁ Kşhayaṁ Hinsām Anapekşhya Cha Pauruşham

Mohād Ārabhyate Karma Yat Tat Tāmasam Uchyate II 25 II

(20) The knowledge, through which one understands the united, indivisible and imperishable principle within all diverse living beings; is called Sāttvic knowledge. (21) The knowledge through which one sees different qualities among all living beings separately is to be considered Rājas knowledge.

(22) However, if one is engrossed in a single object as if it's everything – unreasonably and without knowing the principle, such a trivial knowledge is said to be Tāmas.

[This description of different kinds of knowledge is very broad and indicative. To consider one's immediate family to be everything is a narrow thought and is considered Tāmas knowledge. Rising a little above this and to consider one's society or country to be theirs while considering citizens of different countries to be different is better than Tāmas but still not universal and is Rājas. Rising above this and considering the entire universe to be one and understanding the unity in this diversity is Sāttvic knowledge. Refer to the unification process of knowledge discussed in 9th chapter. This Sāttvic knowledge is the ultimate knowledge there is. This knowledge includes both mental process of unification as well as its effect on the tendency of the person.]

(23) The assigned action that is (dutifully) performed without keeping love or hatred in mind, without attachment, by a person who doesn't keep an expectation for its fruits is called Sāttvic (Karma). (24) However, the action performed with a lot of efforts by a person who has desire for its fruits or is selfish is called Rājas (Karma).

(25) The action initiated with delusion without thinking about its consequences, without knowing one's capability and whether it would cause harm or destruction to others; is called Tāmas (Karma).

[These three types of Karma cover all actions. We've covered in the 11th chapter, why Sāttvic Karma is the best. This is the true 'Akarma' as well. It should also be noted that while assessing whether a Karma is Sāttvic or Rājas or Tāmas, it's always the intellect of the doer which is considered and never the action itself. 25th verse also tells us that doing a Karma without looking at its consequences is Tāmas and not Sāttvic,

Mukta-Saṅgo 'Nahaṁ-Vādī Dhṛity-Utsāha-Samanvitaḥ

Siddhy-Asiddhyor Nirvikāraḥ Kartā Sāttvika Uchyate II 26 II

Rāgī Karma-Phala-Prepsur Lubdho Hinsātmako 'Śhuchiḥ

Harṣha-Śhokānvitaḥ Kartā Rājasaḥ Parikīrtitaḥ II 27 II

Ayuktaḥ Prākṛitaḥ Stabdhaḥ Śhaṭho Naiṣhkṛitiko 'Lasaḥ

Viṣhādī Dīrgha-Sūtrī Cha Kartā Tāmasa Uchyate II 28 II

Buddher Bhedaṁ Dhṛiteśh Chaiva Guṇatas Tri-Vidhaṁ Śhṛiṇu

Prochyamānam Aśheṣheṇa Pṛithaktvena Dhanañjaya II 29 II

Pravṛittiṁ Cha Nivṛittiṁ Cha Kāryākārye Bhayābhaye

Bandhaṁ Mokṣhaṁ Cha Yā Vetti Buddhiḥ Sā Pārtha Sāttvikī II 30 II

Yayā Dharmam Adharmaṁ Cha Kāryaṁ Chākāryam Eva Cha

Ayathāvat Prajānāti Buddhiḥ Sā Pārtha Rājasī II 31 II

Adharmaṁ Dharmam Iti Yā Manyate Tamasāvṛitā

Sarvārthān Viparītānśh Cha Buddhiḥ Sā Pārtha Tāmasī II 32 II

Dhṛityā Yayā Dhārayate Manaḥ-Prāṇendriya-Kriyāḥ

Yogenāvyabhichāriṇyā Dhṛitiḥ Sā Pārtha Sāttvikī II 33 II

Yayā Tu Dharma-Kāmārthān Dhṛityā Dhārayate 'Rjuna

Prasaṅgena Phalākāṅkṣhī Dhṛitiḥ Sā Pārtha Rājasī II 34 II

thus reaffirming that it doesn't mean that one should do anything once they leave the expectation for the fruits.]

(26) One who doesn't have attachment, who doesn't do it as 'me' or 'mine', remains stoic irrespective of whether it's success or failure, (but) remains full of courage and enthusiasm while performing an action; is said to be Sāttvic (doer).

(27) Attached to objects (of desire), greedy, full of happiness and sorrow (with success and failure respectively), craving for achievement of fruits of action, violent and impure – such a doer is said to be Rājas. (28) Undisciplined, ignorant, obstinate, duplicitous, dishonest, lazy, always unhappy and procrastinator – such a doer is said to be Tāmas.

[After explaining different types of Karta (doer), Bhagwān now explains different types of Buddhi (intellect).]

(29) O Arjun! Listen as I tell you three different types of intellect and determination according to Gunas (attributes) distinctly and exhaustively. (30) O Arjun! The intellect that discerns between when to act and when not to, what's appropriate to do and what's inappropriate, what to fear and what not to, what is binding and what is liberating; is Sāttvic. (31) O Arjun! The intellect that can't properly decide between Dharma and Adharma (here righteous and unrighteous), appropriate and inappropriate is Rājas. (32) O Arjun! The intellect which, covered with darkness, considers the Adharmic (here unrighteous) to be Dhārmic (righteous) and derives opposite meanings in all matters is Tāmas.

[After classifying intellect this way, there doesn't remain a separate deity called conscience as held by Adhidaivik but it is classified under Sāttvic intellect. We've elaborated on this in 6th chapter. Now we move on to determination.]

(33) O Arjun! The unwavering determination which, through Yog, sustains the activities of mind, Prāna (life energy) and senses is Sāttvic. (34) O Arjun! The determination which sustains Dharma (here duty), Kāma (pleasure) and Artha (wealth) and that situationally maintains the desire for fruits is Rājas.

Yayā Svapnaṁ Bhayaṁ Śhokaṁ Viṣhādaṁ Madam Eva Cha

Na Vimuñchati Durmedhā Dhṛitiḥ Sā Pārtha Tāmasī II 35 II

Sukhaṁ Tv Idānīṁ Tri-Vidhaṁ Śhṛiṇu Me Bharatarṣhabha

Abhyāsād Ramate Yatra Duḥkhāntaṁ Cha Nigachchhati II 36 II

Yat Tad Agre Viṣham Iva Pariṇāme 'Mṛitopamam

Tat Sukhaṁ Sāttvikaṁ Proktam Ātma-Buddhi-Prasāda-Jam II 37 II

Viṣhayendriya-Sanyogād Yat Tad Agre 'Mṛitopamam

Pariṇāme Viṣham Iva Tat Sukhaṁ Rājasaṁ Smṛitam II 38 II

Yad Agre Chānubandhe Cha Sukhaṁ Mohanam Ātmanaḥ

Nidrālasya-Pramādotthaṁ Tat Tāmasam Udāhṛitam II 39 II

(35) O Arjun! The determination, which by making a person unintelligent stops them from giving up dreaminess, fear, grief, despair and vanity is Tāmas.

[While Dhruti literally means courage, here it doesn't mean physical courage but mental determination. Decision making is the task of intellect. However, determination is the virtue of mind. Thus, mental determination is a function of both intellect and mind. Essentially, the verses classify three types of determination as follows – Tāmas makes one determined to be lazy and sleepy, Rājas makes one determined to be actively seeking action with expectation for their fruits while Sāttvic makes one determined to be established in Yog and driven for action without expectation for their fruits.]

(36) Now O Arjun! Listen as I tell you the three types of happiness as well. Where (one) enjoys with practice and where end of sorrow is achieved. (37) The happiness that (appears) initially like a poison but subsequently like the nectar of immortality, which arises by the pleasantness of intellect rooted in our soul (spiritual bliss), is called Sāttvic. (38) The happiness that arises from the interaction of senses with their objects (physical), is initially like the nectar of immortality but subsequently like a poison, is said to be Rājas.

(39) The happiness which is initially as well as subsequently delusional, and arises from sleep, laziness and negligence (of duty), is called Tāmas.

[Buddhi (intellect) is such an organ that on the one hand looks towards the visible universe made up of three Gunas (attributes) whereas on the other it also fathoms the universal and all-encompassing principle of Parabrahma at the root of everything. Thus, when one takes the attention of intellect from the physical or outer to the spiritual or inner realm, they experience the ultimate bliss. We've discussed this in detail in the 5th chapter.]

Na Tad Asti Pṛithivyāṁ Vā Divi Deveșhu Vā Punaḥ

Sattvaṁ Prakṛiti-Jair Muktaṁ Yad Ebhiḥ Syāt Tribhir Guṇaiḥ II 40 II

Brāhmaṇa-Kșhatriya-Viśhāṁ Śhūdrāṇāṁ Cha Parantapa

Karmāṇi Pravibhaktāni Svabhāva-Prabhavair Guṇaiḥ II 41 II

Śhamo Damas Tapaḥ Śhauchaṁ Kșhāntir Ārjavam Eva Cha

Jñānaṁ Vijñānam Āstikyaṁ Brahma-Karma Svabhāva-Jam II 42 II

Śhauryaṁ Tejo Dhṛitir Dākșhyaṁ Yuddhe Chāpy Apalāyanam

Dānam Īśhvara-Bhāvaśh Cha Kșhātraṁ Karma Svabhāva-Jam II 43 II

Kṛișhi-Gau-Rakșhya-Vāṇijyaṁ Vaiśhya-Karma Svabhāva-Jam

Paricharyātmakaṁ Karma Śhūdrasyāpi Svabhāva-Jam II 44 II

Sve Sve Karmaṇy Abhirataḥ Sansiddhiṁ Labhate Naraḥ

Sva-Karma-Nirataḥ Siddhiṁ Yathā Vindati Tach Chhṛiṇu II 45 II

Yataḥ Pravṛittir Bhūtānāṁ Yena Sarvam Idaṁ Tatam

Sva-Karmaṇā Tam Abhyarchya Siddhiṁ Vindati Mānavaḥ II 46 II

(40) There's nothing on the earth, in the sky or among the gods that's free from the purview of these three Gunas.

[From 18th verse till here is a description which shows different types of knowledge, action, doer, intellect, determination and happiness. We also saw how diversity exists in the universe and how Sāttvic kind is considered the superior and preferred one among them. Among the Sāttvic kind, too, the most superior state is called 'Trigunāteet' state (beyond the three Gunas). According to Gitā, Trigunāteet or Nirguna is not a separate fourth kind but the superlative version of Sāttvic, as we've discussed in the 7th chapter. Now, following verses describe how distribution of Gunas has resulted in the Chāturvarnya (four-tiered) system. It describes what our 'assigned' work is, which hadn't been mentioned anywhere earlier.]

(41) O Arjun! Actions of Brāhman, Kshatriya, Vaishya and Shudra have been separately classified as per their innate Gunas (attributes).

(42) Tranquility, restraint, austerity, purity, peace, candor, (spiritual) knowledge, science and theistic belief are natural Karma of Brahmans.

(43) Valor, glory, courage, dexterity, not fleeing from war, philanthropy and leadership are natural Karma of Kshatriya. (44) Agriculture, dairy farming and commerce are natural Karma of Vaishya while providing service is the natural Karma of Shudra.

[The Guna-defined structure of the four-tiered system isn't unique to Gitā. It's mentioned elsewhere in Mahābhārat with minor variations. The assigning of duties to people according to their innate qualities is followed in this system.]

(45) One who constantly endeavors in their own Karma attains ultimate enlightenment. Listen how one achieves enlightenment by promptly discharging their duties. (46) Worshipping, through one's own duties, the one from whom all living beings have evolved and who's pervaded this entire universe, leads a person to be enlightened.

[According to Gitā, performing one's duties as assigned to them as per the Chāturvarnya system, without any desires and with the feeling of dedication to Parmeshwar, is devotion of the Almighty Parmeshwar

Śhreyān Swa-Dharmo Viguṇaḥ Para-Dharmāt Sv-Anuṣhṭhitāt

Svabhāva-Niyataṁ Karma Kurvan Nāpnoti Kilbiṣham II 47 II

Saha-Jaṁ Karma Kaunteya Sa-Doṣham Api Na Tyajet

Sarvārambhā Hi Doṣheṇa Dhūmenāgnir Ivāvṛitāḥ II 48 II

Asakta-Buddhiḥ Sarvatra Jitātmā Vigata-Spṛihaḥ

Naiṣhkarmya-Siddhiṁ Paramāṁ Sannyāsenādhigachchhati II 49 II

and leads to enlightenment. This duty assigned to someone according to variation of Gunas may appear faulty, sinful, difficult or unpleasant as well. E.g. In the case in point, killing was a duty of Arjun which appeared wrong or sinful to him. However, Gitā insists that one must follow their own duty and not attempt to adopt someone else's duty which is now explained in subsequent verses.]

(47) Even if it's possible to happily perform someone else's duty, it's better to rather perform one's own duty, albeit flawed. Performing duty assigned as per our nature attracts no sin. (48) O Arjun! One must never forego their natural duty even though it is flawed. Because, just as smoke envelops fire, all initiatives (activities) are engulfed with (some or the other) faults. (49) Behaving without attachment, winning over your mind and acting free of desires attains ultimate state of inaction through renunciation (of fruits of Karma).

[Bhagwān summarizes with a few thoughts shared earlier such as – 'it's advisable to accept one's duty rather than assuming someone else's' (Gitā 3.35) and 'it's not necessary to quit action to achieve ultimate inaction' (Gitā 3.4). While Sanyāsi focus on Moksha alone, Bhagwān emphasizes on Moksha along with universal welfare. This easily explains the advice of Shri Krishna. For the welfare and smooth conduct of the universe it's important that everyone performs to their fullest potential which results in progress of society as a whole. If everyone attempts to quit action, the world would come to an end soon. While Sanyāsi (ascetics) are not concerned with such a possibility, Karmayogi are not so parochial. They say that one must perform their duty, however unattractive or flawed it may appear. Whatever task you see, there could be some fault to be found in it. Therefore, instead of complaining about it, one must perform it with full dedication and without attachment to its outcome. One who has recognized the universality of soul would be worthy of Moksha (liberation), whatever be the duty assigned to them, be it of a priest or of a butcher. A person's greatness does not depend on the act but on the Buddhi (intellect or intention) behind it.]

Siddhiṁ Prāpto Yathā Brahma Tathāpnoti Nibodha Me

Samāsenaiva Kaunteya Niṣhṭhā Jñānasya Yā Parā II 50 II

Buddhyā Viśhuddhayā Yukto Dhṛityātmānaṁ Niyamya Cha

Śhabdādīn Viṣhayāns Tyaktvā Rāga-Dveṣhau Vyudasya Cha II 51 II

Vivikta-Sevī Laghv-Āśhī Yata-Vāk-Kāya-Mānasaḥ

Dhyāna-Yoga-Paro Nityaṁ Vairāgyaṁ Samupāśhritaḥ II 52 II

Ahankāraṁ Balaṁ Darpaṁ Kāmaṁ Krodhaṁ Parigraham

Vimuchya Nirmamaḥ Śhānto Brahma-Bhūyāya Kalpate II 53 II

Brahma-Bhūtaḥ Prasannātmā Na Śhochati Na Kāṅkṣhati

Samaḥ Sarveṣhu Bhūteṣhu Mad-Bhaktiṁ Labhate Parām II 54 II

Bhaktyā Mām Abhijānāti Yāvān Yaśh Chāsmi Tattvataḥ

Tato Māṁ Tattvato Jñātvā Viśhate Tad-Anantaram II 55 II

Sarva-Karmāṇy Api Sadā Kurvāṇo Mad-Vyapāśhrayaḥ

Mat-Prasādād Avāpnoti Śhāśhvataṁ Padam Avyayam II 56 II

Chetasā Sarva-Karmāṇi Mayi Sannyasya Mat-Paraḥ

Buddhi-Yogam Upāśhritya Mach-Chittaḥ Satataṁ Bhava II 57 II

(50) O Arjun! Listen as I briefly tell you how one attains the epitome of knowledge, which is Brahman, upon attaining enlightenment. (51) Being endowed with pure intellect, achieving control with determination, giving up sound and other objects of senses, and putting aside love and hate; (52) relishing solitude, having moderate diet, having body, speech and mind in control and always meditative and detached; (53) free from ego, dominance, arrogance, lust, anger and possessiveness; to become tranquil and selfless – one becomes eligible to be one with Brahman. (54) Upon uniting with Brahman, they become blissful and neither crave nor hate anything. And becoming equanimous towards all living beings, they achieve ultimate devotion to me. (55) With devotion they principally attain knowledge of who and how big I am and thus recognizing me in principle they enter my being.

(56) And by taking refuge in me, they attain eternal and imperishable abode through my grace despite performing all actions all the time.

[Above description is of an enlightened Karmayogi. The clear indications in verses 45, 49 and finally 56 explain how Bhagwān insists on continuation with action without attachment and not giving up actions altogether. The description also closely resembles the ideal devotee or Trigunāteet (beyond three Gunas). In fact, a few adjectives are also common. Advocates of Sanyās may claim that this description is of an enlightened Sanyāsi, as the ultimate state attained either through Sanyās or through Karmayog is the same. However, the path of attaining it as given by Bhagwān Shri Krishna in Bhagavad Gitā is most certainly and clearly through Karmayog. Yet, communalistic commentators have tried to twist even these verses, albeit failing miserably once you see the true meaning.]

(57) By dedicating all actions to me through mind and by becoming one with me, always focus on me while taking refuge in the Yog of intellect.

[The word 'Buddhi Yog' or Yog of intellect has earlier been used (Gitā 2.49) and its meaning there as well as here is 'keeping your intellect focused not on the fruit but towards equanimity'. It's meant the same way here, as Karmayog considers Buddhi to be superior to action.]

Mach-Chittaḥ Sarva-Durgāṇi Mat-Prasādāt Tariṣhyasi

Atha Chet Tvam Ahankārān Na Śhroṣhyasi Vinaṅkṣhyasi II 58 II

Yad Ahankāram Āśhritya Na Yotsya Iti Manyase

Mithyaiṣha Vyavasāyas Te Prakṛitis Tvāṁ Niyokṣhyati II 59 II

Swbhāva-Jena Kaunteya Nibaddhaḥ Svena Karmaṇā

Kartuṁ Nechchhasi Yan Mohāt Kariṣhyasy Avaśho 'Pi Tat II 60 II

Īśhvaraḥ Sarva-Bhūtānāṁ Hṛid-Deśhe 'Rjuna Tiṣhṭhati

Bhrāmayan Sarva-Bhūtāni Yantrārūḍhāni Māyayā II 61 II

Tam Eva Śharaṇaṁ Gachchha Sarva-Bhāvena Bhārata

Tat-Prasādāt Parāṁ Śhāntiṁ Sthānaṁ Prāpsyasi Śhāśhvatam II 62 II

Iti Te Jñānam Ākhyātaṁ Guhyād Guhyataraṁ Mayā

Vimṛiśhyaitad Aśheṣheṇa Yathechchhasi Tathā Kuru II 63 II

(58) Once you focus your mind on me, you shall sail through all difficulties with my grace. However, if you don't listen to me because of your ego, you shall perish.

(59) The egoistic belief of yours to not fight the war is futile. Your nature would make you do it. (60) O Arjun! You'd involuntarily end up doing the same thing that you don't want to do out of delusion, thanks to being bound by natural duty. (61) O Arjun! Parmeshwar, by staying within the hearts of all living beings, controls them through his Māyā like operating a machine. (62) Therefore, O Arjun, Surrender to him with all your being. You'd attain ultimate peace and eternal abode through his grace.

(63) I've thus given you the knowledge which is secret among all secrets. Do what you wish to after giving a complete thought to it.

[We've elaborately discussed the involuntary nature of our actions owing to our nature/tendency, in the 10th chapter. While our soul is free, if we look at the happenings in this universe, we see that soul doesn't control it. There are millions of things happening around us without our control or will which also affect us. We end up behaving as a part of it. In such a case, a wise person does it with calm and stoic mind. A foolish person gets entangled in it. All that the ethics or philosophy of Moksha (liberation) could tell you is not to be attached to your actions. This is the explanation from spiritual angle. From the point of view of Bhakti Mārg (path of devotion), Prakruti (nature) is nothing but a part of Parmeshwar and thus Parmeshwar is shown to be our controller in 61st and 62nd verses. Thus, a wise person should devote themselves to Parmeshwar and perform their duties. While Bhagwān Shri Krishna has said at the end of the last verse, 'Do what you wish to…' the meaning is very deep. Once you attain enlightenment through knowledge or devotion, your thought process becomes flawless. In such a case, whatever choices you make become the model acts for the world. Thus, even your free will becomes beneficial for everyone. You'd then have no need to restrict your mind. This is the true meaning behind it.]

Sarva-Guhyatamaṁ Bhūyaḥ Śhṛiṇu Me Paramaṁ Vachaḥ

Iṣhṭo 'Si Me Dṛiḍham Iti Tato Vakṣhyāmi Te Hitam II 64 II

Man-Manā Bhava Mad-Bhakto Mad-Yājī Māṁ Namaskuru

Mām Evaiṣhyasi Satyaṁ Te Pratijāne Priyo 'Si Me II 65 II

Sarva-Dharmān Parityajya Mām Ekaṁ Śharaṇaṁ Vraja

Ahaṁ Tvāṁ Sarva-Pāpebhyo Mokṣhayiṣhyāmi Mā Śhuchaḥ II 66 II

Idaṁ Te Nātapaskyāya Nābhaktāya Kadāchana

Na Chāśhuśhruṣhave Vāchyaṁ Na Cha Māṁ Yo 'Bhyasūtayi II 67 II

Ya Idaṁ Paramaṁ Guhyaṁ Mad-Bhakteṣhv Abhidhāsyati

Bhaktiṁ Mayi Parāṁ Kṛitvā Mām Evaiṣhyaty Asanśhayaḥ II 68 II

Na Cha Tasmān Manuṣhyeṣhu Kaśhchin Me Priya-Kṛittamaḥ

Bhavitā Na Cha Me Tasmād Anyaḥ Priyataro Bhuvi II 69 II

(64) Lastly, listen as I tell you the secret of secrets once again. As I adore you wholeheartedly, I'm going to tell you something for your benefit. (65) Rest your mind in me, be my devotee, worship me and bow down to me. I tell you under oath that you would (thus) become one with me, (as) you're my favorite.

(66) Quit all Dharma and surrender to me alone. Don't fear, I shall free you from all sins.

[Followers of path of pure knowledge don't agree with the devotional epilogue given above and they try to connect the meaning of the above verses to an appeal to put all Dharma and Adharma aside and recognize the Nirguna Parabrahma (formless absolute) beyond. However, the reference they give has a separate and distinct mention of both Dharma and Adharma and it also mentions the Nirguna (formless or without attributes) Parabrahma. We firmly believe that in this verse Bhagwān is referring to his own form which is Saguna (with attributes), as here Gitā is referring to the simpler and straightforward approach of Bhakti Mārg. By Dharma, different ways of attaining Parmeshwar such as Ahimsa Dharma (path of non-violence), Satya Dharma (path of Truth) etc. are referred to and Shri Krishna asks Arjun to leave all these paths and directly surrender to him. By taking an example of Arjun, Bhagwān is here appealing to everyone to surrender themselves to Parmeshwar, devote to it and continue performing their duties which would ensure their welfare, here and hereafter. This is Karmayog and this is the essence of Bhagavad Gitā.]

(67) Don't tell this (secret) to someone who's not austere, who's not devoted, who's averse to listening and who condemns me. (68) The one who communicates this ultimate secret to my devotees, would attain supreme devotion in me and undoubtedly become one with me. (69) There would be no human who would do dearer service to me than this. There would be no one on this earth dearer to me than them.

Adhyeşhyate Cha Ya Imaṁ Dharmyaṁ Saṁvādam Āvayoḥ

Jñāna-Yajñena Tenāham Işhṭaḥ Syām Iti Me Matiḥ II 70 II

Śhraddhāvān Anasūyaśh Cha Śhṛiṇuyād Api Yo Naraḥ

So 'Pi Muktaḥ Śhubhāñl Lokān Prāpnuyāt Puṇya-Karmaṇām II 71 II

Kachchid Etach Chhrutaṁ Pārtha Tvayaikāgreṇa Chetasā

Kachchid Ajñāna-Sammohaḥ Pranaşhṭas Te Dhanañjaya II 72 II

Arjuna Uvācha

Naşhṭo Mohaḥ Smṛitir Labdhā Tvat-Prasādān Mayāchyuta

Sthito 'Smi Gata-Sandehaḥ Karişhye Vachanaṁ Tava II 73 II

Sañjaya Uvācha

Ity Ahaṁ Vāsudevasya Pārthasya Cha Mahātmanaḥ

Saṁvādam Imam Aśhrauşham Adbhutaṁ Roma-Harşhaṇam II 74 II

Vyāsa-Prasādāch Chhrutavān Etad Guhyam Ahaṁ Param

Yogaṁ Yogeśhvarāt Kṛişhṇāt Sākşhāt Kathayataḥ Svayam II 75 II

(70) Whoever studies the Dhārmic (here righteous) dialogue between us two; I would feel that they've worshipped me with Yadnya (sacrifice) of knowledge. (71) Moreover, one who doesn't find faults and listens to it with faith shall be free of sins and join the auspicious abodes which are destined for pious people.

[This concludes the sermon. Now Bhagwān validates whether Arjun has clearly understood it or not.]

(72) O Arjun! Did you listen to this with focused mind? And O Arjun, did your delusional ignorance completely vanish?

Arjun said – (73) O Krishna! With your blessings, my delusion was destroyed and I remembered (my righteous duties). Now I'm completely free of doubts. I shall behave as you said (i.e. fight).

[Advocates of Sanyās have tried to twist this (73rd) verse claiming that Bhagwān Shri Krishna has asked Arjun to quit the familial life to turn ascetic which Arjun corroborated. However, if you check earlier Adhyāyas (Gitā 2.7) Arjun has clearly stated that he has forgotten his Dharma and duty. This verse refers to him remembering this now. Arjun says that he shall now do what Bhagwān Shri Krishna has asked him to. For this, we can give countless references of Shri Krishna having asked Arjun to 'fight the war' (Gitā 2.18, 2.37, 3.30, 8.7, 11.34). This shall put everything to rest. This concludes the dialogue between Shri Krishna and Arjun. Now Sanjay concludes his narration of the Gitā to Dhrutarāshtra.]

Sanjay said – (74) Thus I heard the mystical dialogue between Bhagwān Shri Krishna and great Arjun that gave me goosebumps.

(75) With the grace of Vyās, I could hear this ultimate secret that is Yog (Karmayog), narrated by lord of Yog Shri Krishna himself.

[As said earlier, Vyās had given special vision to Sanjay whereby he could witness the proceedings on the warfront and report them to the blind king Dhrutarāshtra. This Karmayog is referred to as Yog by Shri Krishna, Arjun and Sanjay alike. The same word is also used in concluding line of every Adhyāya as well. Here it carries an even broader meaning. This includes the divine Yog (ability) of Parmeshwar

Rājan Sansmṛitya Sansmṛitya Saṁvādam Imam Adbhutam

Keśhavārjunayoḥ Puṇyaṁ Hṛiṣhyāmi Cha Muhur Muhuḥ II 76 II

Tach Cha Sansmṛitya Sansmṛitya Rūpam Aty-Adbhutaṁ Hareḥ

Vismayo Ye Mahān Rājan Hṛiṣhyāmi Cha Punaḥ Punaḥ II 77 II

Yatra Yogeśhvaraḥ Kṛiṣhṇo Yatra Pārtho Dhanur-Dharaḥ

Tatra Śhrīr Vijayo Bhūtir Dhruvā Nītir Matir Mama II 78 II

through which it manifests itself in visible form over and above the usual meaning of Yog which is the idea/ability to perform actions skillfully. This divine Yog of Parmeshwar is called Māyā in Vedānta.]

(76) O King! I'm heartened again and again by reminiscence of this wonderful and pious dialogue between Shri Krishna and Arjun. (77) and O King! By thinking about the mystical cosmic form of Shri Krishna I'm amazed and delighted again and again. (78) I am certain that wherever there's Lord of Yog Shri Krishna, there's master marksman Arjun and there shall also be prosperity, victory, eternal wealth and righteousness.

[In conclusion, joint efforts of wisdom and power are destined to achieve victory and greatness of all kinds. This is communicated by the last verse. This is why the adjectives 'Lord of Yog' denoting wisdom and 'Master archer' denoting warrior capability are used to describe Shri Krishna and Arjun.]

This concludes the eighteenth Adhyāya **Mokshasanyāsyog** from the dialogue between Shri Krishna and Arjun on Yog Shāstra (Karmayog Shāstra) within Brahmavidyā (knowledge of Brahman) in the Upanishad sung (narrated) by Shri Bhagwān (Shri Krishna).

Author Background

Sarang Tilak, an active spiritual seeker, is also a Management graduate from Jamnalal Bajaj Institute of Management Studies, Mumbai. Having over 15 years of experience in the corporate field, his area of expertise is Sales, Marketing & Strategy. He has a Black belt in Keimoudo®, a Martial Arts system that helps in physical, mental and spiritual growth of an individual. In his spare time, he loves writing, driving, riding, traveling & living life to the fullest. He lives in Thane, Mumbai.

He can be reached on tilak.sarang@gmail.com